American English

How did English become the language it is today? What does the use of language and its diversity tell us about the world around us? This lively introduction to the study of language explores American English and its place within contemporary society, highlighting the role of language in our daily lives. Beginning with a definition of language, the text unpacks the basic concepts used in linguistics, placing them in the context of real-life situations. Using examples from popular culture, the authors show how the study of language is relevant to students' experience. Each chapter includes a "Hot Topic," inviting students to apply what they have learned to the contemporary world they see around them. Teachers and students will appreciate the book's innovative structure, designed to build an understanding of how different aspects of language work together. A variety of exercises – individual, group, discussion, research – is provided to support every teaching style. Imaginatively organized and fun to use, *American English* is the ideal guide to language study for students taking the subject as a general education requirement, beginning undergraduates in linguistics, and future teachers of English.

JULIE S. AMBERG AND DEBORAH J. VAUSE are both Assistant Professors of English and Humanities at York College of Pennsylvania.

American English

History, Structure, and Usage

JULIE S. AMBERG

York College of Pennsylvania

DEBORAH J. VAUSE

York College of Pennsylvania

 CAMBRIDGE
UNIVERSITY PRESS

CAMBRIDGE UNIVERSITY PRESS
Cambridge, New York, Melbourne, Madrid, Cape Town, Singapore, São Paulo,
Delhi, Dubai, Tokyo

Cambridge University Press
The Edinburgh Building, Cambridge CB2 8RU, UK

Published in the United States of America by Cambridge University Press, New York

www.cambridge.org
Information on this title: www.cambridge.org/9780521617888

First published 2009

Printed in the United States of America

A catalogue record for this publication is available from the British Library

Library of Congress Cataloging-in-Publication Data

Amberg, Julie S.
 American English : history, structure, and usage / Julie S. Amberg, Deborah J. Vause.
   p.   cm.
 ISBN 978-0-521-85257-9 (hardback)
  1.   English language–United States–History. 2.   English language–Variation–United States.
3. English language–United States–Grammar.   4.   English language–United States–Usage.
5. English language–United States–Syntax.   6.   Americanisms. I.   Vause, Deborah J. II.   Title.
 PE2808.A63 2009
 427'.973–dc22

                                                                                    2009028997

ISBN 978-0-521-85257-9 hardback
ISBN 978-0-521-61788-8 paperback

We dedicate this book to our families

Contents

Figures

Tables

Preface

American English: History, Structure, and Usage developed from our individual experiences of teaching the subjects of History of the English Language and Linguistics to our students, who were primarily Secondary Education/English majors, Professional Writing majors, and Literary Studies majors. We recognized that the traditional approaches to these two subjects failed to meet the needs of this particular student population. Non-linguistics majors found the international approaches of linguistics study too broad and the content of the History of the English Language courses too narrow. To help students understand the relevance of language studies, the concepts needed to be grounded in the everyday experiences of their lives. To this end, *American English: History, Structure, and Usage* offers undergraduates content and exercises designed to engage them in understanding the forces that shape the production and usage of American English by applying current linguistic concepts and theories to contemporary situations drawn from American culture. Different from other textbooks in language and linguistics, *American English: History, Structure, and Usage* introduces and integrates descriptions of the history of English into explanations of the structure and usage of contemporary American English, revealing the ways in which the language has developed, as well as the ways in which it is constantly changing.

The textbook's goal is to help students learn how to:

- understand the systematic nature of language in general and American English in particular
- recognize that a living language changes and understand how it does so
- gain knowledge of methods of linguistic analysis
- recognize and appreciate American English language dialects
- be aware of the relationship between ideology and the power of language
- understand the historical forces that change language in general as well as the specific forces that have shaped American English.

Chapter 1 defines language and explores the complex ways in which language and identity are interconnected. It also introduces students to basic methods of descriptive linguistic analysis.

Building on notions of language and identity, Chapter 2 offers a history of American English, discussing the unique characteristics that make it different from other English varieties. The chapter defines Standard American English and identifies privileged dialects in the United States. The chapter ends with a discussion of American English as a global language.

Chapter 3 continues the examination of American English by considering its morphology. The chapter then explores word formation and usage in American English.

Chapter 4 continues exploring the history of American English by contrasting the more modern language with Old and Middle English. The chapter explains the effects of geographical and social isolation on the English language over time and the resulting morphological changes.

Chapter 5 explores both historical and contemporary attitudes about English grammar and syntax. The chapter discusses prescriptivist and descriptivist approaches to the study of grammar and asks students to consider the implications of each.

Continuing the study of elements of American English, Chapter 6 introduces students to the basic principles of its phonology. The discussion then turns to the features of the American English spelling system and the fact of sound/spelling divergences.

Chapter 7 introduces students to the field of semantics and the various approaches linguists have taken to studying language meaning. Students consider meaning classification and change, as well as pragmatics.

Turning from the elements of language to its social context, Chapter 8 investigates dialect variation in the United States. After a brief description of linguistic approaches to dialect study, the chapter considers two widely spoken dialects of American English, Chicano English and African American English.

Chapter 9 traces the development of American language policies from the nineteenth century onward, especially as they affected indigenous, Spanish, and Hawai'ian cultures. The chapter then explores the current national debate over mandating English as the official language of the United States.

Finally, Chapter 10 discusses several language topics in education. It begins by reviewing linguistic theories about second language acquisition and learning. It then contrasts two methods of second language learning, bilingual education and immersion programs, and evaluates each within the framework of linguistic study.

In each chapter, Critical Thinking exercises ask students to explore particular chapter concepts in more depth, and a Hot Topic provides a final example of how the chapter's contents are relevant to contemporary life.

An additional resource for students and teachers is the accompanying website (www.cambridge.org/amberg-vause), which includes exercises, research topics, and further resources. Direct links to all URLs listed in the textbook appear on the website as well.

Acknowledgments

We wish to thank first of all our many students who originally inspired us and have motivated us at each step along the way in writing this book. To them, we are deeply grateful for their patience in putting up with a work-in-progress and for their cogent insights into what worked and what did not in the text. We wish to thank York College of Pennsylvania for supporting the project at all stages and allowing us to pilot the text in our classes. The financial assistance of the Faculty Development Committee of York College of Pennsylvania was invaluable, and we thank the committee for the grants they bestowed. We also thank our colleagues, past and present, in the Department of English and Humanities who were willing to discuss various aspects of this text both informally in the hallways and in more formal settings: Dominic Delli Carpini, Dennis Weiss, Victor Taylor, Jim McGhee, Jerry Siegel, Edward Jones, and Paul Puccio.

We acknowledge with gratitude the Syndicate of Cambridge University Press for believing in this project, a work very different from conventional linguistics or history of the English language textbooks. We also extend thanks to our editor, Andrew Winnard, who supported the text from the beginning. We'd like to thank our readers and reviewers, many of whom made extensive helpful comments on early drafts of the work. Finally, we wish to thank our families for their love and support during the writing of the textbook. Julie acknowledges her husband, Stuart Stelly, for his continued encouragement and advice and her son, Daniel Stelly, for his help with Instant Messaging questions. Deborah acknowledges her son, Michael Vause, for his patient explanations of a teenager's language and her husband, Jamie Vause, for his willingness to endure endless questions.

1   Introduction: What is language?

Key terms

Idiolect
Language community
Language
Language conventions
Arbitrary sign
Iconic sign
Fluency
Communicative competence
Critical period
Universal grammar
Linguistics
Descriptive linguistics

Overview

In this chapter you'll learn about the complex relationship between language and identity. Language reflects both the individual characteristics of a person, as well as the beliefs and practices of his or her community. You'll also learn that languages are rule-governed systems made up of signs, so for an outsider to learn the language of a community, he or she must learn which signs are meaningful and which are not. The chapter will introduce you to the study of language and communication, as well as the methods of analysis used by those who work in this field. It also considers the complexity of language by examining various theories about how children acquire language. The fact that small children learn language in a relatively short period of time indicates that people may have innate language capabilities.

Introduction

How much time do you spend thinking about the language you speak? If you're like most people, you probably don't consider it much at all.

Box 1.1 The power of language

- Former Russian satellite countries Estonia and Latvia have made fluency in Estonian and Latvian, respectively, a requirement of citizenship, thus creating a potential problem for millions of Russian-speaking citizens who have lived in these countries for years.
- An Amsterdam city councilor proposed a law mandating that Dutch be spoken in Islamic mosques in his city, even though the traditional language of Islam is Arabic.
- Members of the Israeli Parliament (Knesset) boycotted a speech given in German by former German President Köhler, insisting that German should not be spoken in the Knesset as long as there are Holocaust survivors living.
- The European Esperanto Union has indicated a new trend in the international labor market: advertisements for many jobs in Europe seek only applicants whose mother tongue is English.
- The Executive Branch of the US government has directed all federal departments and agencies to use "plain language" to make the government more accessible and understandable in its communications with the public.

For many of us, speaking is as natural as waking up each day: it's an unconscious action that we rarely notice we're even doing. And as a result, we usually don't imagine our language as something that might wield power, fuel debate, or even cause conflict. In truth, however, language can operate in all of these ways. The recent news stories in Box 1.1 above illustrate how language plays a significant role in people's lives.

As these stories illustrate, language affects many facets of human culture: religious, political, social, and economic. Many of these situations described are provocative. The banning of certain languages or mandating the use of one over another have produced tension and anxiety, charges of isolationism, and even allegations of racism and discrimination. Why do these attempts to control language produce such strong reactions? Throughout this textbook, as you explore further the connections between people and their language, you'll find answers to this question.

Language and communication

Language is foremost a means of communication, and communication almost always takes place within some sort of social context. This is why effective communication requires an understanding and recognition of the connections between a language and the people who use it. These connections are complex: for example, they tell you when to use slang with a friend or formal language with a boss, how to judge a candidate's campaign speeches, and whether to abbreviate an email. All of these acts require knowledge of the language, as well as the cultural and social forces acting on that language. As you work through this textbook, you will study these various forces, especially as they function within the United States.

Social context is a major factor that drives our language choices. For example, consider the language you might have used in an interview situation, perhaps with a prospective employer or college admissions officer. If you are like many other people, in the interview you probably were as much concerned with how you spoke as with what you actually said. You may have even practiced sounding confident, for instance, or intelligent, so that you would make a good impression during the interview. We make decisions every day, or have decisions made about us by other people, based on the language we use. We frequently evaluate a person's education, socioeconomic level, background, honesty, friendliness, and numerous other qualities by how that person speaks. And when we want to make a particular impression on someone else, we consciously choose our language, just as we choose our hair styles or clothing.

Exercise 1.1

The term **idiolect** refers to a person's use of language within a particular context. Think about your own idiolect and consider the ways in which it changes over the course of your day, depending on the needs of your communication contexts. Have you talked on the phone? Helped a friend study? Ordered in a restaurant? Participated in class discussion? Note in writing the similarities and the differences among several moments of communication you have had in the past four hours. Then imagine that you couldn't vary your language from one context to the next, from informal to formal, from personal to impersonal, from home to chemistry class, and so on. Would this hinder your communication or not? Be prepared to share your thoughts with the class.

Language is integrally intertwined with our notions of who we are on both the personal and the broader, societal levels. When we use language, we communicate our individual thoughts, as well as the cultural beliefs and practices of the communities of which we are a part: our families, social groups, and other associations.

Language and identity

Each community, just like each individual, has its own language that expresses the ideas, values, and attitudes of its members. A particular group

Figure 1.1 *A language community at work*

of language users who share the use of a specific language adapted to fit their needs is called a **language community**. Your language communities may be created by your interests, say a sports team or a school club you belong to, by your age group, by your gender, and so on (see Figure 1.1).

Language communities are often identified by geographical region as well. In the southwestern United States, for example, in some towns along the Mexican border, Spanish is the dominant language, not English. In other towns in this region, English dominates. In each geographical area, the relationship between the two languages reflects the history, politics, and unique identity of its population. Study of diverse language communities across the United States contributes to our understanding of what it means to be American, a complex notion. Awareness of the nature of language communities provides insight into a population and will help you be more effective in using language and in understanding the language used by others.

The work of New York conceptual artist Nikki S. Lee illustrates the fundamental human ability to consciously transform one's self. Lee's acclaimed projects document her successful transformation and assimilation into a wide range of subcultures and social and ethnic groups, from sophisticated yuppies to trailer park residents, a hip-hop crowd, skateboarders, swingers, and tourists. Lee fits into these various groups by putting on the characteristics of that group's identity: its fashions, its gestures, and, of course, its language. Her project reveals the variability of individual identity – we can slip in and out of various identities, if we choose, by simply changing our language and dress. If you want to see photographs of Lee's transformations, visit the website of the Museum of Contemporary Photography: www.mocp.org/collections/permanent/lee_nikki_s.php

Exercise 1.2

Work with two or three peers to identify a particular language community you all recognize, such as restaurant servers, college professors, parents, etc. Then write a dialogue for two or more of you to read to your classmates illustrating the language of this community. Do not identify the community by name for the other students in the class but instead focus on the vocabulary, pronunciation, sentence structure, and style of dialogue to convey the community's identity. After you've written the dialogue, list its distinctive characteristics and speculate on how this particular language community might have acquired these characteristics. Be prepared to discuss how these language characteristics differ from the language of your classmates' dialogues.

How we define language

Although those who study language may disagree over a precise definition because they dispute some concepts, such as whether or not language must have a written and/or oral component, they agree that **language** is a rule-based system of signs. Saying that language is rule-based usually makes people think of other kinds of situations where rules are enforced by a particular authority. For example, think about classroom behavior. Students are expected to sit still, be quiet, pay attention, and so on; typically, there are consequences if they don't follow these rules. Language rules, however, are not enforced by any authority figure; language police do not exist. Instead, **language** rules are **conventions**. This means that they come into existence through common practice by users of the language rather than through the imposition of an authority figure. As a result, members who use the **language conventions** of their particular community may not even be conscious of following them.

> Conventions are the unspoken, unofficial rules within a particular community that are accepted and followed by members who may not even be aware of them. The word *convention* originated in the Latin verb *convenīre*, meaning *to come together*, a meaning still reflected in usage today. If we look at the individuals following a particular convention, we see a community coming together through making the same choices in their actions, which includes their use of language. If you drink a *soda*, you probably live in a different geographical region of the United States from someone who drinks *pop*. And if you drink a *coke*, you live in yet another region (see Figure 1.2). All three words refer to the same thing, a sugary, carbonated drink, but users are influenced in their word choice by the preference of their community.

We talk about language as a system of rules or conventions because a single language convention, for example, a single word, a pause, or an alphabet letter, does not tell us much beyond its immediate meaning. Thus, we usually combine these conventions together to convey larger meanings.

Language signs

The most basic convention of any language community is the acceptance of a set of signs that convey meaning. These signs could be sounds or words or punctuation marks on a page or even silence in a conversation; any of these things is able to carry meaning. To be successful, signs work on two different levels. First, signs indicate the phonic or graphic or visual elements, the physical medium that gives a language form, and then on the second level

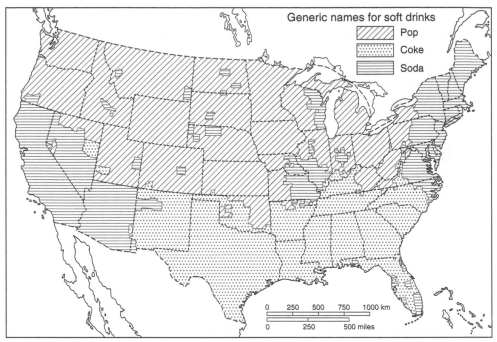

Figure 1.2 *Do you use* pop *or* soda *or . . . ? (After M.T. Campbell 2003,* Generic Names for Soft Drinks by County, http://popvssoda.com:2998/countystats/total-county.html)

the signs portray the message itself, which indicates a particular meaning. To give a quick illustration of this duality inherent in language signs, consider the word *goose*. The alphabet letters represent particular sounds within the American English language system. Then, for the second level, the letters work together to create the word *goose*, which represents the meaning the sign conveys, the concept of a certain kind of bird. The signs of language can come through almost any sensory channel: sounds, like words or music; sights, like a page of text; or even physical movements, like dance. Braille provides an example of signs conveyed through touch.

> Ferdinand de Saussure (1857–1913) was a Swiss linguist. His theories were fundamental in defining the study of language as a science. Saussure's work led to the twentieth-century development of the important linguistic subfield of semiotics, or the study of signs. We'll explore the field of semiotics in Chapter 7.

Types of signs

The signs within a language that convey meaning can be either arbitrary or iconic. An **arbitrary sign** doesn't possess any inherent connection with its meaning. For example, in American English, the word for the object that can open or close a large opening in a wall is *door*. The fact that this word varies from one language to another shows that it is arbitrary: nothing in the word *door* indicates an intrinsic "doorness," or the state of being a door. We only learn

Figure 1.3 *An iconic sign meaning* wheelchair accessible

what this word means through our own individual experiences with other speakers, through reading the word, or through being taught a particular language.

Even words that we consider onomatapoeic, or imitations of the actual sounds, like the *crash* of a box hitting the floor or the *ding* of a bell, are arbitrary within a culture, though we might at first expect them to be the same across all cultures. This illustrates just how closely a culture and its language are linked. What seems to be an objective and literal recording of sound is really the representation of a cultural perspective. For instance, the sound a turkey makes is *gobble gobble* when represented in American English, *glugluglugluglu* in Portuguese, and *krrull krrull* in Albanian. Or think about the *caw* of a crow heard in the United States. In France the same bird would make a *croa-croa* sound and in Sweden a *krax-krax*.

The other type of sign, an **iconic sign**, works on a visual or auditory level to convey its meaning immediately; for example, the picture of a mouse conveys the concept of *mouse* to anyone who looks at it, no matter if the person uses the English name *mouse* or the French *la souris* (see Figure 1.3). No matter what the native language, anyone who hears a rooster crowing will immediately associate the concept *rooster* with that sound. We don't have to learn an arbitrary connection between these iconic signs and the concepts they represent. Table 1.1 illustrates the differences between arbitrary and iconic signs.

Table 1.1 *Arbitrary signs vs. iconic signs*

Arbitrary sign	Iconic sign
Culture-specific meaning	Universal meaning
Learned meaning	Obvious meaning
Example:	Example:
SNAKE	

Exercise 1.3

Identify four iconic and four arbitrary signs from your own experience. Think and write about why each is effective in communicating an idea. Then consider if your process of *reading* an arbitrary sign, of determining the meaning that it conveys, is different from the process of reading an iconic one.

Remember that arbitrary signs carry meaning through convention, through habit or accepted usage. That is, a group of individuals who regularly communicate with each other, a language community, will begin using a particular sign to represent a particular concept and then continue to use the sign consistently to convey that particular meaning. Recognizing the role that conventions play within a language is crucial; without conventions, language wouldn't exist. Let's now explore more fully some of the conventions one has to know in order to be an effective language user.

Fluency in language

When you were a child, you might have had fun with your friends or family inventing a special language to be used just by your circle. Maybe it was a code – signs or made-up words that you substituted for real words. Or maybe you created a made-up language by transposing sounds in some way: *idday ouyay vereay seuay igpay atinlay?* No matter what the structure of your language, it probably took a lot of work for you to produce it, remembering those words or sounds that substituted for others and the special flourishes that made it unique. To have any kind of conversation, you'd have had to really think before you spoke and then wait a while for your friend to formulate his or her answer.

We bring up these childhood games to contrast this scenario with what we usually do when we use our native languages. If you're like most people, you probably never even think about how you produce language, but merely accept as a given that you know it. But what does it really mean to "know" a language? In fact, most of us have very little knowledge about the complex processes we go through just to produce sound and construct meaningful sentences. Do we think about, for instance, how air must leave our diaphragms, enter our mouths, and vibrate behind our closed lips to produce the sound "m"? Do most of us know that when we state a sentence, such as "I gave her the book," that "her" is the indirect object and in this sentence must occupy the position following the verb and no other? In actuality, very few people have this kind of language knowledge, and yet they possess **fluency**. They are able to comprehend and to produce language easily, aware of the many subtleties of its use. So "knowing" a language or being fluent in a language is very different from "having knowledge" of a language, as Figure 1.4 illustrates.

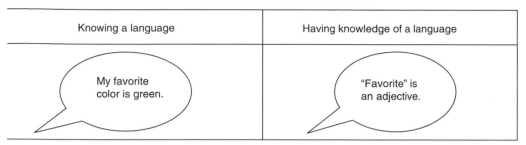

Knowing a language	Having knowledge of a language
My favorite color is green.	"Favorite" is an adjective.

Figure 1.4 *Knowing a language isn't the same as having knowledge of a language*

Word systems

Knowing a language means knowing its word structures and meanings. Native speakers of English know the meanings of many words and know how to combine these words together. They also know how to coin new words in English. For instance, if someone gave you something and called it a *krip*, even though you might not know the word's meaning, you could ask for two of them by adding *-s* to *krip*, creating *krips*; in addition, you could also use the word in sentences: *Do you have any* krips *today? Where are my* krips*?* and so on. The ability to use language includes knowledge of the ways in which words are formed. We will discuss word formation in Chapter 3.

Sentence structures

Native speakers also know how to construct sentences. And they intuitively know when a sentence sounds "wrong." Note that constructing sentences goes beyond just putting strings of words together. As one famous linguist pointed out with his example sentence, *Colorless green ideas sleep furiously*, a sentence may be grammatically correct, but that does not mean that it is well-formed, or meaningful. Sentences must conform to certain rules of language, including rules about meanings. Chapters 5 and 7 will explore in more detail sentence structures and their meanings.

Sound systems

Knowing a language means that speakers know how to produce sounds in their native languages and that they understand which sounds are meaningful and which are not. So, for instance, while guttural sounds made in the throat area are common to many languages, including French, Arabic, and German, American English speakers know they are not a part of the American English sound corpus. In addition to intuitively knowing the sounds that comprise their language, speakers also know the ways in which sounds can be combined. For example, words in English cannot begin with the consecutive sounds represented by the two letters *ts*, so native speakers of English would not expect these two sounds together at the beginning of words. Initial *ts* does occur, however, in other languages, like Japanese. This is why English speakers have trouble pronouncing a word like the Japanese *tsunami* because they are not used to this initial sound combination. In Chapter 6 we'll be discussing more of the sounds and sound patterns of American English.

Context

Finally, being fluent means being able to use language in appropriate ways within particular social contexts. Our ability to use language in this way is called our **communicative competence**. When we respond appropriately to questions, tell jokes, use polite forms, give directions, and so on, we reveal our competence in language. Chapters 7 and 8 discuss language use in context.

Exercise 1.4

To test your inherent knowledge of well-formed English words, sentences, sounds, and communicative responses, look at the following list of words and phrases. Decide if each item conforms to your idea of what is appropriate or well-formed language. Explain why you find some items inappropriate.

1. The lawyer had went to Albany before.
2. He slept through the night.
3. He slept the airplane for ten hours.
4. A new product name: Sbaxn.
5. Will you sleep over at my house?
6. Will you drive over at my house?
7. Will at my house you come?
8. Singular: shelf; plural: shelfs.
9. A woman asks a man, "Do you know Mayor Smith?" The man replies, "I just moved to the city last month."
10. A woman asks a man, "Where do you live?" The man answers, "More than 50 percent of the time."

Considering the complexity of language systems, you can see that being fluent is an amazing ability; even more amazing is the speed and age at which we acquire this ability. If you have ever been around young children, you probably will have noted that they gain communicative competence in their native languages quite early, long before their brains and bodies mature, and do so without making a conscious effort. The fact that we become fluent within the first few years of our lives seems remarkable given the many, many elements and nuances of language use. What can account for our acquiring this broad knowledge in such a short space of time?

Language innateness

Researchers studying children's language learning have observed that the process starts early: typically, most children are able to form one-word units by around eighteen months of age, two-word units by twenty-one months, and so on. And scientists have observed this same process for children across different language cultures, no matter what socioeconomic level, ethnicity, or native language. It seems, then, that the best possible time to acquire a language, the **critical period**, is during the first few years after birth (see Figure 1.5).

These observations about a critical period lead researchers to theorize about the process through which children acquire their mother tongue. Language acquisition obviously depends to some extent on the physical growth and maturation of the child, such as the development of motor skills and cognitive thinking. Children cannot speak until they are physically capable of forming speech sounds and until they have mental processes that provide something for them to communicate.

But this doesn't explain why children acquire their language at such a young age, regardless of their culture or environment. For this reason, many scientists theorize that human beings are born with an innate ability to acquire language. This innate ability may include the awareness that language has patterns; some researchers even speculate that it includes innate knowledge of elements common to all languages, such as the distinction between nouns and verbs.

Theories about innateness, however, do not completely explain the acquisition process. If they did, all children would acquire a language, regardless of their upbringing. Yet we know

One of the most influential linguists of modern times, American Noam Chomsky, became recognized when his theories about innate language capabilities appeared in the 1950s and 1960s. He was the first to hypothesize the notion of a **universal grammar**, a set of characteristics common to all languages. Chomsky's theories concerning "natural" language acquisition, as opposed to behaviorist theories that suggested all language was learned, have profoundly influenced many subfields of linguistics, including psycholinguistics, cognitive linguistics, and theoretical linguistics (see Figure 1.6).

Infancy	Infants learn to recognize sound patterns, helping them to identify units of meaning.
Age 1	Babies produce individual words in isolation and show understanding of a few individual words, as well as basic commands/questions.
20 months	Toddlers begin building basic sentences, occasionally producing two-word strings.
Age 2	Toddler lexicon consists of more than 50 items, and their knowledge of sentence-building allows the creation of unique phrases rather than mere repetition.
Age 3	Children's increased vocabulary, around 1,000 words, and grammatical knowledge allows increasingly longer and more complex sentences. They understand almost everything that is said to them.
Age 4	Children use and understand the language of the adults around them.

Figure 1.5 *Approximate timeline for first language acquisition*

Figure 1.6 *Noam Chomsky*

that some children, such as those who do not hear speech from others and those whose caregivers do not respond to their attempts to communicate, do not acquire language proficiency. Because children must interact through language with others, practicing both listening and speaking in order to acquire fluency in language, we know that social and cultural contexts also play a role in acquisition.

Contemporary researchers, such as Catherine Snow at Harvard University, theorize that social interactions play a primary role in helping children learn language patterns. These scientists offer evidence that, rather than possessing innate knowledge specifically about language itself, as the "Chomsky-ites" argue, children possess the "innate ability" to develop certain cognitive capacities to support language acquisition. Both of these positions suggest that children are born with their brains already programmed to support language learning; they diverge, however, in what form that "programming" takes. Thus researchers disagree about the roles biology and culture play in helping children learn their native tongues. The story of Genie in Box 1.2 illustrates that a relationship exists between innate linguistic ability and acquired language knowledge when children learn language.

The fact that humans know their language systems without consciously having to learn them intrigues those people who study language and communication. These professionals, called linguists, attempt to account for our linguistic competence as part of their general work of explaining the structures and functioning of human language. You might say that much of a linguist's work is to discover how we know what we (unconsciously) know about our native

---

Box 1.2 The story of Genie

In 1970, a social worker in California discovered "Genie," a 13-year-old who had been kept locked in a room by herself for most of her life. This extreme neglect had left her mentally and emotionally handicapped. In spite of her age, Genie was only at an infant's level of development, with no language other than the coos that infants make. Linguists worked intensively with Genie over several years, teaching her basic elements of language like a simple vocabulary, but she never acquired the ability to combine simple phrases together into sentences. Because of her age, Genie's case study creates questions about the critical age for language acquisition. She was able to acquire some language, which suggests that the critical age may extend as late as puberty, but she never became proficient in her native tongue.

---

tongues. In the following pages you will learn some of the principles that guide linguists in their study of language.

Studying language

Linguistics, the scientific study of language and its use, is classified primarily as a social science, in the same category as psychology, sociology, anthropology, and the other disciplines that study human behavior. There are many branches of linguistic study, such as sociolinguistics, the study of language as it affects and is affected by social relations, and psycholinguistics, the study of the psychological factors that allow humans to acquire, use, and understand language. We will begin our study of language in this book by practicing **descriptive linguistics**, which is the study of a language as it is actually used within a particular language community. Descriptive linguists study both a language's structure and its specific differences from languages of other communities.

Like other social scientists, linguists maintain as objective a perspective as possible in their work, and so, for example, when they describe particular language structures, they avoid making judgments. This means that a descriptive linguist would examine elements like pronunciation or sentence structure by analyzing what is actually said in conversations rather than by turning to the rules in a dictionary or in a handbook of some kind. Since you yourself will be acting as a linguist throughout this course, you'll also need to be objective about language and language use. You may find this difficult at first, particularly if you have had teachers, parents, and other authorities correct

In popular culture, we frequently use the words *language* and *speech* as if they were interchangeable, even though they signify two very different concepts. While language is a system of meaningful signs, speech is language conveyed through a particular *medium*, in this case through our speech sounds. *Sign language*, a language conveyed through the medium of physical hand gestures, also illustrates the difference between language and its medium (see Figure 1.7). Signing, like writing or speaking, is a mode of transmitting meaning. For information on American Sign Language, see the website of the National Institute on Deafness and Other Communication Disorders: www.nidcd.nih.gov/health/hearing/asl.asp

Figure 1.7 *Arbitrary sign for* American Sign Language used here

your language because it was "wrong." Just remember that, from a linguist's point of view, no language is either good or bad, better or worse.

Notice also that the term *linguistics* doesn't refer to a particular kind of tongue or language and so does not privilege one over another. Linguists study all languages as equals. They analyze language by looking for patterns. They do not identify the "correct" pattern and then seek to impose it on the language. Box 1.3 suggests the process to follow when analyzing language.

The following exercise will give you practice in linguistic analysis of the kind that we've described above. You will be asked to look at a set of sentences and draw conclusions about the rules that govern their use.

Exercise 1.5

Analyze the use of the underlined adjectives *smart* and *intelligent* in the following sentences. Can you identify at least two rules of English that seem to govern their use?

1.   Richard is a smart student.
2.   Richard is smarter than Josh.
3.   Wilma is an intelligent student.
4.   *Wilma is intelligenter than Sandra.
5.   Wilma is more intelligent than Sandra.
6.   Richard is the smartest student in the class.
7.   *Wilma is the intelligentest student in the class.
8.   Wilma is the most intelligent student in the class.

Note: The asterisk is used before sentences that speakers regard as unacceptable. We will use this notation throughout the book.

An important aspect of this course is learning to think like a linguist. In the following chapters, as we begin examining American English, we will be using, and encouraging you to use, the principles of linguistic analysis below. In this way, you will become more aware of the ways in which language works in your lives and will be able to use that understanding both now and in the future.

Box 1.3 Guidelines for linguistic analysis

Analyzing a language is a difficult task. To be successful you must use your language precisely to convey exact meanings, and you must examine objectively the language you choose to study. To help you establish an objective viewpoint, we suggest that you apply the following guidelines:

1.   **Describe** language use rather than judge language. For example, instead of saying, "The speaker used an incorrect form to create a negative statement," say "The speaker used a double negative to create a negative statement." Never use judgmental words like *correct*, *proper*, *wrong* and so on; instead, be objective.

2.   **Examine** actual language usage rather than make an assumption. In other words, don't let cultural stereotypes or your own expectations mislead you in your judgments about language use. For example, don't assume all people living in the southern United States speak with a traditional southern accent.

3.   **Analyze** language in generalizations. Linguists make conclusions based on statistical evidence, not on the personal experiences of one individual. You could draw conclusions based on the usage of a majority of interviewees but not on the usage of your next-door neighbor.

Chapter summary

In this chapter you have learned that all speakers possess individual **idiolects**, which may change according to the **conventions** of their different **language communities**. You have also learned that **linguistic** methodology requires linguists engaged in **descriptive** analysis to remain objective about the **languages** they study. Language consists of a **system** of **arbitrary signs** whose meaning is agreed upon by members of a **language community**. The chapter reviewed innateness theories that suggest humans possess innate capabilities that allow them to develop **communicative competence** without conscious knowledge of the rules governing their languages.

Critical Thinking exercises

1.   There are three basic modes of linguistic communication – oral (speaking, singing), visual (writing, graphics), and gestural (signing). Get with a partner and discuss the advantages and disadvantages of each mode. To help you think about this, put them into a context: for instance, ask yourselves what the disadvantages and advantages are of telephoning, or writing a letter, or using sign language with a friend. Next, you and your partner should each interview three people outside

of your class, asking them their impressions of these three types of communication. Note down and then compare their responses. Based on what they have said, draw some conclusions about these modes and their uses, and describe these in a one-page response. You may also wish to consider what linguists might answer when asked their impressions of the three modes, and then compare these with your other answers (after Finegan 2003).

2.   Think about the type of language used in each of the following situations, and then write out a sample dialogue between two of the individuals in each scenario. Next, write a comparison/contrast of the language conventions used in each. Be sure to consider how things are said, as well as what is verbally communicated. For instance, is the speech loud or soft? Do speakers take turns? Add any other patterns you can identify.

    a.   players in a basketball game

    b.   students in a college chemistry class

    c.   a driver caught speeding

    d.   friends at a birthday party.

Now consider your analysis. How, as a speaker, do you know what the appropriate language will be in any situation? What sort of cues might you consciously or unconsciously pick up on?

3.   In an application for a position as a teacher's aide in an elementary school, a young woman listed as one of her qualifications, "taught my children language." Drawing on what you have learned about language acquisition in this chapter, write two or three paragraphs in which you respond to this statement. Before you begin writing, you may want to define what you think this young woman means by "taught" and then compare that meaning with how the word has been used in this chapter. You'll obviously want to consider what is taught and what is acquired in language.

Hot Topic: Fitting language to a language community

Religious texts present an interesting study of the relationships between languages and their respective language communities because every specific religious language is both well-known and revered in its community. So when the language of the religious community changes over time, as all living languages do, questions arise about how these changes affect the original language of the religious text. For example, some contemporary scholars are re-examining and re-translating both the Torah and the Bible into gender-neutral American English, attempting to avoid assigning a gender to God or specific gender roles to each of the sexes, believing that an all-powerful God would not be limited to a particular gender or would not favor one human gender over another. Other members of these faiths find this sort of language change offensive because they reject the changes in perception such language carries.

Because this Hot Topic exercise cannot address every one of the many language controversies swirling around religious texts, we'll focus on examining just a few contemporary American English translations of the *Bible*. We chose the *Bible* rather than the *Torah* or the *Koran* or another religious work because more translations exist of the *Bible* in American English than of these other texts and because information about these translations is easily accessible through online sources.

Working with a peer group, analyze one of the translations below to identify ways in which the language of that particular translation has been adapted to fit the needs of one specific language community. You'll want to begin with a little research online about the text, starting with the website given. What organization or person has made the translation? What were the author's/authors' purposes in creating the translation? Who is the target audience for this translation? What need did the translator(s) see in the target language community?

Once you've determined this background information, choose a fairly short passage of text from the link(s) provided on the website, no more than twenty to thirty lines long. Read the passage carefully and describe as fully as possible the language of the translation. Consider elements like word choice, word order, word combinations, length and complexity of sentences, tone, use of figures and symbols, and anything else that stands out in the text. (If you have difficulty identifying differing language elements, try comparing/contrasting your chosen passage with its matching passage from the King James Bible at www.king jamesbible.com. How does it differ from this earlier, formal translation?)

Finally, analyze the translation for its effectiveness, given its purposes. What might be its effect on the intended audience? What assumptions might the translator have made about the intended language community? For example, does this community share a certain level of education? A vocabulary indicating a shared cultural background or job type or age range, or other characteristic? Do they listen to the Bible being read or do they read it for themselves? Is one gender or one job or one personality favored over others? Does the language imply some sort of hierarchy among audience members?

Important reminder: As you work, remember that you should be developing generalizations about language use, rather than making judgments about its correctness. In addition, stay focused upon the language: avoid straying off into discussions about the religious ideas presented.

Translations

The Message
www.biblegateway.com/versions/?action=getVersionInfo&vid=65

God's Word Translation
www.godsword.org/cgi-bin/gwstore.cgi?cart_id=6602673_24128&page=
books.htm

The Cotton Patch Version of the New Testament
http://rockhay.tripod.com/cottonpatch/index.htm

NETBible
http://bible.org/netbible/index.htm

The Amplified Bible
www.biblegateway.com/versions/index.php?action=getVersionInfo&vid=45&lang=2

Learn more about it

The study of language

Aronoff, M., and Rees-Miller, J. (eds.) 2003, *The handbook of linguistics*, London: Blackwell.
This collection of essays summarizes the nature of the field of linguistics, including reports from both theoretical and applied research.

Banich, M. T., and Mack, M. (eds.) 2003, *Mind, brain, and language: Multidisciplinary perspectives*, New Jersey: Lawrence Erlbaum.
Banich and Mack bring together essays that explore the relationship between brain, mind, and language. Essay topics include language development, language processing, and the neurological bases of language.

Language acquisition

Gleitman, L., and Landau, B. (eds.) 1994, *The acquisition of the lexicon*, Cambridge, MA: MIT Press.
This anthology brings together specialists from a variety of academic disciplines to discuss their research exploring issues related to the processes by which children acquire their lexicon so quickly and are then able to use it so creatively.

Hulit, L. M., and Howard, M. R. 1993, *Born to talk: An introduction to speech and language development*, New York: Macmillan.
This study traces language development stage by stage, attempting to reveal how culture, place, and identity interact as formative influences.

Jackendoff, R. 1994, *Patterns in the mind: Language and human nature*, New York: Basic Books.
The author lucidly explains contemporary theories about the structure and acquisition of human language.

Pinker, S. 1994, *The language instinct: How the mind creates language*, New York: HarperPerennial.
Psycholinguist Steven Pinker provides a basic introduction to the production and uses of language.

2   Defining American English

Language variety
American English
Prolonged language contact
Standard American English or SAE
Privileged language
First language
Second language
Linguistic relativity

Overview

This chapter asks you to explore the concept of American English by considering the historical connections between a nation's language and its national identity. You'll learn that the United States is a collection of diverse language communities, each using a variety of American English. You'll also realize that language is tied to social status. The languages of communities with high status, or power, in a society are privileged over the languages of other, less powerful communities. Finally, the chapter offers a view of American English in the world and how it is changing to fit the needs of diverse language communities. The Hot Topic asks you to explore the use of politically correct language in American English.

Introduction

Did you know that there is a long history of regarding American English as a "lesser" language? In colonial times, speakers of British English considered American English to be merely a corrupt version of their own language. In 1735, for example, the British tourist Francis Moore complained about the "barbarous" American use of the word *bluff* to describe a river bank, a meaning not employed in Britain. In 1887, one of Oscar Wilde's fictional characters in *The Canterville Ghost* comments, "We have really everything in common with America nowadays except, of course, language." Even more recently, in 1995, *The Times* quoted His Royal Highness The Prince of Wales complaining about the corrupting quality of American English.

Is American English really just a bad version of British English? Despite its detractors, you know this can't be true since, as you learned in Chapter 1, languages are not intrinsically "good" or "bad." A national language simply reflects the identity of a nation's people. In this chapter we'll examine how American English defines and expresses the national identity of the United States. As we begin to explore this complex topic, we ask you to first consider the examples of usage in Box 2.1.

Box 2.1 American English?

Examine the following sentences and identify the one(s) in American English:

1.	"Let's redd-up the room."
2.	"Don't block the box."
3.	"El restaurante esta mucho busy today."
4.	"How's by you?"
5.	"She ask him but he busy."
6.	"You go up in through there."

Actually, all of these sentences are American English, even though the vocabulary or the sentence structure might not be immediately recognizable to many of you. The first three sentences use vocabulary that's probably unfamiliar to the majority of American English speakers. We can easily identify the communities in which these usages are common. "Let's redd-up the room" comes from Pennsylvania Dutch country, where "redd-up" means that the speaker wants to clean up, in this case to clean up the room. You probably recognize all the words in the second sentence, "Don't block the box," but might not recognize what they mean in this particular usage. It's a message for drivers in New York City, warning them not to drive into an intersection until the way out of that intersection is clear. And the third sentence, "El restaurante esta mucho busy today," might be labeled "Spanglish" because it follows English sentence structure but combines Spanish and English vocabulary.

Although the words in the last three sentences are more commonly recognized than the words in the first three, each uses a sentence structure that many Americans might not understand. The fourth sentence, "How's by you?," might seem to be missing a word or two, but this sentence simply asks "How are you?" for natives in Wisconsin. Americans familiar with the language in urban areas or with the African American English dialect would recognize that, in sentence five, "She ask him but he busy," a woman has asked a man a question, but he was too busy to fulfill her request. Texas is represented in the sixth sentence, "You go up in through there," with the speaker giving directions by listing

Figure 2.1 *Do you prefer dippy eggs, sunny-side-up eggs, or eggs over easy?* (©iStockphoto.com/Juanmonino)

prepositions in a way that a non-Texan would undoubtedly find confusing. So as you see, each of these six sentences is tied to a specific American language community.

These sentences reveal that American English is extremely varied, differing in both vocabulary and sentence structure from one part of the country to another, and from one ethnic heritage to another (see Figure 2.1). (Chapter 8 discusses such language variation in more detail.) Because linguists recognize that all languages exist in varied usages rather than in a single unchanging form, they commonly discuss **language varieties**, a term that recognizes the diversity existing within a language, such as American English, without ranking these variations into some sort of imposed order. The fact that American English has specific varieties within it helps to define its uniqueness because other kinds of English, such as British English or Australian English, don't contain the same variations. Examining its varieties may help us to understand the composition of American English, yet this study doesn't define the language as a whole. What do we mean when we refer to "American English"? Let's try to answer this question below.

What is American English?

If we think about defining American English in terms of geography, we might claim that American English is the language that's spoken in the United States of America. This is obviously wrong, though, because many languages are spoken in the United States in addition to American English. For example, think about all the Native Alaskan languages, or Spanish, or Russian, or any other of the languages spoken in America on a daily basis. Gordon (2005) lists the United States of America as having 162 living languages spoken within its borders. This number includes the languages spoken by immigrants and American English varieties of languages, such as Pennsylvania Dutch, as well as native languages such as the Aleut spoken in Alaska.

Claiming that American English is the English spoken in America is also wrong. Many other kinds of English are spoken regularly in the United States. Just think about all the British, Canadian, Scots, Irish, Australian, and other English speakers inside American borders who would be quite surprised if we were to claim they were speaking American English. Furthermore, American English speakers also exist in other countries around the world. Thus we have to conclude that using geography to identify American English doesn't provide a valid basis for a definition.

If we think about defining American English in terms of nationality, we might claim that it's the language spoken by Americans. Yet this definition, too, is flawed. Americans speak a wide variety of languages in addition to English; in fact, many Americans either don't speak English at all or are learning English as their second language. So identifying a speaker's nationality also fails to help when defining American English.

> An example of the differences between American English and other varieties of English can be seen in the popular Harry Potter series. You may not know that these volumes have been "translated" for their American audience: Author J.K. Rowling worked with her editors to rid the books of British words and British grammar usage that would be unfamiliar to American readers. For example, in the United States, the first book is known as *Harry Potter and the Sorcerer's Stone*, while in Britain the title is *Harry Potter and the Philosopher's Stone*. The American version of Harry eats bags of chips and candy, rather than the British packets of crisps and sweets.

Having rejected the previous approaches, let's turn to a historical point of view, which might help us out. We can define **American English** as one of the many types of English, like Canadian English or Australian English or British English or Indian English and so on, that originated in England and traveled to America with British colonists. (See Figure 2.2) American English differs from the other types because it adapted over time to fit the needs of its speakers in the United States. This perspective is more helpful than the previous two approaches to defining American English because it gives us a way to describe the language. It also guides us toward thinking about its connection with the community that uses it and its important role in shaping a national American identity, as well as the identities of individual Americans.

> The US Census Bureau (2006b) reports that one in five Americans speaks a language other than English in the home.

The history of American English

The history of the American English language reflects the history of the nation itself, which teaches us that the United States has always been a land

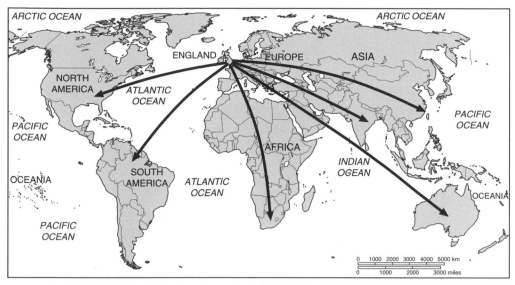

Figure 2.2 *British colonization carried English around the world*

of immigrants. And because immigration brings new peoples and languages into contact with each other, it has always been a dominant force of change on American English. The term **prolonged language contact** refers to the way that a language will change over time as a result of the users of one language interacting with the users of another language. Early colonists first brought English to America, and later waves of immigration brought new words and new influences, creating new prolonged language contacts for American English and so changing the language.

Exercise 2.1

Trace the history of your own personal language use by examining your family history and your geographical region. Where has prolonged language contact come into play in your own history? Be sure to consider the following questions:

1. Ancestry – What languages have shaped speakers in your family? What role has race and/or ethnicity played in these languages?
2. Geography – What regional variations have influenced the way you speak and the way earlier generations spoke?

Write up your findings in a two or three page report, giving examples of the language you and your family use.

American English initially appeared when British colonists took up life along the eastern coastline of North America. From the moment the first colony was settled in Jamestown, the colonists found that their native language was no longer sufficient. The New World had animals, plants, peoples, and terrain

Figure 2.3 *The Old Mission Church in Zuni, New Mexico, built in 1776*
(Credit: T. H. O'Sullivan/The Library of Congress, LC-USZ62-50460)

never before seen by the British, so new words had to be learned. Many times
these words came from the Native Americans: *opossum*, *raccoon*, *skunk*, *hickory*, *pecan*, and *squash*, for example. And as new words were added, older
words became obsolete. In addition, American English pronunciation began
subtly altering as well, because the colonists would not have heard the same
speech sounds that their family and friends in Britain heard on a daily basis.
So even the first generation of colonists to the New World was already using
a language different from that of their mother tongue.

By the time of the American Revolution, almost 3 million people of European
and African descent lived in North America. Although the majority were native
English speakers, almost one-fourth had European first languages such as
German, French, and Dutch. And approximately one-fifth of the total population was African American, primarily slaves, with a variety of African native
languages. Many common words today, such as *levee*, *boss*, *cookie*, and *noodle*,
first entered American English as a result of prolonged contact with immigrants
speaking other languages during the colonial period. When we also add interaction with the Native American languages to this mix, we see that English
in America was able to expand in many different directions due to its constant
exposure to other languages.

Later periods saw different waves of immigrants, each with its own separate
influence. The Irish Potato Famine and the failed German revolution of the
1840s resulted in approximately 3 million new Irish and German immigrants.

The second half of the nineteenth century saw Scandinavians settle in the upper Midwest. The early twentieth Century brought large numbers of immigrants from Southern and Eastern Europe, including Italians and Jews. More recently, Hispanic and Asian peoples have swelled immigration numbers. While each of these groups was learning American English, it was also bringing changes to its new language.

A similar type of prolonged language contact occurred during the years when the United States expanded westward to the Pacific and brought American settlers into a region where many Spanish speakers already lived. Figure 2.3 illustrates the presence of Spanish speakers in early America. Here, though, instead of new settlers bringing another language into contact with the established language of American English, the new language in the West was American English. Because of its prolonged contact with the Spanish already in use on the West Coast, American English gained vocabulary and usages reflecting this western cultural addition to the American identity.

Exercise 2.2

As you now know, the development of American English is integrally intertwined with the development of its population. Each group of words below entered American English from the first language of an immigrant wave. As you work with a partner, examine these lists to identify the cultural contexts in which American English speakers might have learned these particular words from an immigrant population. You might find that a little research into the period and culture is also helpful. For example, a number of words for food items might indicate that a specific wave of immigrants owned or worked in a lot of restaurants or, in an earlier period, got jobs as cooks, so that those outside their particular language community learned to enjoy their native dishes.

French (before 19th century)	Native American (before 19th century)	Spanish (by early 19th century)
portage	totem	lariat
prairie	moccasin	lasso
rapids	tepee	ranch
bayou	wigwam	mustang
crevasse	powwow	burro

In more recent times, political conflict and wars have created yet another type of prolonged language contact for American English. The actual contact between peoples of different cultures created when Americans leave the United States to live in another country, as well as the media coverage of this type of contact, have brought many new usages into the language. For example, the Gulf Wars in recent years have expanded the American English vocabulary with Arabic words and phrases, such as *jihad* and *burqa*.

Today British and American Englishes differ from each other because American English has been shaped by its history. But we have to remember that they also differ because British English has been changing as well, just in different ways from its American cousin. It has not remained the same as it was when the earliest colonists immigrated to the New World. In some cases, an aspect of British English has changed since colonial times while Americans have retained the older usage. This might make even contemporary American English seem a bit archaic from the British perspective. For instance, some Americans preserve pronunciations that British speakers have lost, like pronouncing the initial vowel sounds in *either* and *neither* like the first sound in *eat*. The British, instead, pronounce this sound as *i* as in the vowel sound found in *kite*. And of course some of the British vocabulary has shifted as well. In other cases, British English has remained the same while the American usage has changed.

This brief discussion of American English history gives you a broad overview of the language's development. Future chapters will examine specific aspects in more detail. Chapter 4 looks at other forces that shape language change. Chapter 8 explores regional, social, and other varieties in American English, giving you the chance to consider language variation in more detail. But now that you have a better understanding of American English itself, let's consider the relationship between the language and national identity.

American English and American identity

At first, language use itself didn't receive much attention from the early colonists. After all, they were busy trying to survive. But as the political identity of America began to develop, American English was recognized as part of that identity. After ending the Revolutionary War with Britain, the early United States Congresses debated for another six years the appropriate system of government for the new nation. During this period early statesmen, as well as common citizens, also deliberated on the language of their recently created country. Some objected to the continued use of English in America since the nation had just fought, and won, a war against Britain. They wanted to mark their independence by severing all connections, including those linguistic, to England. Others were concerned about the identity of the new nation as a whole and worried that continued use of English would inhibit the growth of nationalism and a sense of unity in the population. Other languages suggested to take the place of English included Greek, French, and German. None of these alternatives, however, was ever seriously considered as a replacement for American English as the nation's primary language.

Commentators such as author and educator Noah Webster took note of the importance of language in nation-building. In his *Dissertations on the English*

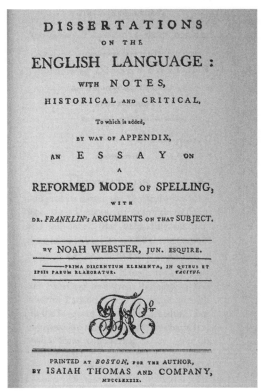

Figure 2.4 *Noah Webster's* Dissertations on the English Language *shaped attitudes toward American English*

Language, Webster ([1789] 1951, pp. 20–21, see Figure 2.4) defended the use of English by suggesting that Americans deliberately employ American, and not British, English:

> Our political harmony is therefore concerned in a uniformity of language. As an independent nation, our honor requires us to have a system of our own, in language as well as government. Great Britain, whose children we are, and whose language we speak, should no longer be our standard; for the taste of her writers is already corrupted, and her language on the decline. But if it were not so, she is at too great a distance to be our model, and to instruct us in the principles of our own tongue.

So although English continued to be the primary language of the newly created United States, it was recognized and valued as American English, different from British English.

In 1828, Noah Webster published his most influential work: *An American Dictionary of the English Language.* His earlier writing had revealed his strong interest in the English language, particularly in American usage, and this publication attempted to capture the lexicon of everyday Americans. It contained approximately 12,000 American words not previously used in British English. Chapter 6 discusses Webster's role in shaping American English spelling.

Exercise 2.3

You're probably aware of some of the stereotypes people around the world hold about Americans. Let's use these preconceptions to examine the way that language and identity reflect each other on a national basis. The following list describes several usages common to American English:

- shortening words (math, fridge)
- preferring the informal and the personal (oral instead of written)
- avoiding titles and courtesies common in other languages (use of first names)
- using euphemisms (*restroom, washroom*, or *powder room* instead of *toilet*)
- having a tendency to exaggerate (the *Super Bowl* of American football, the *World Series* of American baseball, the *America's Cup* of international yachting)

What sort of stereotypes might people of other nationalities make about Americans based on these characteristics of their language? Think about both positive and negative judgments. Now think about other nationalities from an American perspective. Can you think of any stereotypes that seem to be supported by particular language use common to a particular nation? How valid are conclusions about national character that are drawn from language usage? Be prepared to discuss your conclusions with the class.

Today Americans are interested in these earlier concerns about American English for what they might say about the role of language in creating national unity, still a matter of concern. But the worries about establishing an American English no longer exist. American English, like Americans themselves, now has its own identity. It's not confused in any way with British English, Indian English, or any other kind of English spoken in the world. Defining American English is still a complicated task, but unlike what America's founders experienced, the complications today have nothing to do with the British.

Standard American English

Some of the Americans concerned with clarifying the separation between British and American English in the late eighteenth century focused on deliberately changing American English themselves rather than waiting for the language to change over time. These individuals wanted their national language to be truly national, with only one variety used by all Americans. And they also wanted their language to be respected around the world rather than considered a corrupt version of British English. Future President John Adams even proposed establishing "The American Academy for Refining, Improving, and Ascertaining the English Language," with its authority to control the language coming directly from Congress (see Figure 2.5). Although these may have been good political ideals, your own linguistic understanding of how languages change reveals why such an organization of "language police" would ultimately have been powerless to affect the development of American English. After all, language doesn't change because of the imposition of rules but because language changes over time.

Figure 2.5 *John Adams (Credit: The Library of Congress. LC-USZ62–133304)*

Although an "American Academy" has never been established, one specific variety of American English, **Standard American English** or **SAE**, has become the expected norm for communications in a public forum, such as in the government, education, or media. Thus it is the socially privileged language variety in the United States.

> You can read Adams' thoughts on language for yourself in this collection of excerpts from his letters: www.pbs.org/wgbh/amex/adams/sfeature/sf_letters.html

From a linguistic perspective, as you know from Chapter 1, all languages are considered equal; one is not considered more valuable or "better" than another. So linguists haven't named SAE as the *standard* variety because it's the best; SAE is not a judgmental term. Instead, it recognizes that this particular variation is widely used in educational and political institutions, the institutions of power, within a certain language community. When we talk about Standard American English, we aren't identifying the "correct" version of the language. *Standard* in this usage means something that is widely used or accepted rather than a model by which to judge others. For example, when a builder talks about a *standard ceiling height*, he's referring to the most commonly used distance between the floor and the ceiling rather than the *correct* distance. Similarly, *Standard American English* refers to the language variety that is the most commonly recognized as the preferred model for use in public institutions.

Perhaps the best way to describe SAE is to contrast it with other American Englishes. Language varieties might be marked by geographical boundaries, such as Southern or Minnesotan, by cultural boundaries, such as Chicano or Navajo-English, and so on. Since all people, not just Americans, speak a language shaped by factors such as their geographical location, gender, race, socioeconomic class, etc., we can safely say that no one in America speaks SAE naturally; in fact, SAE is a learned variety of American English, different from the language we naturally acquire when we first gain language. And because of this, SAE also tends to refer to the written, rather than spoken, form of American English. As we continue to discuss Standard American English throughout the rest of this textbook, remember that we're speaking from an objective, linguistic perspective rather than a judgmental one.

Since SAE is the language of national institutions, it's associated with the politically and socially powerful people who use it. And the human desire for power of all kinds is also extremely important in shaping language. In most human relationships, one entity has power over others, whether through economic, political, physical, social, or some further means of control. The choices we make about language usage define who we are by indicating the specific status or role we possess. For instance, imagine that you own a successful computer software company. You decide to expand your business by buying a rival company located in Brazil. Even though your new Brazilian employees use their native language of Portuguese to communicate with each other, they use American English when dealing with you. You might have required them to use American English because you're not fluent in Portuguese, but they might also have made this change voluntarily. Who would want to risk their job by using a language the new boss doesn't understand? In instances like this, accepting the language choices of others means that these employees have accepted a subordinate position; they have acknowledged your authority. This is just one instance of many ways in which language exerts power. The next section explores the relationship between language and power in more depth.

> Unlike Standard American English, which stresses the written form of the language, Standard British English also stresses the spoken form, identified as *Received Pronunciation*. *Received* in this instance means *accepted*, so Received Pronunciation means the pronunciation that would be expected and used among the educated (see Figure 2.6). Most Americans would consider Received Pronunciation a "typical" British English variety because of the British Broadcasting Corporation's (BBC's) influence in the United States, although this is changing as the BBC has increased the range of language varieties it broadcasts.

Figure 2.6 *Buckingham Palace – site of the* Queen's English (©iStockphoto. com/S. Greg Panosian)

Language and power

Most people are unaware of the more subtle ways in which our language becomes a tool in power negotiations in our society. Because language is closely allied with social attitudes, speakers with social power also become speakers with language power, that is, the power to control how others express themselves. This expression of power might be as simple as allowing an individual to talk, like when someone screens phone calls to decide whether to answer or not. It can also be as complex as determining how others can use language, such as when workplaces mandate certain written conventions regarding word choice or tone.

When one speaker's language dominates because that person holds control of the larger social situation, we identify the speaker's language as privileged. A *privilege* is a benefit or an advantage granted to a small number of people, so a **privileged language** is one that receives advantages not granted to other languages. In other words, one speaker has advantages over others because of the language she uses. We see these advantages being illustrated in a variety of ways. If certain members of a group are allowed to spend more time talking, or are permitted to interrupt other members of that same group, we can see that their language is privileged. On a larger level, one community's language may be privileged over another community's. For example, dealing with the Internal Revenue Service requires a taxpayer to become familiar with the bureau's language so that he can understand the questions and explanations related to his taxes. The IRS does not take the time to learn the language of a hairdresser or a history teacher because the organization has power over the individual (see Figure 2.7). Thus the responsibility falls on the individual, who must take the time to learn the IRS bureaucratese. Language both carries and conveys, then, the power markers of human relationships.

Figure 2.7 *The teacher controls language within the classroom*

And when we consider even larger language communities, we can see the role that privileging plays in shaping an entire community's language. At the national level, Standard American English holds the privileged role among all the varieties of American English because it is used by those who possess power in American society. For this reason, learning SAE in school is considered extremely important; without this knowledge, individuals might not be able to get jobs or interact appropriately with others who use SAE professionally. And we see the same dynamics of privileging at work when two different languages and cultures come into contact. Just think about the early nineteenth-century contact between American English and Spanish speakers in what would become the state of California. Although it absorbed some Spanish vocabulary due to the contact between the two cultures, American English became the dominant language as American English users came to hold political, economic, and social power, and Spanish and Spanish speakers held more subordinate positions.

The relationship between power and language in American school systems came to national attention in 1979, when African American parents successfully sued the Ann Arbor, MI School District Board, claiming that their children's language use had led to discrimination by the schools, which in turn resulted in the children receiving an inferior education. Research has since shown the truth behind this charge. The fact that cultures privilege one kind of language over another means that speakers of the less privileged language are frequently judged to be less intelligent than those who speak the privileged language. A child's use of a minority language variety can lower the quality of his or her education (Labov 1972).

Exercise 2.4

On your own, brainstorm about other situations, either in the past or in your daily interactions, where you see evidence of the relationship between language and power. To get started, consider some of the different roles you play throughout the course of your daily life: student, employee, child, parent, consumer, and so on. How are power relations displayed through language in your interactions with others? Be prepared to talk about these situations in class.

Given its place of privilege, why doesn't every American choose to use SAE all the time? Why do so many varieties of American English exist? To answer these questions, think once again about the relationship between language and identity. We learn our first language as very young children from our families and caregivers in our homes. Deliberately choosing another language may seem like a betrayal of the others in our first language community, like we're trying to be "better" than they are or are trying to assume a new identity. Many people are unwilling or unable to make such a choice. Instead, they might move back and forth between language varieties as they change language communities. So, for example, a speaker who uses a regional variation with a family member might then use SAE at school or with a boss. In this way speakers can negotiate among different language communities. The fact that American English users change their language depending on the community demonstrates that English is not one single language but consists of varieties. And the interaction between varieties means that each is constantly influencing the other. No living language exists in a vacuum.

We've been focusing on American English as it has developed over time within the boundaries of the United States. But these same principles of prolonged language contact and language privileging shape usage on the global level as well. Because American English is now used in countries around the world, part of its identity in the twenty-first century is as a global language. Let's now consider language change and identity on the international level.

American English as a global language

Obviously the wide use of both British and American English around the world attests to the power that English users have held in the past and continue to hold in the present. A country's history as a colony of England or the United States might mean that government agencies, law courts, and even schools continue working in English. Today, roughly one-fourth of the world's population uses some variety of English, as shown in Figure 2.8. And American English holds as much or more influence as British English in many parts of the world because the United States has become so powerful in terms of political, economic, and cultural forces. Americans control most of the world's television programming, and American English is the language of Hollywood, the computer industry, business, air traffic control, and the scientific community. For these reasons, American English can truly be called a global language: it's used around the world. Just as we see variations in American English usage in the

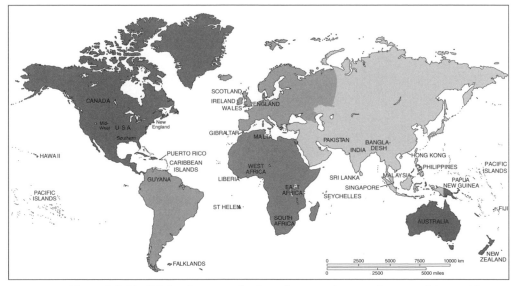

Figure 2.8 *English has become a dominant language in countries around the world*

United States, though, we note its many varieties elsewhere in the world. Let's now consider the forces at work in shaping American English as a global language.

One of the primary factors affecting a global language is the reason people have for using it. In many countries, such as Australia, English is learned as a **first**, or native, **language**. Roughly 400 million people around the world have English as their first language. In other countries it's learned as a **second language**, in addition to an individual's native language, because it is widely used in business, education, and/or political contexts. Some estimate that over 1 billion individuals around the world use English as a second language. These numbers mean that, currently, English is probably the most widely spoken language in the world, but only because of its use as a second language. In other words, global users rely on English for specific, immediate purposes, rather than learning and using any sort of standardized American or British English. In fact, a recent study by David Graddol (2004) suggests that the use of English as a first language is actually declining, down from 9 percent of the world's population in the mid twentieth century to about 5 percent by 2050 (see Table 2.1).

Table 2.1 *Projected changes in global language communities: 1995–2050 (after Graddol 2004)*

Top ten global language communities of native speakers in 1995	Number of native speakers (in millions)	Top ten global language communities of native speakers aged 15–24 in 2050	Number of native speakers (in millions)
Chinese	1,113	Chinese	166
English	372	Hindi/Urdu	74
Hindi/Urdu	316	Arabic	72
Spanish	304	English	65
Arabic	201	Spanish	63
Portuguese	165	Portuguese	33
Russian	155	Bengali	32
Bengali	125	Russian	15
Japanese	123	Japanese	11
German	102	Malay	10

Obviously English is still being privileged on the international level because it's important enough to be learned as a second language, but it's no longer increasing as a first language. And because a second language has a different purpose from that of a first language, users might not need as thorough a vocabulary or range of sentence structures as native speakers do. In addition, second languages are used differently from first languages. Individuals using English as a second language typically alternate between their two languages, depending on their particular circumstances. Such close contact between two languages enables the one to exert a strong influence on the other, with users importing lexical elements in the knowledge that others will easily understand them. This is creating new varieties of English fairly quickly. In Japlish, for example, English words are used along with Japanese words, syntax, and even pronunciation. Such mixtures can be difficult to understand for people who don't use both Japanese and English, yet its widespread use in Japan shows that it's a successful language of communication.

Exercise 2.5

Speakers who use American English as their first language tend to be scornful of international Englishes such as Japlish, regarding them as corrupt imitations rather than "real" languages, much the same attitude that British English speakers have had about American English. To give you an idea of how widespread they are, here are a few more examples of these international Englishes:

Taglish – Philippines (Tagalog and English)
Chinglish – China, Hong Kong, Taiwan (Chinese and English)
Hindish – India (Hindi and English)
Konglish – Korea (Korean and English)
Swenglish – Sweden (Swedish and English)
Franglais – France (French and English)

Make a list of pros and cons, reasons why such international Englishes have a positive purpose, as well as reasons why they might be harmful.

The fact that English is so widespread leads some linguists to speculate on the future development of a new variety, World English. They recognize that satellite broadcasting, travel, world markets, multinational corporations, and other established international organizations will encourage a core of vocabulary, grammar, spelling, and pronunciation to develop, enabling successful communication in English anywhere in the world by any speaker of English. And many times business communications take place in English between non-native English speakers. For example, a Japanese importer might conduct negotiations with an Argentinian exporter in English, even though neither speaks English as a first language. Yet a uniform global English that would simplify such transactions doesn't currently exist. Even the Englishes spoken as first languages differ enough to cause communication breakdowns. As an illustration, imagine that your boss leaves you a message to meet with him at *half nine* to discuss your request for a promotion. If you're American, you probably don't whether

Globish is a 1,500-word, extremely simplified variety of English created specifically for the business world. Its creator, Jean-Paul Nerrière, was an IBM vice president in International Marketing. Nerrière, whose first language is French, used English in professional conferences and meetings. He noticed that meeting with non-native English speakers, such as Koreans and Japanese, was much more efficient than meeting with native English users. Even though their purpose was to conduct business, native English users wouldn't use the basic English adopted by their peers, instead using vocabulary and phrasing too complicated for their international peers to comprehend easily. So after retiring from IBM he designed *Globish*, intended only for international communications, not to convey the culture of a national language: www.globish.com

this means 8:30 or 9:30, while if you're British, you know that your boss will be expecting you at 9:30. Using a World English would minimize the potential for such conflicts.

Culturally, though, the desire for national identity might oppose the development of an internationally uniform variety of World English. Each country has its own natural and cultural features, each with its own lexicon for describing these unique aspects. And each nation has its own desire for independence and autonomy. Accepting a World English might mean giving up unique aspects of a nation's English language usage.

Exercise 2.6

Write about the positives and negatives of a single, uniform World English. Why would it be useful to be able to communicate anywhere in the world in one language? What would native language speakers have to give up or change in order for a world language to come into existence?

How will these international tensions be resolved? David Crystal (2003) suggests a few possibilities. If all the major international institutions adopted the same variety of English, that variety would automatically become the World English. Or a new variety could be intentionally created and put into use to serve this specific purpose of functioning as the World English. Crystal even suggests that English speakers of the future may find themselves moving between a regional English, such as southern American English, a national English, such as American English, and World English, comfortable in all three varieties. Other researchers disagree with Crystal's suggestion, finding quite optimistic the idea that English could transcend its history and belong to the entire world without privileging one culture over another. As we've discussed in this chapter, language almost always implies power, and therefore some forms of English are bound to be privileged over others.

Now that you're more knowledgeable about American English, its history and its future, you're ready to examine its elements. Chapter 3 begins this examination by considering the words of English.

Chapter summary

This chapter has defined **American English** as a language with its roots in Britain, which has adapted over time to fit the needs of its speakers in the United States. The linguistic forces created by immigration, bringing contact between diverse cultures and their languages, have been particularly significant in shaping American English. You have learned that there are many **varieties** of American English and that some of these, typically the language of the socially or politically empowered, are **privileged** over others. And you've thought about how English is used in countries around the world.

Critical Thinking exercises

1.   Fighting over language? Because the history and culture of Quebec are more closely connected with the French than with the British, during the 1960s and early 1970s the political factions supporting the sovereignty of Quebec resented the legal privileging of English and English users in their province. Bombings, strikes, and even kidnappings and the declaration of martial law marked the height of this discord. In 1977, the Charter of the French Language was enacted, which not only declared French the official language of Quebec but also identified the legal rights of both French and English users to prevent future discrimination. Today, examining this cultural conflict helps us identify some of the same positions in other language conflicts around the world. Working with several classmates, explore the history of Quebec's language law. You'll find the CBC's archive of radio and TV news broadcasts, *Fighting Words*, particularly useful in understanding the attitudes of all sides in the debate. Once you understand the issues involved in this particular conflict from the past, think about the current growth of English as a global language. Do the non-English peoples who are beginning to use English as a second language for economic reasons risk dealing with the same problems that the citizens of Quebec faced, or are the situations completely different? Be prepared to take a position.

2.   Those of you who intend to pursue teaching careers after you complete college may very well encounter classrooms in which there is a range of socioeconomic, ethnic, foreign, and other language varieties. You have learned in this chapter that language and identity are closely interconnected, and so working with students who use diverse American English varieties will take care and sensitivity. To anticipate how you might handle a diverse classroom, consider now your own attitudes toward the range of existing varieties, including SAE. How might these attitudes come into play in the ways in which you present material, plan lessons, manage classroom behavior, and all the other work you would do as a teacher? Next, think about the populations you will serve: the students, parents, principal, and community at large. What might be their attitudes toward language and language teaching? Summarize your ideas in an exploratory essay of one or two pages that shows you have considered a range of opinions.

3.   Pay attention to world news reports, making special note of any news items that deal with English used internationally. Although these stories might not deal directly with language, any sort of

interaction will obviously require its use. You might find relevant news stories dealing with business, technology, science, politics, even the media itself. Quickly summarize the news items. Then analyze them carefully in terms of contacts between cultures and language and/or the privileging of one language over another. Be able to explain to the class how your news stories illustrate either or both of these two concepts.

Hot Topic: Politically correct language and the Sapir–Whorf hypothesis

As you are learning, language and culture are closely intertwined. If we define culture as a set of behaviors, accepted practices, and beliefs, then we can say that defining American English means, to a large extent, defining American culture. While most people understand the notion that language reflects our cultural beliefs, some scholars have argued that language not only reflects but also determines to some extent how we think about things, a hypothesis called **linguistic relativity**. This belief in the power of language to shape one's reality, sometimes called the Sapir–Whorf hypothesis, was introduced by linguist Edward Sapir in the 1930s, and then later enlarged upon by his student, Benjamin Whorf. Whorf compared some Native American languages and cultures with English-speaking cultures and hypothesized that cultural perspectives were in large part determined by their language. In one example, he noted that western, English-speaking cultures, like the United States, regard time in a linear fashion, a fact underscored by the English verb tense system of future, present, and past. In contrast, the Native American Hopi culture conceives of time as continual, regarding the past and future as ever a part of the present. In the Hopi language there are no past or future tenses. Whorf suggested that the languages of these two cultures produced the distinctions between their speakers' concepts of time.

Since Whorf's time, linguists have contested his hypothesis, questioning his translations of Native American languages, as well as his analysis of their grammars. And, more recently, cognitive linguists, who study the processes of language in the brain, argue that language and thought are not the same thing at all, but that we think in a "language" of thought that is different from any one language we speak. Despite these disagreements with Whorf's ideas and methodology, though, most contemporary linguists do accept a weaker form of the Sapir–Whorf hypothesis, which recognizes that we perceive the world in certain ways because of the way that our language orders ideas. If we live in a world, for example, in which electronic technology is at our fingertips, then we are bound to have many words and phrases in our vocabularies to refer to these items. And this same language may appear in contexts that are decidedly un-technological: have you ever used phrases such as *The team is all charged up*, *The* <u>interface</u> *between the high school and college students has improved*, and so on? While language does not confine or limit our thoughts, then, it does influence how we think about things and how we express ourselves.

Politically correct language, the practice of replacing negative terminology with more emotionally neutral language, illustrates a current application of linguistic relativism in American culture. One purpose behind using politically correct language is to shape the general public's attitudes toward people who have been disregarded or treated negatively in the past. For example, a recent usage guide put out for reporters and news people by a media group suggests that reporters use descriptors such as *differently abled*, *physically challenged*, and *physically disabled*. It explains that even though individuals might refer to themselves as *gimpies* or *crips*, such terms carry negative judgments and so should not be used in objective reports.

For this assignment, look at the following list of some politically correct terms and consider their invention – why did these words enter into American English? What made them go out again? See if you can create a history of some of the words – what earlier forms were used to describe the same group or thing? Think of possible reasons for the changes that have come about in the ways in which groups have been identified. Then decide for each word whether ideas and/or attitudes about that group or thing might have been changed because of the language. Write up your research and conclusions in a paper to be handed in to your instructor.

1.   Orientals
2.   mentally challenged
3.   colored people
4.   people of color
5.   the poor
6.   physically challenged
7.   ladies
8.   queer

Learn more about it

American English

Algeo, J. 2001, "External history," in John Algeo (ed.), *The Cambridge history of the English language*, vol. VI: English in North America, Cambridge: Cambridge University Press, pp. 1–58.
Algeo examines the development of American English by tracing the influence of historical and cultural events on the language.

Dillard, J. L. (ed.) 1980, *Perspectives on American English*, The Hague: Mouton De Gruyter.

This collection of essays examines the social and historical contexts for the development of American English and its many varieties.

MacNeil/Lehrer Productions 2005, *Do you speak American?* [Television documentary], New York: Thirteen/WNET.

This public television documentary examines the dynamic state of American English; its accompanying website provides helpful explanations and resources for further study: www.pbs.org/speak/

Language and power

Milroy, J. and Milroy, L. 1991, *Authority in language: Investigating language prescription and standardization*, 2nd edition, London: Routledge.

Milroy and Milroy examine judgments about language and the consequences of such judgments in society and in the daily lives of individuals.

Schmidt, R. 2000, *Language policy and identity politics in the United States*, Philadelphia: Temple University Press.

Schmidt compares and contrasts two different approaches toward language policy in the United States: language assimilation and language pluralism.

Thomas, L., Wareing, S., Singh, I., Peccel, J., Thornborrow, J., and Jones, J. 2004, *Language, society, and power*, 2nd edition, London: Routledge.

This wide-ranging text discusses in a number of contexts the ways in which language functions and influences thought.

English as a global language

Crystal, D. 2003, *English as a global language*, 2nd edition, Cambridge: Cambridge University Press.

This brief text, written for the general public, provides an overview of how English came to be used around the globe, as well as speculation about its role in the future.

Graddol, D. 2004, "The future of language," *Science* 303:1,329–1,331.

In this article, Graddol examines the rapid changes affecting the world's languages, pointing out that English may not be the dominant language of the future.

3 American English morphology

Key terms

Lexical meaning
Grammatical function
Morpheme
Root
Stem
Affix
Prefix
Suffix
Inflectional morpheme
Derivational morpheme
Lexicon
Etymology
Loanword
Synonym
Coined words
Compound
Initialism
Acronym
Clipped word
Back formation
Eponymy
Blend

Overview

Chapter 3 examines the basic structure of American English words. You will learn about the conventions American English speakers follow to combine meaningful elements together into words. These building blocks of the American English language system allow speakers to communicate effectively, even when conveying complex information. The chapter also explores how words come into language. What are the many ways in which the wordbank of American English has expanded or contracted through time? Finally, the Hot

Topic asks you to examine the language of advertising as you explore the effects of product naming.

Introduction

As you know from Chapter 1, all native speakers of a language have an inherent knowledge of its structure and usage. To see how this works for American English, let's imagine a group of friends who are big fans of Bruce Lee, the Kung Fu hero of many Hollywood movies. One day these friends are sitting around when one of them, John, does a couple of fake karate moves aimed at the dog. If another friend yelled out, "John's Bruce Lee'd Fido!" everyone present would know what was meant: John has performed some Bruce Lee-like moves at the dog (see Figure 3.1). The friend who said this has created a new word, perhaps one that will never be used again, but one that is immediately understood, given the communicative competence of native speakers. Notice that no one had to ask what the speaker meant. Instead, the new sentence was easily comprehended through complex, unconscious, language processes. Of course, the ability to produce this unique word also came from communicative competence.

Let's now look closely at this newly coined word to see which rules of English word construction the speaker unconsciously employed. While we'll explain the terms presented here in more technical detail later in this chapter, for right now we'll just examine the speaker's communicative competence at work. Obviously the sentence contains a new verb: "Bruce Lee'd." Which conventions about forming English verbs were followed to arrive at this new term?

Words in English are categorized depending on their forms and functions. These word categories, or parts of speech, include those terms familiar to many, such as nouns, verbs, adjectives, prepositions, and so on. In turning the proper noun (a name designating a unique thing or entity), "Bruce Lee," into a verb

Figure 3.1 *Giving a* Bruce Lee

Table 3.1 *Lexical vs. grammatical word categories*

Lexical categories	Examples	Grammatical categories	Examples
Noun	Mousepad	Determiner	This
	Women		The
	Lawn		That
	Building		A
Verb	Carry	Preposition	To
	Shred		At
	Listen		For
	Laugh		In
Adjective	Large	Conjunction	And
	Soft		But
	Blurry		Or
	Careless		Nor
Adverb	Easily	Comparative	Better
	Slowly		More
	Repeatedly		Less
	Well		Worse

(typically the word or phrase expressing the action of a sentence), the speaker has followed the conventions for English verb formation. If we analyze the phrase, we see that she's employed the present perfect tense, one of the tenses associated with verbs. The present perfect tense is formed with the auxiliary *has* (contracted here to *'s*) plus the past participle ending *-ed* on the verb. Although the words *Bruce Lee'd* are original when used as a verb, they were understood by the group because the language follows the rules for English verb formation.

Note that while a new verb was created in the sentence above, the word endings are familiar to us. This reveals something else about language: words contain various elements that carry meanings. Linguists have classified these elements into two categories: **lexical** elements, which carry an identifiable meaning or express the content of what we wish to communicate, and **grammatical** elements, which indicate how words function in a sentence when combined with others (see Table 3.1). Let's now look more closely at both kinds of elements.

Word structure of contemporary American English

Morphology

Definition of morphemes

In attempting to describe the word structures of a language – always already intuitively known by a native speaker – linguists usually break down the language into its smallest linguistically significant parts. They have proposed that all words contain at least one **morpheme**, a minimal unit of linguistic meaning. Just like the categories we've seen for words, morphemes can be lexical, having an identifiable meaning, or they can be grammatical, indicating how morphemes in a word or sentence are related to one another.

The sentence below contains both lexical and grammatical morphemes:

The teacher previewed the test material in the help sessions.

In this sentence, the morphemes *teach, -er, pre-, view, test, material, help* and *session*, are lexical, that is, each one has a particular meaning. We know the different meanings of *teach, view, test, material, help*, and *session* respectively; the lexical morpheme, *-er* on *teacher* in this case, indicates the person who does the act of teaching, and the lexical morpheme *pre-* on *view* indicates when or in what manner the material was viewed.

The other morphemes in the sentence, *the, -ed, in,* and *-s*, are grammatical morphemes. These morphemes give information about grammatical function by indicating the relationships between lexical morphemes: the article *the* announces that a noun or noun phrase will follow; the verb ending *-ed* indicates the tense of the verb, thus indicating the time in which the subject performed the action of the verb; the preposition *in* connects the verb *previewed* to the place where the action took place; and the *-s* on the end of *sessions* indicates plurality or more than one of whatever noun comes before it.

Classification of morphemes

Other distinctions are also made among morphemes. For instance, all morphemes can be classified according to whether they are free or bound, in other words whether they can stand alone or must be attached to another morpheme to have linguistic meaning. The group of free morphemes includes lexical morphemes and thus comprises most of the nouns and verbs in English – *school, pupil, book, teach, study, write*, and so on. Many free morphemes are also called **roots**. Roots are morphemes that cannot be analyzed further into smaller units of linguistic meaning. A root such as *boy*, for instance, cannot be further broken down into shorter morphemes, and so it can stand alone. The free morpheme *boy*, however, can have other morphemes attached to it, such as we see in the words *boys, boyfriend, boyish*, and so on. When a root has other morphemes attached, then we refer to the root as a **stem** (see Table 3.2). Notice that a word can be made up of two free morphemes, as in the word *boyfriend* above, or can consist of a free and a bound morpheme, as in the word *boyish*.

Other free morphemes are grammatical, such as prepositions like *in, at*, or *on*, determiners like *the* or *a*, and conjunctions like *since* or *and*. These morphemes express grammatical relationships between other lexical morphemes in a sentence.

In contrast to free morphemes, bound morphemes must be attached to another morpheme. The bound morphemes in English include all of the bound roots, roots that cannot stand on their own, and all of the affixes. **Affixes** are

Table 3.2 *Adding different stems to the same root*

Morpheme classification	Example	Part of speech
Root	Boy	Noun
Stem	Boy + ish	Adjective
Stem	Boyfriend	Compound noun

comprised of **prefixes**, morphemes added to the beginning of a root, and **suffixes**, morphemes added to the ending of a root. Affixes can be attached to both bound and free roots.

Affixes can be both lexical and grammatical bound morphemes. Lexical affixes change the meaning of the root to which they are attached, seen, for example, in the words *dis-please* or *pre-view*. Affixes that solely indicate relationships between morphemes, such as the *-ed* on past tense verbs, are grammatical morphemes. Affixes are important building blocks of the English language. In the following section we will discuss some of their special attributes.

> Many word games depend upon the player's knowledge of affixes: *Words in a Word* (finding other words in one word); *Word Morph* (forming one word from another by changing only one letter); and *Word Jumbles* (unscrambling letters to form words). (See Figure 3.2.)

Unscramble the following words, all having to do with protection:

tysafe	venpretion	tyicurse
fyforingti	ableimmeper	fensede

Figure 3.2 *Example of a word jumble*

Affixes: Inflectional and derivational morphemes For purposes of study, linguists have classified English affixes as either **inflectional** or **derivational morphemes**. All prefixes are derivational morphemes, while the group of suffixes has been divided into both inflectional and derivational morphemes. Linguists have made the distinction between inflectional and derivational affixes because they recognize that these morphemes act in different ways when joined to others. Let's first consider inflectional morphemes.

You've seen in the previous discussion that grammatical morphemes provide information about both the word functions and the relationships of morphemes in a sentence. **Inflectional suffixes** are all grammatical morphemes because they provide information about grammatical functions, as Box 3.1 illustrates.

Inflectional morphemes are always suffixes in English. They only carry grammatical meaning, such as number or tense, by indicating how words connect to each other. Inflectional morphemes never change the basic meaning or the word category of a word. And remember that English only has eight inflectional morphemes.

Box 3.1 Inflectional morphemes

In English there are eight inflectional suffixes:

1. *plural marker -s*
    book, book*s*
2. *possessive marker 's*
    baby, baby*'s* cry
3. *third person singular marker -s*
    I take
    you take
    he/she/it take*s*
4. *past tense marker -ed*
    we enter
    we enter*ed*
5. *part participle marker -ed or -en*
    we wait
    we have wait*ed*
6. *progressive marker -ing*
    you make
    you are mak*ing*
7. *comparative marker -er*
    hard
    hard*er*
8. *superlative marker -est*
    smooth
    smooth*est*

Notice that these inflectional morphemes are carrying out grammatical functions such as indicating tense (*-ed, -ing*), number (*-s*), possession (*'s*), or comparison (*-er*). In and of themselves they have no meaning, but their importance is that they indicate relationships between morphemes in a sentence: *Susan is taller than Jared.* *He judged the art show last week.*

Derivational morphemes differ from inflectional morphemes because they may change the word category, as well as the meaning, of a word. For instance, when the lexical morpheme *-er* is attached to the verb root *play*, the word changes word categories from a verb to the noun *player*. The meaning also changes as well, from an action to an actor. Note that not all additions of derivational morphemes cause changes in word categories. Here are some that do not: *dis* + *like* (verb to verb); *prince* + *ess* (noun to noun); *yellow* + *ish* (adjective to adjective).

Derivational morphemes are a very important part of our language because they foster our linguistic creativity, allowing us to derive words from our mental **lexicon**, our mental inventory of morphemes. The same morpheme *-er* from *player* above can be attached to many roots to create new words, for example, *writ-er*, *sew-er*, *announc-er*, *produc-er*, *design-er*, and so on. Derivational morphemes are part of our language's structural rules for word formation: suffixes and prefixes can be added onto roots to give additional meaning to a root.

The group of derivational morphemes is large, and potentially infinite, given that new words are coming into our language every day and many of these words are made up of derivational morphemes. At the same time, their application may be limited. Think for example of the derivational morpheme *-tex* indicating a type of fibrous material. How many words can you think of with this morpheme? *Gore-tex*,[TM] *Cordtex*,[TM] and maybe just a few more, which are also brand names. The derivational morpheme *-tex* is not productive, that is, it does not combine with many other morphemes to produce words. Its range is limited.

Other derivational morphemes are very productive because they can be used to create a large number of words. Consider, for instance, the *-al* on many adjectives: *manual*, *topical*, *final*, *patriarchal*, *subliminal*; the *-ist* on nouns: *pianist*, *artist*, *anarchist*, *hypnotist*; and the *-ify* on many verbs: *qualify*, *pacify*, *modify*, *amplify*, *horrify*, and maybe even some seen in popular writing but not yet accepted into standard dictionaries: *countrify*? *cozify*? Box 3.2 analyzes the use of other derivational morphemes.

Box 3.2 Derivational morphemes

Derivational morphemes may be either prefixes or suffixes in English. They change the root word's meaning and may also change its grammatical category. The examples of words in Figure 3.3 demonstrate the differences between derivational and inflectional suffixes. In examples 1 and 2, the bolded suffixes are inflectional. Notice that these suffixes change the stem's grammatical relation to other words in the sentence, but not the stem's category. That is, the stem *sign* is a noun and remains a noun when the plural *-s* or the possessive *-'s* is attached; the stem *act* is a verb and remains a verb when the present continuous ending *-ing* or the past tense ending *-ed* is added. In contrast, in examples 3 and 4 the bolded derivational suffixes change the categories of the stems: *-ify* added to *sign* changes the word from a noun to a verb; the addition of *-cation* onto the verb then changes it back into a noun; *-or* on *act* changes the stem from a verb to a noun. The same change happens when we add *-ion* to the stem.

1. sign   sign**s**   sign**'s**

2. act   act**ing**   act**ed**

3. sign   sign**ify**   signifi**cation**

4. act   act**or**   act**ion**

Figure 3.3 *The difference between derivational and inflectional suffixes*

Exercise 3.1

A. Divide the following words into morphemes where possible. Identify them as free or bound, and as inflectional or derivational. Explain your classifications.

1.	biology
2.	heeded
3.	careful
4.	transfigure
5.	carrying
6.	rude
7.	motivation
8.	modernize
9.	unhappily
10.	boys'

B. Consider the following words of a made-up language and identify all of its morphemes, both lexical and grammatical. You should have a total of 11. Once you've identified the morphemes, write out the rules of word formation for this language.

seebo	"house"	sento	"boy"
aseebo	"houses"	memko	"mother"
pokimbo	"church"	merko	"sister"
apokimbo	"churches"	furato	"king"
tanto	"husband"	furako	"queen"
atanto	"husbands"	furasento	"prince"

Translate the following English words into this made-up language:

princess
mothers
girl

As you now know, morphemes are the building blocks of words. Our study of morphemes helps us to understand how words are formed, and how words come into our language. Let's now look at the various word formation processes at work in American English.

Word histories

Linguists who study a language's lexicon attempt to identify each word's **etymology**, that is, its origin and history. The study of word etymologies reveals that our lexicon, like our grammar, is constantly changing. New words are coming into the language all the time as other words drop out. Historically, the very first English spoken was the Germanic language brought by the Angle, Saxon, and Jute invaders when they entered England in the fifth century CE. The longer these speakers and their descendants remained separated from other Germanic speakers on the European continent, the more dissimilar their vocabularies grew. Even though the lexicon of the very first generation of English speakers varied little from that of its Germanic parents, it still possessed some differences. After all, life in England was different from life on the continent in the geography, the resources available for daily living, and the political and social climate; new things needed to be expressed by new words. So from the very beginning, the English lexicon began to differ from its mother tongue.

American English has developed along a similar pattern. It started with the English spoken by the first colonists and then immediately began adding new words to describe new ideas, new practices, and new trends. Each age, to paraphrase Ralph Waldo Emerson, must write its own words, that is, each generation typically can be associated with a language all its own. We can see this fact by looking at changes in the American English lexicon that have occurred in the last century. The current baby-boomer generation (those over 50) might recall having used the words *groovy*, *cop out*, and *hip*. For the boomers' parents' generation, now outdated words might include *copacetic*, *clamdiggers*, and *doll* (meaning a pretty girl). And for that generation's parents? Perhaps the word *cheaters*, used to describe a pair of glasses, or a *sinker* (another name for a doughnut), and surely many other words that for a variety of reasons have passed out of the language. You've probably seen in your own lifetime several words that have already entered and exited daily use.

Exercise 3.2

Think of words that you use or that you've heard used today that did not exist perhaps five, ten, or twenty years ago. Where did these words come from? Which ones might be likely to remain in use in the future? Perhaps looking at magazines from previous years might help you with this task. Write down the words you've discovered and compare your findings with those of your classmates.

In the exercise above you probably had no trouble identifying at least a few new words that have come into your language in your lifetime and perhaps others that have already passed out of use. These additions and deletions in such a short period illustrate how a lexicon is in a constant state of change. Now let's examine in a more detailed way how these changes come about.

Borrowings

Many words in English are borrowings, or **loanwords**, from other languages, adopted through frequent exposure to a foreign lexicon. Because such language contact might occur through trade, travel, media coverage, migration, or any number of other ways, these borrowings are called popular loanwords (see Figure 3.4).

Figure 3.4 *An example of two popular loanwords*

American English speakers *rendezvous* with their friends, wear *chic* clothing, dance the *salsa*, eat *sushi*, *nosh* on a *bagel*, go to the *bazaar*, *schuss* down the ski slopes, *shampoo* their hair, and do many other things that they describe with borrowed words. Think of a recent phenomenon in contemporary American society that was brought from another culture, and you probably will see many borrowings from that culture's language into English. The current popularity of Japanese cartoons in America, for instance, has introduced new terms such as *manga* (comic books), *anime* (Japanese animation), and *otaku* (obsessive fans of anime). (See Table 3.3.)

In many parts of the United States today American English and Spanish are in close contact with each other, due to the number of Hispanic immigrants who have entered the country. This increase in the number of Spanish loanwords and its effect on American English worries some Americans. Historically, though, English survived a much more extensive cultural contact when French became the privileged language in England after the Norman Conquest in 1066. Scholars estimate that French affected as much as 60 percent of the Anglo-Saxon lexicon. Chapter 4 will discuss these changes in more detail.

Scholarly loanwords enter our language for intellectual reasons. As writers and speakers, we may deliberately search for words in a foreign language that capture our ideas more precisely than anything in our native English. In addition, borrowed words can be easily understood by speakers of other languages. Scientists, for instance, frequently use Latin when naming new discoveries or inventions because it can be understood by an international audience. We see this practice in the naming of newly found elements, plants, stars, and other scientific discoveries. Words such as *abdomen* and *cancer* and others are all loanwords from Latin.

And when Latin does not contain a needed word, we are still able to use Latin morphemes to create a new word. New plant names, drug names, disease names, and other scientific names are formed by combining Latin morphemes, creating

Table 3.3 *American words borrowed from other cultures*

Borrowed word	Meaning in American English	Language borrowed from	Original meaning
Bagel	A ring-shaped roll that is boiled and then baked	Yiddish	A ring-shaped roll that is boiled and then baked
Pajamas	Loose garment for sleeping	Hindi	Leg-garment
Robot	A human-like mechanical device	Czech	Compulsory labor
Tycoon	A wealthy and powerful businessperson	Japanese	Great lord

words considered neo-Latin. *Microscope* illustrates this use of Latin loan morphemes. The prefix *micro-* means *small* and *scope* means *to see*, so *microscope* means *to see small things*. Even though the Romans themselves could not have used this word, because they did not have the technology, it entered modern American English through our borrowing of Latin morphemes. Another advantage of using Latin morphemes is that they are so productive. How many English words can you think of that begin with *micro-*? *bio-*? What other Latin morphemes are frequently used as either prefixes or suffixes in American English?

Advantages of loanwords

No matter their source, loanwords provide a means of constantly updating the lexicon. If American English could not adjust to reflect changes in knowledge and understanding, it would quickly limit users rather than serve them. For instance, consider the Anglo-Saxon word *brȳdlāc*, which translates to *bride* + *lock*, or *marriage*. This word went out of use after the Norman Conquest, when the French word *marriage* began appearing. Today we use the word *marriage* for a variety of combinations, not just for the union of a husband and wife. For example, in cooking we might say we marry basil and tomato in a sauce. Note that this usage gives a certain importance to each element, unlike *brȳdlāc*, which suggests a particular power arrangement between a husband and wife.

But borrowings do not always replace words. English sometimes retains both words, giving the English lexicon **synonyms**, terms that have the same or similar meaning. This practice creates a vocabulary with extremely broad and subtle variations. Let's consider some examples. The Anglo-Saxon word *doom* did not disappear from use when the French word *judgment* entered the language. Instead, *doom* came to mean a specific, negative judgment or a bad end. *Judgment* indicates an objective decision rather than a specific positive or negative decision. So the retention of both words enables us to convey implications about the type of decision rendered. The differences between the words

Table 3.4 *Examples of loanwords that allow subtle distinctions in meaning*

Originated in English	Borrowed from Latin	*Originated in English*	Borrowed from French
Lord	Master	*Sweat*	Perspire
Harbor	Port	*Lamb*	Mutton
Climb	Ascend	*Simmer*	Stew

house (Anglo-Saxon) and *mansion* (French) are undoubtedly familiar to you, even though both words refer to a dwelling for humans. English even contains some triplets, where words from French and from Latin have been added to their Anglo-Saxon counterpart: *holy/sacred/consecrated* and *fire/flame/conflagration* (see Table 3.4).

Although Norman French has had the most extensive influence on English to date, contact with other languages also added, and continues to add, a variety of loanwords to the language. The following exercise illustrates this point.

Exercise 3.3

Working with a small group, divide the following excerpt from Abraham Lincoln's *The Gettysburg Address* so that each individual is responsible for only a few words. Then research the etymology of each word and, if you can, identify the century in which the word first appeared in English. Focus on each root word, although you can also explore the etymologies of prefixes and suffixes if you wish. Was the word borrowed from another language? Maybe it passed through several languages on its way to English? You'll need to use a fairly comprehensive dictionary, such as the *Oxford English Dictionary* or the unabridged *American Heritage Dictionary*. You can also check for etymological dictionaries online. When you finish, combine the group's sections together so that you can examine the etymologies for the entire passage. Then consider the implications of your research. Do you see any patterns? Perhaps certain kinds of words all come from the same language? Or words came into use during the same century? Discuss your analysis with your group and prepare an oral report for the rest of the class.

> Four score and seven years ago, our fathers brought forth upon this continent a new nation, conceived in liberty, and dedicated to the proposition that all men are created equal. . .
>
> It is for us, the living, rather, to be dedicated here to the unfinished work which they who fought here have thus far so nobly advanced. It is rather for us to be here dedicated to the great task remaining before us. . . that from these honored dead we take increased devotion to that cause for which they gave the last full measure of devotion.   (Lincoln 1863)

Were you surprised by the origins of any of the words in this passage? Or by their age? One of the great strengths of American English is its flexibility: it easily incorporates new words and ideas.

Coined words

Some words that enter the English lexicon are newly **coined**, meaning that they are words that have never existed before and have been created to fulfill a new need. Many new product names are coined words, such as *Jello*, *Tums*, *Swiffer*, and *Windex*. Other new words come into the lexicon through new discoveries and inventions. Just look at a few recent additions to our everyday vocabulary: *Segway* (a two-wheeled electric propulsion system), *gardenburger* (a vegetarian patty), and *swoosh* (a trademarked logo). Note that newly coined words almost always follow the rules for English word formation; if they didn't, they would be hard to use and thus wouldn't enter into the popular lexicon.

Compounds

Many words have originated in English through **compounding**, which is the process of joining two or more words together to form a new word. Words like *milkshake*, *downsize*, *cross-trainer*, *mallrat* and so on have all been created by combining words. This characteristic of English existed when the language itself came into being about 1,600 years ago, when the first Germanic speakers landed on the island that would later become England. The opening lines of the Old English text *Beowulf*, for instance, demonstrate this practice of compounding words. A word found there, *ymbsittendra*, combines the words for *around* and *sitting* to make *neighboring people* (or those who are literally sitting around the place where we are). This compounding ability demonstrates in yet another way the great flexibility of the English lexicon.

Notice that compounds can consist of nouns, verbs, adjectives, or even prepositions. Notice also their various contemporary spellings: compounds typically start being written as two separate words, eventually become hyphenated, and finally become one word. The word *boldfaced* underwent this process: it was originally written *bold faced*, became *bold-faced*, and then finally became the form it is today.

Initialisms

Language users tend to abbreviate what they're saying for faster communication. One way they do this is by abbreviating things down to their initials. Consider how cumbersome it would be to have to state every time the Federal Bureau of Investigation instead of FBI, or the Young Men's Christian Association instead of YMCA. When a phrase is reduced to its initials and referred to by these, it is called an **initialism**, or alphabetic abbreviation. Like other parts of our language, initialisms go in and out of use, usually depending on the frequency with which the phrase is required. As an example, one of the cited reasons for the 2003 US initiation of war with Iraq was the fear that then Iraqi President, Saddam Hussein, had weapons of mass destruction. Because of the seriousness of this threat and the resulting war, the phrase *weapons of mass destruction* came to be used repeatedly by government officials, the media, and the general public. Finally, by the third month of engagement, an initialism had appeared, *WMD*, and there was now a convenient way to refer to this threat.

Computer technology has produced an explosion of new initialisms. In addition to the many technical terms that have been reduced to their initials, including *WWW* (*World Wide Web*), *URL* (*uniform resource locator*), and *HTML* (*hypertext markup language*), users have also developed a shorthand of initialisms that convey further information. These include *btw* (*by the way*), *lol* (*laughing out loud*), *faq* (*frequently asked questions*), *bbfn* (*bye-bye for now*), *imo* (*in my opinion*), and many more. We see that as technologies are developed to give us more ways to communicate quickly, we will find more ways to abbreviate our communications.

Acronyms

Like initialisms, **acronyms** are created to save time and cut down on awkwardness. Acronyms differ from initialisms, though, because they are pronounced as words created from the initial letter of each word in a phrase. Instead of saying United Nations International Children's Educational Fund, for example, we say UNICEF, instead of Acquired Immune Deficiency Syndrome we say AIDS. Their origins are often forgotten as acronyms become standard parts of the language. Few Americans probably recall that *radar* stands for *radio detecting and ranging* or that a *nimby* position represents a *not-in-my-backyard* stance. To be most effective, an acronym should have a strong link to the meaning or purpose of the group or thing it stands for. *MADD* (*Mothers Against Drunk Driving*) is highly effective, since it both indicates the group's name and expresses the sentiments of its members. Other effective acronyms include *GAS* (*Gentlemen Around Sixty* – a men's social club), *CARE* (*Cooperative for Assistance and Relief Everywhere, Inc.*), and *STOPP* (*Stop the Oppressive Power Plant*). As it did for initialisms, computer technology has contributed many acronyms to our language over the past twenty-five years, including *MUD* (*multi-user domain*), *DOS* (*disk operating system*), *RAM* (*random access memory*), and countless others.

Notice that both initialisms and acronyms require literacy. If someone cannot read or write English, and so has no idea of the spelling of the words being referred to, she will not be able to understand either an initialism or an acronym.

Clipped words

Just as we reduce words to initialisms or acronyms for ease in writing and pronunciation, so do we clip words. **Clipped words** are shortened forms of words, for example, *fridge* for *refrigerator*, *mums* for *chrysanthemums*, *cords* for *corduroys*, and so on. Often the clipped version has become so ingrained in our vocabulary that we forget its source: think of the words *exam* and *note*, which are shortened from *examination* and *notation*, respectively. Notice that clipped words don't change their part of speech, just their length.

Back formation

Some words come into English through mis-analysis of their morphological roots. This happens when native speakers create a word based on an assumption of the word's history that does not match the reality. Take for instance the word *televise*, which entered American English shortly after television became popular. Speakers coined this verb because of their intuitive familiarity with the common derivational process in English of forming nouns from verbs. Nouns such as *animation*, which originates from the verb *animate*, or *emancipation*, which comes from the verb *emancipate*, are examples. In this case, however, the word *television* was coined for this specific invention and was not derived from a verb form *televise*. But since the majority of American English speakers were unfamiliar with the true etymology of the noun, they easily created a verb form through their own creative competence with the language. Word creations such as *televise* are examples of **back formation**, when words come into the language through mis-analysis of their morphological histories. Back formation is an interesting language phenomenon because it demonstrates speakers' intuitive knowledge of word formation rules.

Eponymy

Many words have found their way into our language from people's names, or through **eponymy**, because the thing being referred to becomes associated with a specific name. Rudolf Diesel, German automotive engineer, was the inventor of what we now call the *diesel engine*. A teacher of the blind, Louis Braille, invented the *Braille* reading and writing system. The last name of the founder of Pennsylvania, William Penn, was combined with a Latin-derived word, *sylvan*, to form the compound proper noun *Pennsylvania*, or "Penn's woods." The word *spa* comes from the resort town of Spa, located in western Belgium. Proper names aren't just nouns but may become verbs, adjectives, and other parts of speech as well. To describe a day that's going badly, someone might say, "It's a Charlie Brown day," drawing upon the well-known cheerless days of the hapless *Peanuts* comic strip character.

Blended words

Words can also come into the language by the **blending** of the parts of two or more words. This is how we have *brunch* (*a meal coming between breakfast and lunch*), *motel* (*a convenient drive-in hotel*), *chortle* (*a combination of a chuckle and a snort*), and *telethon* (*a marathon telephone* *fundraising*). Notice that blends are different from compound words in that the parts usually cannot stand by themselves and so are not morphemes. The word, *ch-ort-le*, for instance, is made up of three parts that by themselves have no significant meaning. Other common blends include *fantabulous* (*fantastic* + *fabulous*), *travelogue* (*travel* + *monologue*), *guesstimate* (*guess* + *estimate*), and *Chunnel* (*Channel* + *tunnel*).

Exercise 3.4

Read the following list of words and identify how each has come into the English language. Choose from the ways discussed above, such as blending, initialisms, back formations, etc. To discover the origins of words you aren't sure of, refer to a dictionary.

1.   gym
2.   NASA
3.   hovercraft
4.   morph
5.   NAACP
6.   plaza
7.   info
8.   PIN
9.   sandwich
10.   brainwash

Chapter summary

This chapter explains the basic structuring principles of English words. **Morphemes**, the minimal units of linguistic meaning that make up words, may be bound or free and may be **roots**, **stems**, and **inflectional** or **derivational affix**(es). You have also learned many of the ways in which words come into the English language, such as through **blending**, **clipping**, **compounding**, and other means. The chapter has shown how many words in English are borrowed from other languages, usually due to immigration, occupation, revolution in technology, and other phenomena.

Critical Thinking exercises

1.   Among the 10,000 new additions to the latest *Merriam-Webster Collegiate Dictionary* is the term "McJob," defined as "low-paying and dead-end work." Discuss with a partner how the morpheme *Mc-* has been used here. Where did it come from? *Mc-* is potentially a very productive morpheme. What other words or morphemes could it be applied to? What would their meanings be? Think of

other morphemes that have recently entered our language and that have the capacity to be very productive. We'll start you off with a few: *e-*, as in *e-commerce, e-zines, email*; *-gate*, as in *Watergate, Irangate, Monicagate*; and *Reddi-*, as in *ReddiWhip*,™ *ReddiServe*,™ *ReddiMix*.™

2. One idea you might have thought about as you read this chapter is the fundamental linguistic concept that words are arbitrarily assigned meanings, that is, that words are solely signs and have no intrinsic relationship to the things that they represent (see Chapter 1 for discussion of this concept). A *table* could just as easily be called a *chair*, a *house*, or a *tree*, for example. This fact of arbitrariness allows people to name new things coming into our culture, an action that endows the namer with a certain power.

    Unless you're in a particular profession or occupy a certain prestigious position, you probably won't have occasion very often in your lifetime to name or give words to things, besides perhaps naming babies or pets, or maybe a business or company. Yet, there are some people in our society who do have the power to name, sometimes frequently. Converse with two or three other students in your class and come up with a list of people who have the power to name. You may wish to consider historical figures as well. In your discussion, consider the following questions: In our society, who has the power to name? Whom do we allow to make up words for us? In what situations does naming occur? What are the effects of allowing others to name things for us? Be prepared to share your ideas with the class.

3. How do new words enter your personal lexicon? Try keeping track of your own language for a few days and making a note of new words that you catch yourself using, either in writing or speech. Do they come from class? From TV? From friends? From reading? Then identify how these words came into existence: compounds? initialisms? borrowings? What does this say about the influences on your personal language? Compare notes with others in your class to see if you can identify any similarities. Does this say something about the factors that affect your age group's language? Write a short report explaining your analysis and conclusions.

Hot Topic: The language of advertising

Everywhere we go we are bombarded with advertisements urging us to buy particular products. The names of these products, intended to convey reliability or quality or exclusiveness or some other desirable trait, are carefully chosen by marketing specialists to encourage us to choose one brand over another. If a product is particularly successful, the brand name may enter the national lexicon as a new word. *Xerox* or *Kleenex*, for example, are brand names that have become generic nouns in American English. The subfield of linguistics that studies names and the naming process, onomastics, is an essential element of today's business world.

Product names, brand names, and company names all create a particular identity for a product. And advertising campaigns convey that identity to the consumer. Just think about the insurance and banking giant, the *Prudential* Company. That company name was not selected by chance but was chosen to convey certain characteristics that its owners wanted associated with their business.

Examining such names linguistically can reveal information about the product, its manufacturer, and even its intended market. For an example, let's consider just two brands of cell phones: T-Mobile and Nextel. Identifying the etymology of these names is not difficult. Both are blends, and both incorporate some clipped aspect of the word *telephone* in their name. Each also evokes a particular aspect of cell phones that makes it superior to older telephones. *T-Mobile* obviously emphasizes mobility, while *Nextel* emphasizes *next*, for *next generation* or *next new technology*. These names also indicate slightly different intended markets for these phones: T-Mobile would appeal to a slightly older community who want to be more mobile, while Nextel appeals to a slightly younger market who would be concerned with having the newest technology.

Work with a peer group to choose a product and then gather as many brand names for that product as you can. Identify the etymology of each name – eponym, initialism, clipping, etc. – and then analyze the identity conveyed by that name. Can you predict long-term success or failure based just on the name? Prepare to share your research with the rest of your class.

Learn more about it

Morphology

Bauer, L. 1983, *English word formation*, Cambridge: Cambridge University Press.
Bauer discusses theories of word formation and their relevance to other subfields of linguistics, drawing primarily upon materials in English as examples.

Carstairs-McCarthy, A. 2002, *An introduction to English morphology*, Edinburgh: Edinburgh University Press.
The author explores various approaches to understanding English word meaning and structure.

Matthews, P. H. 1991, *Morphology: An introduction to the theory of word structure*, 2nd edition, Cambridge: Cambridge University Press.

Applying a range of contemporary linguistic theories, Matthews examines how different languages construct words from morphemes.

Pinker, S. 1999, *Words and rules: The ingredients of language*, New York: Basic Books.
   Pinker explains how we convey meaning through words by using linguistic conventions and by making associations.

Etymology

Baugh, A. C. and Cable, T. 2001, *A history of the English language*, 5th edition, Upper Saddle River, NJ: Prentice Hall.
In an approachable, yet comprehensive, style, this introductory-level text explains the historical development of the English language within its context of cultural change.

Crystal, D. 1995, *The Cambridge encyclopedia of the English language*, Cambridge: Cambridge University Press.
This text is an encyclopedic survey of the English language, which includes several chapters on how words have entered the English lexicon.

4   The historical roots of American English

Synthetic language
Analytic language
External change
Internal change
Geographical isolation
Cognates
Danelaw
Inflectional decay
Leveling
Vernacular

Overview

      In this chapter, you will learn more about the forces that cause language change by tracing the historical roots of Modern American English. American English is a member of the Indo-European family of languages and so shares a history with languages such as German, French, and Greek. You'll discover that it has other elements in common with these languages as well. And you'll understand the process through which American English evolved from the Old English used in England 1,400 years ago to its structure today. The Hot Topic asks you to examine the history of gender-neutral pronouns in American English in order to contrast natural language change with deliberate attempts to impose new language usage.

Introduction

      What have you found to be the single most difficult aspect in your study of a foreign language? If you're like most American college students, you probably answered, "memorizing inflectional endings." European languages such as German, French, and Spanish rely on inflectional morphemes to indicate tense, person, number, and/or case for nouns, pronouns, verbs, adjectives, adverbs, and so on. This is different from contemporary American English, which, as you just learned in Chapter 3, has only eight inflectional morphemes. As a result of this difference, American students frequently find memorizing this aspect of a foreign language tedious and time-consuming.

> You're probably familiar with the term *case* from your studies of a second language, and so you know that it refers to the different roles that nouns can fulfill within a sentence, such as the subject or the object. Different languages have different numbers of cases. Finnish, for example, has fifteen cases, while Modern German has four. Old English had five: nominative, accusative, genitive, dative, and instrumental.

Obviously other languages besides European ones use inflections, but we specifically want you to think about the relationship between contemporary European languages and American English. These languages all have the same ancestor, Proto-Indo-European, used about 6,000 to 8,000 years ago in southeastern Europe. And as recently as 1,000 years ago, English was an inflected language, just like its European cousins. Why does such history matter today? It illustrates that all aspects of a living language, even the most basic elements of its morphological structure, are constantly changing. And understanding how and why this change took place in the past helps us understand the kinds of language change American English is undergoing now or might undergo in the future.

The following brief description of a ninth-century Viking raid from *The Anglo-Saxon Chronicle* illustrates the loss of inflections in English over time. The Old English line is in italics; the Modern English translation is immediately underneath each word:

þā	*Deniscan*	*āhton*	*wælstōwe*	*gewald.*
the	Danes	had	of the battlefield	control.

(after Thorpe [1861] 1964, p. 136)

You can immediately see that the word-for-word Modern English translation would seem odd to contemporary readers because the words appear out of order. Old English users relied on the inflections at the end of the words, rather than the word order, to tell them how the words linked together. Sometimes a Modern English translation requires several words to indicate the meaning of a single word of Old English. Here, for example, Old English uses the word *wælstōwe*, where the Modern English version uses *of the battlefield*. This difference occurs because of the loss of inflections. Separate prepositions and articles don't always appear in Old English: instead, the inflection carries their meaning.

Because Old English relied on inflectional morphemes to indicate relationships between words (see Chapter 3), linguists call it a **synthetic language**. In contrast, Modern American English is called an **analytic language** because it depends primarily on word order, rather than on inflections, to indicate word functions. So even though our modern language is a direct descendant of Old English, its structure differs dramatically. What happened? Why did a synthetic language become an analytic language?

You know from our discussion in Chapters 2 and 3 that the vocabulary of a language changes over time for a number of reasons, such as immigration, new inventions or discoveries, cultural contacts of different kinds, and so on. But you probably didn't realize that the structure of a language changes over time as well. Understanding this shift in the structure of the English language requires examining how **external change**, an action of human behavior, such as moving, trading, learning, etc., which changes a language community, ultimately creates **internal change** within the language itself. These internal changes occur within language structures such as word and sentence forms. Once we understand some of the external changes that caused the word and sentence structures of English to change in the past, we can identify similar forces at work on the word and sentence structures of contemporary American English.

To *synthesize* means to combine separate elements into a unified whole. So a *synthetic language* is one that combines roots and inflectional morphemes together into words. To *analyze* means to separate a whole into its basic elements, the exact opposite of *synthesis*. An *analytic language* uses several words together, which are then analyzed individually to reveal their relationship to one another. In a synthetic language such as Old English a single word standing alone can be identified by its function, such as the subject or object of a sentence, because of its inflection. In an analytic language, however, such as Modern American English a single word standing alone can only be identified by its word category: noun, verb, etc. A more specific function such as the subject or object of a sentence can only be indicated when several words are used together.

The history of English

Geographical and social isolation

Let's start at the very beginning of English language history, so that we can see how external actions of human behavior force language change. One of the most basic of these forces occurs when speakers of a language separate themselves from other members of their language community through a geographical move, resulting in **geographical isolation**. Geographical isolation creates change in language use because the day-to-day reinforcement of other language users disappears. In other words, geographical isolation causes social isolation from the original language community. And since the two groups no longer maintain close contact with each other, neither is aware of language changes the other is undergoing. The longer the communities remain geographically isolated from each other, the more different their languages will grow (see Figure 4.1).

Here's a hypothetical example. Imagine that you move a thousand miles away from your family and friends, and don't communicate with them for thirty years. When you finally come back for a visit, you'll still be able to understand members of your old language community, but your language will be subtly different from theirs. You'll probably pronounce a few words differently because you haven't been hearing the same speech sounds that your family and friends have been repeating to each other. You'll also have some different words in your vocabulary for new things such as animals or plants or geographical features

Figure 4.1 *Geographical barriers create isolation from other speakers*
(Credit: The Library of Congress, LC-USZ62–119941)

that don't exist where you grew up. And, of course, the language of your family will have changed as well to incorporate the new ideas, trends, and so on of their own geographical area. These sorts of changes might take place over the course of a lifetime. Now imagine that you move away and never return to your childhood home. Your children will learn the pronunciation and vocabulary that you teach them, and will also incorporate other variations into their language during their own lives. After a few generations, the language that your descendants speak will be quite different from that of the descendants of your childhood friends who never moved away. The following exercise asks you to consider the impact of geographical isolation on the development of American, British, and Australian English.

Exercise 4.1

Locate word and sentence structure differences between American English and British and/or Australian English. For example, you might look at magazines, newspapers, websites, even movies or TV shows. What sort of differences can you find? How might geographical isolation have helped these specific differences develop?

Proto-Indo-European

Just like many other contemporary European languages, English is considered a member of the Indo-European family of languages. The name indicates the geographical area this group of languages serves: India and

Europe. Based on historical study, linguists hypothe-size about the existence of a single ancestral language for the Indo-European family, called Proto-Indo-European. About 6,000–4,000 BCE in southeastern Europe, Proto-Indo-European speakers were probably nomadic, traveling around in search of the best food and living conditions they could find. Over time, groups of these speakers slowly separated from each other and from the geographical location of the larger group, either through choice or through chance, moving in different directions. As you've already seen, geographical isolation among members of a language community creates differences within that language, first in the vocabulary and then, over a longer period of time, in the structure. Over many generations, each of these Indo-European-speaking groups developed its own unique language as a result of initial geographical isolation from its mother tongue. Thus the individual branches of the Indo-European family came into exist-ence, named, like their parent, for the contemporary geographical region that they serve: Albanian, Arme-nian, Baltic, Celtic, Germanic, Greek, Indo-Iranian, Italic, and Slavic.

Some scholars hypothesize about languages and language families in existence before Proto-Indo-European, asking themselves how this ancient language itself developed and how it relates to the ancestral languages of the world's other ancient language families such as the Altaic family of Central and North-East Asia and the Uralic family of Northern and Eastern Europe. One line of research speculates that Proto-Indo-European may be one branch of an even older language family, called Nostratic, which included Proto-Altaic and Proto-Uralic. A few scholars are even trying to trace linguistic history back to an ultimate single language, Proto-World, from which all the world's language families have developed. Since no examples of languages this old have survived, definitively proving such a history for the Indo-European family of languages is unlikely to ever be accomplished.

English belongs to the Germanic branch of the Indo-European family of languages. Over time, as the Germanic speakers subdivided and became geographically isolated from each other, they became the ancestors of the speakers of modern-day Swedish, Norwegian, Icelandic, German, and English, as well as of many other languages. The families of Germanic speakers who crossed into what we now call England were the first speakers of the English language.

Cognates

You may be wondering how linguists and historians know that such vastly different languages as Russian and Spanish, for example, are related to each other. Table 4.1 provides a few examples of lexical similarity between old and modern European languages. As you can see, these words from different languages, called **cognates**, share similar forms and meanings. Cognates occur when languages share the same ancestral language; over time, these words have developed in differing ways from the ancestral words. A large number of lexical similarities like these are unlikely to occur from random chance, particularly if a system of similarities can be identified. Instead, they provide evidence of historical relationships among the ancestors of these modern languages. Box 4.1 illustrates some examples of cognates from the Indo-European family.

Box 4.1 Cognates from the Indo-European family

Compare the examples in Table 4.1 taken from different descendants of Proto-Indo-European. As you can see, this table follows a chronological progression across the page, from the most recent words on the left to the oldest words on the right. Since no written records from the Indo-European period survive, identifying the definitive ancestor of a particular word is impossible. So linguists have theorized a reconstruction of Indo-European based on similarities among its descendants. The asterisk symbol * before the Indo-European word in the column above indicates that it is a reconstruction rather than an actual recorded word from that language.

Table 4.1 *Indo-European cognates*

Modern English	Modern German	Old English	Latin	Greek	Indo-European
brother	*bruder*	*brōþor*	*frāter*	*phrātēr*	**bhrāter-*
name	*name*	*nama*	*nōmen*	*onoma*	**(o)nomen-*
wolf	*wolf*	*wulf*	*lupus*	*lukos*	**wlkwo-/wlpo-*

Exercise 4.2

Based on your own experience or exposure to European languages through study, friends, even television or film, identify cognates in other languages to add to the table above. For example, do you know the word for *brother* in Spanish or Italian? Or can you think of other cognates not included above, such as words for *mother* or *thank you*?

Then analyze your extended table for other sorts of relationships between languages. For instance, just with the few words listed above, you can see that Greek and Latin seem to be more closely aligned than English and Latin. Can you identify other groupings based on geography or culture or period? After you've completed your analysis, you might find visiting the interactive *Proto-Indo-European Demonstration and Exploration Website*, sponsored by the University of Texas at San Antonio, helpful in providing more evidence to support the conclusions you've already identified: www.colfa.utsa.edu/drinka/pie/pie.html

Geographical and social isolation are external changes, changes that take place outside the language itself. They force cultural changes, which, in turn, force internal, language changes. Other external factors have affected the development of English as well.

Language privileging

Another change that affects language occurs when one language becomes privileged over another. You learned this concept in Chapter 2; now we'll examine some historical examples of it so that you'll be able to recognize the implications for language due to these power relationships.

When Germanic-speaking tribes the Angles, Saxons, and Jutes moved into what we now call England, they moved into a land inhabited by speakers of non-Germanic languages, including Celtic and Latin (see Figure 4.2). These Germanic tribes were mercenaries, hired in 449 CE by the Celtic leader, Vortigern, to protect his people. Then, when the Germanic invaders saw how weak the Celts were, they decided to move in permanently. These invaders brought their native language with them, a descendent of Proto-Indo-European known as West Germanic. The moment when the Angles, Saxons, and Jutes began using Germanic in England marks the earliest form of English. The language that is spoken today in the twenty-first-century United States developed from this beginning in England approximately 1,550 years ago.

In 43 CE, several hundred years before the Germanic tribes arrived, the Romans had invaded and occupied Britain, dominating the native Celts. Because of the Romans' dominance, Latin became privileged over the Celtic language. However, because the Romans did not push the Celts out but instead cohabited Britain with them, the Celtic language and culture continued to survive. Then, in 410 CE, the Roman legions were officially recalled to defend the Roman Empire in Europe against the Huns. With the Roman withdrawal, the Celts were once again dominant, at least until the West Germanic tribes invaded.

Over the next hundred years or so, more and more groups of these Germanic tribes arrived, settling in slightly different areas and continually expanding the region of England under their control. Looking at the resolution of the conflict

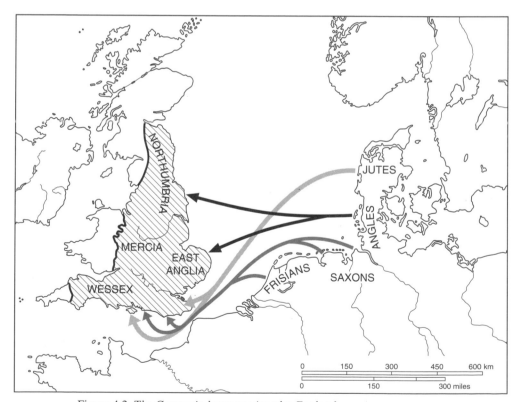

Figure 4.2 *The Germanic language invades England*

between the invading Germanic tribes and the native Celts illustrates once again that the language of the politically powerful is always privileged over the language of the subjugated. According to the *Oxford English Dictionary*, the earliest form of the word *England* is *Engla land*, referring to the land settled by the Angles. So when we use *England* and *English* today, we are privileging the Germanic invaders.

Other names we use when speaking about this historical period also reflect the power and success of the Germanic invaders in England, as well as our own tendency to privilege our contemporary perspective. We refer to these invaders and to their culture as *Anglo-Saxon*, from the names of two of the major Germanic tribes, the Angles and the Saxons, ignoring the contributions of other groups such as the Jutes. We call the language of the Anglo-Saxons *Old English*, reflecting our own twenty-first-century perception that it's the earliest recognizable form of our contemporary English language.

In *The Cambridge Encyclopedia of the English Language*, author David Crystal (1995) points out that our name for the descendants of the Celtic peoples that the Anglo-Saxons defeated over a thousand years ago is *Welsh*. It derives from the Anglo-Saxon name for the Celts: *wealas* or *foreigners*. When you remember that the Celts were the occupied and the Germanic speakers the invaders, you can immediately recognize how power affects language. Because the Anglo-Saxons were the dominant force, their word became privileged. *Wealas* became *Welsh* over time. If the Celts had been successful in defending their land against the Germanic invaders, we would surely not be calling them *foreigners* but instead a name of their own choosing.

Exercise 4.3

As you've just seen, the invaders or the persons in power get to rename places they inhabit. The study of names and naming, onomastics, includes the examination of all kinds of naming: place names, personal names, object names, and so on. Working on your own, spend a little time exploring this discipline by choosing a place name in the area where you attend school. You could choose a town name, a road name, the name of a geographical feature, such as a lake or a hill, a building name, any place name that catches your interest. Research this name through local or state histories, through interviews, or through online sites. You might find a foreign language dictionary helpful, as well as a local librarian. Do other places in the region or in the country share this name? Determine where the name came from, who actually applied this name to the place, and why this particular name has been retained.

Then, share your research with your classmates. Can you create categories of place names in your area? Do any patterns emerge? Whose language seems to have been the most privileged in this geographical location?

Old English

Over time, the language of the Angles, Saxons, and Jutes developed into what we now name *Old English*. The individual language varieties of Germanic originally spoken by the small invading groups gradually disappeared as each group lost its distinctive identity and recombined to form larger

You might be wondering how linguists can determine the number of language varieties in Old English. Well, writers today often indicate a variation by spelling a word as it is pronounced rather than by following the standardized spelling. So we might

Figure 4.3 *The four distinct varieties of Old English*

language communities. From surviving manuscripts, we can tell that eventually four distinct varieties of Old English developed: Kentish, spoken in the area settled by the Jutes, West Saxon, spoken in the area settled by the Saxons, and Northumbrian and Mercian, spoken in the areas settled by the Angles (see Figure 4.3). These variations remind us that, even though we speak about Old English as if it was one distinct entity, it wasn't. Just like American English today, it consisted of several varieties.

The following exercise asks you to consider American English history in comparison with what you now know about early British English history.

see a written sentence like *Pahk the cah* as an attempt to indicate what the sentence *Park the car* sounds like when said by a speaker from Boston. Writers before the fifteenth century spelled words as they sounded because the printing press, and the concept of spelling standardization, had not yet come into existence. So comparing/contrasting spellings for the same words in different manuscripts is one of the markers that historical linguists use in discovering sound differences and thus identifying varieties for languages like Old English that are no longer spoken.

Exercise 4.4

Reflect on what you know about American history, immigration, colonization, and so on. Do you see any similarities between the Germanic tribes' ultimate conquest of England and the European colonization of America, or are the two completely different? Where, and when, did immigration, travel and eventual occupation occur? How has that affected American English? Where and when have different cultures mixed? Did any of the native peoples have their language and cultural practices restricted or otherwise affected by contact with the European colonists? Can you identify some of the ways in which these external changes have affected internal changes in American English? Be prepared to discuss your observations in class.

Once Old English became geographically fixed in England and thus isolated from other languages spoken on the European continent, we see another basic force at work, changing the language. As you remember from our earlier discussion of American English in Chapter 2, prolonged language contact occurs when speakers of two or more languages interact with each other for an extended period of time. Prolonged contact always causes a culture, and a language, to change.

This sort of change took place through three different types of contact during the Old English period. Old English first came into prolonged contact with another language when Roman Catholic missionaries brought Latin with them to Britain. Later, Scandinavian invaders introduced Old Norse. In 1066 the Norman Conquest forced contact with Norman French.

Prolonged language contact

Latin In 597 CE, St. Augustine led a group of forty missionaries into England with the goal of converting the Anglo-Saxons to Christianity. And since Latin was the language of the Roman Catholic Church, these missionaries used Latin in their religious practices. When Augustine was successful in his efforts, the Church presence expanded quickly. With the Church came the need for the Christian Anglo-Saxon communities to understand Latin, or at least enough to follow the liturgy. Because of this need, the Old English lexicon quickly grew to include Latin words. Obviously, words dealing with practices and concepts of the Roman Catholic Church, such as *martyr*, *ark*, *canon*, *nun*, *shrine*, *temple*, and so on, entered the Anglo-Saxon vocabulary at this time. In addition, the Church also brought knowledge about the practices and products of life in other places, so words such as *cap*, *sock*, *millet*, *fever*, *lily*, *anchor*, and a wide range of others entered Old English. Equally important, the Church brought formal education in reading and writing Latin into the country.

Old Norse The second language that shaped Old English through prolonged contact was Old Norse. In approximately 787 CE, almost two hundred years after St. Augustine's arrival in Kent, conflict between the established Anglo-Saxons and Norse-speaking Vikings began when the Vikings began making raids along the coastline of England. The violence intensified as large numbers of these Scandinavians invaded England and began moving

Figure 4.4 *Alfred the Great* (© iStockphoto.com/Macatack)

inland. The Anglo-Saxon king, Alfred the Great, finally ended this fighting in 886 CE by making a treaty with the Scandinavians (see Figure 4.4). Alfred's treaty geographically divided England, giving the Scandinavian invaders the northern part of England or the **Danelaw** and saving the southern part of England for the Anglo-Saxons (see Figure 4.5).

This obviously created prolonged contact between the two cultures and their languages of Old English and Old Norse, through business affairs like trading and political negotiations, as well as in social affairs like marriages.

Since the Scandinavians' language, Old Norse, was also a descendant of Germanic, it already shared a lot of similarities with the Old English language even before its speakers moved to England (see Box 4.2).

Once the Scandinavians settled in England, the common vocabulary made social and economic interaction fairly easy, but the pronunciation and the inflectional system of Old Norse differed from Old English. This difference leads some scholars to speculate that it encouraged the rate of morphological change already taking place in Old English.

Scholars date the composition of the great Old English epic, *Beowulf*, to the time of the Norse invasions of England. This poem has long been a staple of high school English courses in the United States, even though American students read translations of the original, since Old English would be as unfamiliar to them as any foreign language. Through the years there have been many translations of *Beowulf* created specifically for juvenile audiences; perhaps the most recent form has been the graphic novel, a fictional narrative that is told through the use of limited text and many illustrations, often in comic-book-like form. This latest version of *Beowulf* shows us how this classic text has once again been reinterpreted for contemporary culture – yet another example of how language is always in the process of change. To see sample pages of one *Beowulf* graphic novel, go to www.thecomic.com/

Figure 4.5 *The Danelaw*

Box 4.2 Similarities between Old Norse and Old English

Modern English	Old English	Old Norse
child (bairn)	bearn	barn
floor	flór	flórr
door	duru	dyrr

How could prolonged language contact have an effect on morphology? Imagine trying to communicate with someone who isn't from the same language community. You'll probably tend to emphasize what you share and de-emphasize what's different in order to ensure communication. Thus the Anglo-Saxons and the Danes might have de-emphasized the pronunciation and inflectional differences between their language varieties. This means that the inflectional endings would have lost their distinct and different pronunciations, a process termed **inflectional decay**. Inflectional decay takes place over time naturally, but now its rate increased significantly because of the prolonged language contact. As the Old English inflections began to sound alike, they lost the ability to indicate the relationships between words. And when inflectional endings lose their individuality, speakers stop distinguishing among them, in other words stop using them to indicate how the words within a sentence function together.

Figure 4.6 *Preserving the past*

Because of inflectional decay, Old English speakers began relying more and more on word order to indicate the relationships between words. We can trace this decay through the spelling of words because, as the inflections lost their distinction, we see spellings change from distinct case endings such as *-um* or *-os*, with a distinct function in each sentence, to the neutral *-e*, which served as a placeholder with no function at all. You've probably seen store names, such as *Ye Olde Clock Shoppe*, that try to convey the feeling of antiquity by using this decayed case ending (see Figure 4.6).

Norman French Another even more dramatic instance of prolonged contact began in 1066, when the Norman Conquest brought speakers of yet another language, Norman French, into contact with Old English and so forced it even further from its Germanic roots. After the decisive Battle of Hastings won England for the Normans, William, Duke of Normandy, took control of all England, changing its political, legal, social, and religious institutions. This clear-cut and immediate external change in English culture marked the end of the Anglo-Saxon period in English history and so brought about the internal change that marks the end of the Old English period. William's victory brought a sudden influx of an elite of Norman French speakers into England and thus began a period of intense contact between Old English and Norman French. The earlier contact between Old English and Old Norse had been geographically

Box 4.3 Privileging French

This selection from *Robert of Gloucester's Chronicle*, written in approximately 1300 CE, reveals the Norman conquerors' attitudes toward the native English language of their new land. A word-for-word translation of the Middle English is immediately underneath each line, and a Modern American English translation follows.

þus come, lo! Engelond, into Normannes honde.

Thus came, lo England, into Normans' hand.

And þe Normans ne couþe speke þo bote her owe speche

And the Normans nothing could speak then except their own speech

And speke French as dude atom, & here chyldren dude al so teche.

And spoke French as [they] did at home, and their children did also teach.

So þat heymen of þys lond, þat of her blod come,

So that high-men of this land, that of their blood come,

Holdeþ alle þulke speche, þat hii of hem nome.

hold all the-same speech, that they from them took.

Vor bote a man couþe French. me tolþ of him wel lute.

for unless a man knows French. one counts of him very little.

Ac lowe men holdeþ to Englyss. & to her kunde speche 3ute.

but low men hold to English. and to their own speech yet.

[MODERN AMERICAN ENGLISH:

Lo, thus England came into the Normans' hand, and

the Normans could speak nothing except their own

language and spoke French as they did at home, and

also taught their children French. So those high-men

of this land [England] that come from their blood, all

hold the same language that they [the English] took

from them [the Normans]. For unless a man knows

French, one counts him for very little. But the low-

men hold to English and to their own language yet.]

limited to some extent by the Danelaw. William, however, conquered all of England, and so no limitations existed on the geographical spread of Norman French.

The language of William's court was Norman French, so it immediately became privileged. Any English speakers who wished to interact with the new ruler needed to speak in French rather than in English. In fact, after William, England had several Anglo-Norman kings who didn't speak English at all. As we see in the following passage, the people with political power during the early Middle Ages spoke French and were not interested in learning English themselves. Box 4.3 illustrates this attitude.

When the Normans took political control of England, they did not restrict the language and culture of the native English speakers, as had happened with the earlier Germanic and Norse invasions with regard to the native Celtic peoples. Instead, they relied on the native English speakers to do the work of the country. So English remained the daily language of those who did not have immediate contact with the new Norman rulers: speakers in the lower socioeconomic classes and speakers in the geographically remote regions of England. And even though the English speakers who dealt with aristocrats quickly learned to speak French, they still spoke English to their families, friends, and co-workers. The Normans who wanted to communicate with the English also became bilingual. So the new culture that developed after 1066 made a place for both languages. The result was that both French and English were being used regularly during the early Middle Ages. And the term *Middle English* refers to the English language that developed as a result of this prolonged contact with Norman French. As Box 4.4 indicates, English finally became recognized as the dominant language in England again almost 400 years after the Norman Conquest only after significant political and cultural shifts had taken place.

Box 4.4 The rise of English as the national language

English took a little over 400 years, from 1066 to 1489, to once again become the national language of England:

1066 Norman French replaces English as the privileged language of the land.
1272–1307 Edward I is the first English king to speak English fluently.
1362 Chancellor opens Parliament in English rather than in French.
1362 Parliament dictates that lawsuits should be in English and so officially recognizes English.
1489 French is eliminated as the language of Parliament.

And of course the English of 1489 was vastly different from the English of 1066 as a result of its prolonged exposure to both French and Latin and to all of the cultural changes that had taken place.

Morphological change: leveling

The prolonged contact with French after the Norman Conquest finalized the loss of Old English inflectional morphemes. Because Norman French was now the dominant language, the inflectional endings of Old English went through a **leveling** process, where they all became *level*, exactly like each other, and then eventually disappeared completely (see Box 4.5).

By the time Chaucer was writing *The Canterbury Tales* in the late fourteenth century, nouns had lost the distinctive Old English case endings, their inflectional morphemes. This inflectional loss continued the decaying process that had begun many centuries earlier when Proto-Indo-European began changing into Germanic. Unbound inflectional morphemes such as prepositions and auxiliary verbs became standard, replacing the disappearing bound morphemes or inflections. As a result of this change process, Middle English depended on word order to convey relationships between the words in a sentence. By this time, English had become an analytic language.

Have you ever wondered why English uses one word for an animal and another word entirely for the food that comes from that animal? Beef comes from cows, pork from pigs, and so on. These terms came into use during the early Middle Ages because of the split in language between the upper class and the lower class of English society. The upper-class aristocrats spoke French and so ate food with names that originated in their native French: beef, mutton, pork. The lower-class Anglo-Saxon peasants worked to raise the animals for slaughter, so they used names from their native Old English: cow, sheep, pig. Aristocrats would never have labored with the animals, and the peasants would never have eaten with the court, so both names stayed in use, eventually entering our American English vocabulary.

Box 4.5 The loss of inflectional endings in English

Old English inflections	Middle English leveling	Modern English loss
clawu	clawe	claw
heorte	herte	heart
drincan	drinke	drink
nama	name	name

In these examples, you can clearly see the distinctive Old English inflections undergoing the process of leveling so that, in Middle English, they are no longer being pronounced or spelled distinctively. (And in Middle English, these final vowels would have been pronounced.) Then, in words like Modern English *claw*, *heart*, and *drink*, the inflectional ending has completely disappeared. In other words, such as *name*, the Middle English leveled inflection -*e* survives as a silent letter in Modern English, being preserved only in the written form.

A national language: Early Modern English

During the Early Modern English period, beginning in the late fifteenth century, many significant external changes were taking place. And once again, we see these cultural changes reflected in the language. One of the most obvious appears in the privileging of English over Latin. Throughout the Old and Middle English periods, the frequent political upheavals and the reliance upon oral communication for the majority of the population meant that Latin was the language of education, of religion, of literature – of permanence. At the end of the Middle Ages, though, a growing sense of nationalism encouraged English speakers to become interested in their own language. English then emerged as the recognized national language of England as the result of varying forces working within English culture:

1.   *The Renaissance* encouraged intellectual growth through exposure to classical works and to translations of those works into the **vernacular**, or everyday speech of the people. This gave English speakers easier access to learning and literacy because they didn't need to learn Latin to access the intellectual community.

2.   *The Protestant Reformation* empowered vernacular languages and supported the spread of literacy. One of the ways in which the Reformation challenged Roman Catholicism was by encouraging its followers to learn to read the Bible for themselves rather than relying on a priest to do so for them.

3.   *The establishment of the printing press* in England in the late fifteenth century by William Caxton supported the intellectual changes taking place by providing less expensive and more numerous printed works for literate society to read.

4.   *The growth of English nationalism* developed from the political and economic growth of England during these years and strengthened the English people's perceptions of themselves and their language.

5.   *The rise of the middle class* gave native English speakers more voice in local and national affairs. This meant that the English people didn't need to learn French or Latin to speak with superiors, making the English language itself more authoritative and powerful. Its use didn't automatically mark one as a member of a lower socioeconomic class.

As you already know, the Early Modern English period also saw the birth of American English. During the sixteenth century, English explorers began investigating the New World, bringing back descriptions of new places as well as new plants, animals, foods, and peoples. In his essay "American English: Its Origins and History," Richard W. Bailey (2004) argues that American English first appeared with these explorers' use of Native American words in descriptions of their discoveries for English audiences. Then, when the colony at Jamestown was established in 1607, American English was firmly established in what would become the United States. Since then, of course, during its history in the United States, American English has developed its own unique identity. And it continues to change today, adapting to fit the needs of its users.

Exercise 4.5

You've already thought about the roles that geographical isolation and prolonged language contact have played in the historical development of American English. Now think about changes that you see happening in the language you use today. Are you using new words or abbreviations? Why? Is American culture privileging a particular type of language or language use? Are any of the eight remaining inflections changing or even disappearing? As you consider these changes, be sure to think about both spoken and written American English.

Now you understand the basic structural elements, the morphology, of American English and the history that have made it so different from its European cousins. Chapter 5 examines word order, the structuring devices that Modern English uses in place of inflections.

Chapter summary

As you might know from reading Chaucer or Shakespeare, the language we speak today differs greatly from that of earlier periods. English morphology and syntax have changed over time, caused by **geographical** and social isolation, as well as by **prolonged language contact**. This chapter has primarily focused on examining the **external history** of early English, that is, the political, religious, intellectual, social, and other kinds of events that change the identity of a language community and so affect its language. But these events do not occur within the language itself. The **internal history** of a language records the changes that have occurred within the language itself, like morphological or lexical change, as a result of the external history. These changes transformed English from a **synthetic** into an **analytic** language. By the end of the Middle Ages, English had transformed into the language we recognize today. For example, many of our words today can be traced back to Middle English and the influence of Norman French. In addition, our contemporary word and language structures reflect the **leveling** that took place as a result of **language decay**. Thus modern American English is an analytic language rather than a synthetic one.

Critical Thinking exercises

1.   Reflect on your own knowledge of languages other than English, such as ones you may have studied in school or are familiar with through family or social activities. You don't need to be fluent in another language to have a little familiarity with it. Then compare/ contrast the structure of the words and/or sentences of this language

with English. Is this an analytic or a synthetic language? Be prepared to share your analysis with the class.

2.   Work with a group of peers to identify some of the contemporary external events that are forcing our current language toward change. Be sure to discuss why these events in particular might change our language, as well as identify some specific ways you think it will change (or that you've seen change already). Choose the single event that you think will have the most significant effect in terms of the future of American English; then write a one-page rationale supporting your choice.

3.   A verb's *tense* is the expression of time in which the action of the verb is happening. Modern American English has only one inflectional morpheme to indicate past tense: the tense marker *-ed*. Identify at least three other ways in addition to this inflection by which American English users indicate past time. Write sample sentences as illustrations. Then be prepared to discuss the pros and cons of such variety. How would a synthetic language differ in indicating verb tenses?

Hot Topic: Gender-neutral pronouns

This chapter has examined some of the ways in which language changes over time as a particular culture changes. Although these changes have come about as a result of human activities, such as war or trade, they have not been conscious goals. Let's now examine a movement currently underway in the United States to see if conscious endeavor can produce change in a nation's language use.

Like the historical examples explained in this chapter, the current use of gender-neutral pronouns is tied to a significant culture change, specifically with the rise of the women's liberation movement beginning in the 1960s in the United States. American English has always contained gendered pronouns. These free morphemes, however, make a large number of people dissatisfied with our language for a variety of reasons. Some resent the need to always identify an individual's gender, especially in situations where it is totally irrelevant. Others worry that the traditional English use of male references, such as the generic *he*, creates different expectations for men's and women's abilities because it omits women. Still others dislike some of the effects of trying to avoid using gendered language, such as the increased sentence length created by dually referencing *his or her* rather than using just a single pronoun.

While more people are aware of writing in gender-neutral ways, with professional and academic style guides to help them, the question remains whether our language is really changing as a result. In fact, many American English users resist using gender-neutral pronouns because of their artificiality or because of their desire to avoid politically charged language.

Work with your peer group to assess the effectiveness of this reform movement to date and make a prediction for its future. Will it truly change our language, or will we always need to have style guides telling us how to achieve gender-neutral language? The following list of websites may help you gather information:

The Epicene Pronouns: A Chronology of the Word That Failed
www.english.illinois.edu/-people-/faculty/debaron/essays/epicene.htm   This collection by Professor Dennis Baron at the University of Illinois at Urbana-Champaign provides a chronological list of gender-neutral pronouns proposed over the last 150 years or so.

The LSA Guidelines for Nonsexist Usage
www.lsadc.org/info/coswl/coswl.gls.htm This website from the Linguistic Society of America provides a brief explanation and then suggestions for ways to make language more gender-neutral.

Non–Sexist Language: Some Notes on Gender-Neutral Language
www.english.upenn.edu/~cjacobso/gender.html   This website, by Carolyn Jacobson, a graduate assistant at the University of Pennsylvania, provides a history and rationale for the use of gendered pronouns.

As you work with your group, consider the following questions:

1.   Compare/contrast this reform movement with the historical change of English from a synthetic to an analytic structure. Do the general linguistic concepts of language change outlined in Chapter 4 lead you to think this movement will succeed or fail?

2.   Reflect on the usage of gender-neutral language that you personally observe in the course of your day. What sort of evidence of actual usage do you notice?

Learn more about it

A developing language: Old English

Aitchison, J. 1998, "Language change: Progress or decay?" in V. P. Clark, P. A. Eschholz, and A. F. Rosa (eds.), *Language: Readings in language and culture*, New York: St. Martin's Press, pp. 431–441.
The author explores the inevitability of language change and its effects.

BBC World Service 2000, *The routes of English*. Retrieved June 30th, 2006 from www.bbc.co.uk/radio4/routesofenglish/storysofar/series1.shtml
This multimedia site from the BBC includes transcripts, maps, behind-the-scenes diaries, games, and much more in a celebration of 1,000 years of English. Series 1 examines significant moments in the history of the language.

Crystal, D. 2004, *The stories of English*, New York: Penguin.

As the title indicates, this work traces the history of the English language by addressing its diversity rather than focusing on an idealized standard.

Trask, R. L. 2006, "Where did English come from?" in H. Luria, D. M. Seymour, and
   T. Smoke (eds.), *Language and linguistics in context*, Mahwah, NJ: Lawrence
   Erlbaum Associates, pp. 143–146.

In this comprehensive, short introduction to the study of language, Trask gives a concise history of the development of Germanic languages, including English.

A national language: Early Modern English

Bailey, R. 1991, *Images of English: A cultural history of the language*, Ann Arbor,
   MI: University of Michigan Press.

In a reader-friendly narrative, Bailey examines the relationship between attitudes about the English language and the culture in which those attitudes are expressed.

Bailey, R. 2004, "American English: Its origins and history," in E. Finegan and
   J. R. Rickford (eds.), *Language in the U.S.A.: Themes for the twenty-first century*,
   Cambridge: Cambridge University Press, pp. 3–17.

Stressing the linguistic diversity of America, Bailey traces the origins and history of American English. The author examines in particular the historical linguistic input from Caribbean, Native American, African, and other languages.

Baugh, A. C. and Cable, T. 2001, *A history of the English language*, 5th edition,
   Upper Saddle River, NJ: Prentice Hall.

In an approachable, yet comprehensive, style, this introductory-level text explains the historical development of the English language within its context of cultural change.

Burnley, D. 1992, *The history of the English language: A source book*, New York:
   Longman.

This book includes a wide range of original texts, grouped by historical period and introduced with a brief essay on the linguistic developments of that period.

5 American English grammar and syntax

Key terms

Grammar
Prescriptive grammar
Mental grammar
Descriptive grammar
Traditional grammar
Nonstandard variety
Syntax
Constituents
Syntactic categories
Phrase structure rules
Generative grammar
Transformation rules

Overview

This chapter discusses various definitions of the term *grammar* and explains a few of the most widely accepted approaches to the study of grammar conventions. These approaches include descriptive rules about American English phrase and sentence construction, as well as theoretical models of a speaker's inherent grammar knowledge. To remind you that all languages are systematic, the Hot Topic asks you to analyze the grammar of an electronic discourse.

Introduction

Have you ever heard your friends or classmates say something similar to the following?

"I'm no good at public speaking because my grammar is bad."

"I hate grammar, but I know it's something I have to learn to be a good teacher."

"You're an English Major, so I'd better watch what I say."

These three statements represent the opinions of many undergraduates today. Notice the common perspective among them. The speakers believe that grammar is something they should know in order to be successful in other skills, but they feel inadequate in their grammar knowledge and so dislike activities that they think will require "good" grammar. Unfortunately, this negative attitude is not limited to students. Many adults share the same anxieties. Even though the word *grammar* has seven letters, our society tends to react as if it were a four-letter word. Why do people react in these negative ways?

An answer may be found if we think about the first time many of us heard the word *grammar*. Typically, this was in a classroom when a teacher tried to help us become more proficient in self-expression, usually by correcting our grammar. Ironically, the teacher's good intentions may have ended up creating the exact opposite effect: rather than becoming more proficient, we actually learned to doubt our own language abilities! After all, no teacher ever says, "The grammar in that sentence is lovely." Instead we hear, "Fix your grammar," or "You're not saying that correctly," or some other negative reaction to our use of language. No wonder people cringe or feel self-conscious when asked to think about *grammar*.

People might also have negative associations with grammar because they are confused by its rules: users often disagree about what these entail. This disagreement over grammar rules sometimes happens because of language change, which, as you've learned in earlier chapters, is an ongoing process. Even SAE is always in the process of changing. Sometimes change occurs quite quickly; in other cases, change takes place very gradually, over many decades or even centuries. The following exercise will show you some of the changes that have taken place over time in American English grammar.

Exercise 5.1

Divide into groups and then, working as a group, choose one of the following "grammar rules" to investigate. A sample sentence for illustration follows each "rule" below:

1.   *Ain't* is not a word. "*I ain't gonna be there.*"
2.   Never begin a sentence with "because." "*Because I was late for school, I ran quickly down the hall.*"
3.   Never split an infinitive. *The mission of the Star Ship Enterprise was "to boldly go where no man had gone before."*
4.   Never use a double negative in a sentence. "*He ain't gonna do nothing.*"
5.   Never begin a sentence with *But*. "*But what's the matter with that?*"
6.   Never end a sentence with a preposition. "*Why'd you have to go and do that for?*"

Explore the history of the rule you've chosen by examining usage handbooks and guides. You might, for example, go online to www.bartleby.com/usage/, a site that offers several different guides to language usage. You'll also want to explore your campus library as well. Try to look in older, as well as contemporary, guides so that you can compare and contrast perspectives of different periods. What did you discover? Are these, in fact, rules that always have been and always must be followed? What do your research and your own personal experiences tell you about these "rules" and the concept of language change? Be prepared to discuss your research with your classmates.

Box 5.1 explains yet another conflict over the rules of grammar.

Box 5.1 Conflict over American English grammar

In the spring of 2003, a high school teacher in Maryland challenged an answer to one of the questions in the English Writing Skills section of the widely distributed Preliminary Scholastic Aptitude Test (PSAT), an academic evaluation tool published by the Educational Testing Service (ETS) and used to select exceptional students for college admission and scholarship awards. The question asked students to correct the grammar of a sentence by selecting one out of several possible answers. The teacher disputed the correct answer given by ETS, contending that two correct choices were possible within the conventions of Standard American English grammar. After newspapers across the country picked up the story and printed the sentence in question, dozens of people, including English teachers, retirees, 10th graders, presidents of language societies, and others, wrote in to their local papers with their own views on the "correct" response. Some agreed with the teacher, citing grammar rules they'd learned in elementary school or from "definitive" grammar books. Others disagreed with the teacher's choice and cited yet other rules to support their selection of a different answer.

Eventually, ETS decided that there was no definitive, correct answer to the question and so declined to give credit for either answer choice. Instead, it dropped the flawed question from the test, even though this meant that almost 500,000 tests had to be rescored (see Figure 5.1).

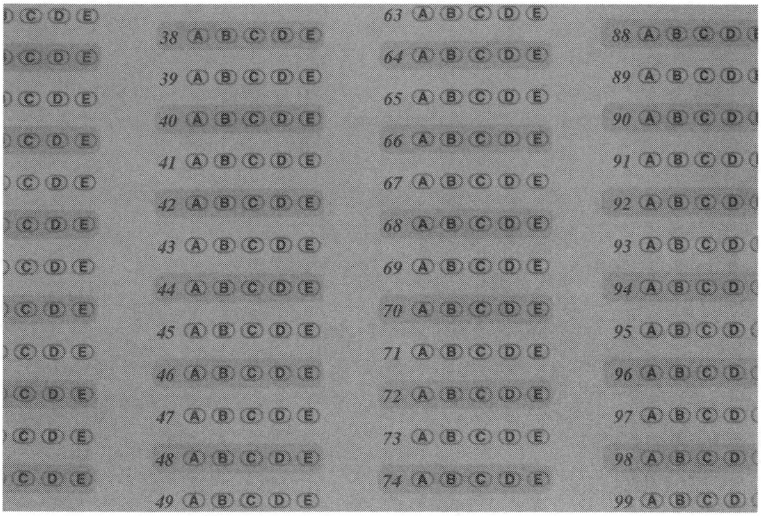

Figure 5.1 *Which answer is correct?*

Definitions of grammar

Another possible source of conflict when discussing grammar is that the definition of "grammar" varies, depending on who is using the term. Teachers, scholars, and writers may use the word to mean different things. To some, it means punctuation, to others, spelling, or word order, or pronunciation, or some combination of all these different concepts. Linguists broadly define **grammar** as the system of rules that govern a language, yet they understand that various ways exist to describe such a system. You may be most familiar with **prescriptive grammar**, the language rules that you learned in school. A prescriptive grammar is usually a set of rules representing a privileged language within a culture whose use is widely mandated within its institutions, such as in schools and government. The rules of a prescriptive grammar are derived from the concept of an ideal language usage and are intended to help users "improve" their language. Prescriptivists strongly believe in the notions of correctness and error, and thus may argue that the grammar of the privileged language is "better" than the grammar of a nonprivileged one.

A grammar isn't merely a set of rules to be memorized, though. As you've learned in this textbook, young children acquire their native languages in relatively short periods of time without any formal instruction at all. That they can do this suggests that humans possess a **mental grammar**, or inherent knowledge about the rules of their language. These rules concern the structures and combinations of sounds, words, and sentences, as well as their assigned meanings. Although speakers of the same language may have similar rules in their mental grammars, the details of these rules will vary because of individual differences.

When linguists attempt to describe people's inherent linguistic knowledge, they create a descriptive grammar, a set of rules that accurately describes a language as it is actually used. Unlike a prescriptive grammar, a **descriptive grammar** does not teach users to "improve" their language use. Instead, it enables study of the language itself by describing its structures. Most linguists describe rather than prescribe grammar rules in an attempt to remain as nonjudgmental as possible about language use.

Exercise 5.2

Decide which grammar type – prescriptive, mental, or descriptive – is suggested by each statement below. Be able to explain your answer.

1. Students must go to school to learn correct grammar.
2. Most children use two-word sentences by twenty-one months of age.
3. In SAE, adjectives immediately precede the noun they modify.
4. A complete sentence has a subject and a predicate.
5. Some linguists argue that English does not have a future tense form of the verb but instead indicates future time through other verbal constructions.
6. Every speaker knows how to use nouns and verbs.

Let's now explore in more detail the historical backgrounds of prescriptive and descriptive types of English grammar.

Prescriptive grammars

The term *grammar* came into use in England during the Middle Ages and originally referred to the study of Latin by learning its rules. Because Latin was the language of scholarship during this period, the term eventually came to mean learning in general. *Grammar schools* were schools that specifically taught Latin, the language of learning throughout medieval Europe; learning Latin was considered the first step toward attaining an education. Our use of the term *grammar school* today in American English derives from this early usage, but now it means the beginning years of academic study, the years that provide a base for more specialized study, rather than the specific study of Latin.

Studying grammar was an important element in a medieval education, and since Latin was the language used in education, the grammar studied was that of Latin. Because the purpose of this study was to ensure the "proper" academic use of Latin, students learned

Use of the Latin grammar as a template to study English grammar received a boost in the first half of the sixteenth century when William Lily published *A Shorte Introduction of Grammar*, which explained Latin grammar in English. Even though Lily was merely continuing the same prescriptive methods as his predecessors, he used English rather than Latin terminology. This text changed the practice of teaching grammar to such an extent that Henry VIII (see Figure 5.2), and later his son Edward VI, declared Lily's *Grammar* as the approved national guide to learning Latin grammar.

Figure 5.2 *Henry VIII*
(Credit: T.A. Dean/The Library of Congress, LC-USZ62-93719)

Latin grammar in the tradition of classical grammarians. In later periods, when Latin was no longer the language of education and the English language itself was being studied, students continued to use the Latin grammar as a template because Latin was still considered a more "learned" language than English.

The eighteenth century and the prescriptive approach

British English Continuing the privileging of Latin that had taken place in earlier centuries, eighteenth-century grammarians developed specific rules that they believed would improve English by making it more like Latin. For example, when analyzing Latin verbs, they realized that the Latin infinitive is always one word while the English infinitive is always two, since English lacks the inflectional suffix that Latin has. For instance, the English infinitive *to love* is the single word *amare* in Latin. In order to make English grammar parallel to that of Latin, these grammarians decided that English users should never separate the two parts of the infinitive in a sentence. Most of you will recognize this as the "split infinitive rule" still sometimes taught today, and which you may have researched in Exercise 5.1.

In addition to differing from Latin, another flaw found in English by eighteenth-century writers was the fact that it had changed over time. In his *A Proposal for Correcting, Improving and Ascertaining the English Tongue*, written in 1712, Jonathan Swift complained about the way that English was constantly changing – for the worse (see Figure 5.3). He proposed establishing an English Academy with the authority to correct and then maintain an official English in its "proper" form. Because Latin had been the privileged language for centuries, Swift wanted English to become like Latin: permanent and unchanging. Swift, and others who took this position, failed to recognize that Latin was no longer spoken by a living culture and therefore was no longer able to change; in contrast, a living language like English simply cannot be this settled.

One of the causes of the degeneration of English, according to many writers in the eighteenth century, was its use – or rather misuse – by the lower socioeconomic classes. Samuel Johnson's translation of the Roman Quintilian's adage "Language is the dress of thought" reflected this period's belief that one's language reflected one's rank in society. Poorer people "naturally" spoke a poorer sort of English while wealthier people used the correct form. This attitude even influenced Parliament. As Olivia Smith (1984) explains in *The Politics of Language*, in the eighteenth century petitions from lower-class British citizens for reforming the voting system were dismissed because of their "vulgar" language. Today we consider language "vulgar" if it contains profanity or obscenities, but these petitions were quite proper from a modern point of view. In the eighteenth century, however, they stated a vulgarity: the notion that members of the working class had rights as citizens. This incident clearly shows one of the ways in which the language of the upper socioeconomic class was privileged.

American English Underlying the prescriptivist approach in the eighteenth century was the British assumption that a majority of English speakers used their language incorrectly. Many writers in the newly created United States held this assumption as well and thus sought to prescribe a standardized grammar. Different from the British, though, who wanted English grammar to resemble Latin grammar, American grammarians wished to standardize American English in order to clarify its distinction from British

Figure 5.3 *Jonathan Swift (Courtesy of Project Gutenberg)*

English. Many of these writers believed that the newly formed country would best be served by a prescriptive language standard, enabling all Americans, regardless of socioeconomic class or geographical location, to write and speak the same language.

The prescriptivist approach today

Today, the prescriptivist approach continues to dominate the study of English grammar within American education. Most elementary and secondary schools in the United States teach grammar from this perspective and, although the emphasis on various elements of grammar has varied over the decades, the foundation on which its rules rest has been essentially the same since the late seventeenth century. Because of its longevity and continuity, this approach has come to be known as **traditional grammar**.

Methods in teaching traditional grammar have changed little over the years: students learn the parts of speech, or word categories, including nouns, verbs, adjectives, prepositions, and others, and then go on to learn how these parts are put together in sentences, thus studying word functions, such as subjects, predicates, modifiers, and so on. While supporters of the traditional grammar system, typically those teaching in school systems but also a lot of parents and others interested in "good"

The strong surge of nationalism supporting the independence of the United States also appeared in discussions of its language. Some wanted to discontinue the name *English* because they had just won a war against the English. A new name would mark a beginning for the language, as well as for the country. Lexicographer Noah Webster supported the name *Federal English*; *American* was another proposal. Neither of these suggestions received lasting support, so today Americans still use *American English* and *English*. The use of these names today, though, differs from the time of the Revolution because *American English* now has a distinct identity. Regardless of the name, no one today would confuse it with *British English*.

language, celebrate it as a systematic, coherent model, in fact if we look more closely at its formulation, we can see the ways in which it departs from consistency and completeness.

Exercise 5.3

You are probably familiar with the type of exercise below from your own middle- or high-school experience. It appears straightforward and clear, with a distinct right/wrong answer, yet, as you work through the exercise, we think you'll find that a traditional grammar system does not always provide clear-cut answers. As you respond to each sentence, note possible questions or confusion you experienced in reaching your answer.

This exercise is divided into two parts. Part A asks you to identify parts of speech in the sentences listed, choosing from the categories Noun, Verb, Pronoun, and Preposition. Part B asks you to identify which words function as subjects or predicates in the sentences listed.

Here are a few traditional definitions of parts of speech and of their functions to help you out:

Noun – A noun is a person, place, or thing that functions as a subject or an object in the sentence.

Verb – A verb is an action or a state of being that functions by indicating what the subject is doing.

Pronoun – A pronoun refers to the preceding noun and functions by providing a short
   replacement for the noun.

Preposition – A preposition is a grammatical marker that functions by indicating the relationship
   between words in a sentence.

Subject – A subject is the word or phrase that a sentence is about.

Predicate – A predicate is the action of a sentence and all its modifiers.

A. Identify each of the underlined words in the following sentences as a Noun, Verb, Pronoun, or Preposition:

1.   The <u>dog</u> lives outside most of the year.
2.   <u>It</u> has its own doghouse.
3.   <u>It</u> is going to rain this afternoon.
4.   It's been <u>raining</u> all afternoon.
5.   <u>Raining</u> every day on my vacation is not my idea of fun.
6.   I took the bill <u>up</u> in my hand and gasped at the total.
7.   I ran the bill <u>up</u> in the bar and drowned my sorrows.

B. Circle the subjects and underline the predicates in the following sentences:

1.   We often leave for the stadium at 3:00 a.m. to get a good spot in line to buy tickets.
2.   Make sure to leave early enough for the game tomorrow.
3.   The team, which had just flown in from Los Angeles, was eager to play.
4.   There was a hush as the fans learned of the coach's retirement.
5.   When will the coach work again?
6.   "Never!" exclaimed the coach.
7.   It is a sad day for baseball when a beloved coach retires.

How did you do on the above exercise? Did you have any trouble identifying the parts of speech in part A? What about the subjects and predicates in part B?

A good classification system should be precise and consistent, with mutually exclusive categories. And it should also be complete, that is, fully descriptive. Chances are, in the exercise above, you found identifying the parts of speech and functions difficult because of inconsistency, lack of clarity, and overlapping classes. In fact, we see from this exercise that this rule-based system of traditional grammar does not fully describe the language. Is *It* in part A, sentence #3 a pronoun? Did you identify *up* in part A, sentence #7 as a preposition? What did you do with the *There was* construction in part B, sentence #4? If traditional grammar tells us that every sentence needs a subject, what do we do, then, with sentence #2 in part B where there doesn't appear to be one? You may be surprised to learn that even among traditional grammarians there is a lack of agreement on the names of parts of speech and the functions of many of these words.

Does it dismay you to think about the fact that traditional grammar – something you may have been tested and retested on all through school – is not an exact science? (See Figure 5.4.) In fact, English grammar rules have been in constant change as the language has changed. It's hard to pin down, then, one "correct" grammar, since language change happens at different rates in different places.

REPORT CARD

Smith City High School
Rt 3, Box 777
Smith City, U.S.A. 88888

Social Security # 111-11-1111
Allen Jones
47 Country Town Rd.
Smith City, Arkansas 88888

Teacher	Course	Marking Period	Final Grade
Lettis	Algebra II	66	71
Joast	Chemistry	88	91
Lee	English Grammar	38	42
Horrol	Physical Education	73	78

Figure 5.4 *Did you study grammar in school?*

Exercise 5.4

Make a list of different kinds of judgments that have been made about grammar as described in the previous discussion of grammar perspectives through history. For instance, you might note the belief that proper English grammar should follow a Latin template. Once you've listed these judgments, ask yourself if these attitudes still exist today. Are you aware of any other judgments that might be made today about grammar? Be prepared to discuss your ideas in class.

Descriptive grammars

Although for several centuries now prescriptivism has been the dominant approach to English grammar study in both England and America, already in the

Figure 5.5 *Noah Webster (Credit: The Library of Congress, LC-USZ62-78299)*

seventeenth century opposition to this method began appearing. Those opposed to prescriptivism believed that learning grammar should require studying English as it is being used, rather than describing the language as it should be. This approach did not gain much popularity in either country, though, until the early nineteenth century, when, in 1828, American Noah Webster (see Figure 5.5) published *An American Dictionary of the English Language*, which identified American English vocabulary and language practices based on the actual usage of the time. In addition to showing skeptical Americans and Britons that American English possessed its own identity, this important work validated a descriptive approach to language.

Descriptive approaches to grammar came to be much more widely used in the mid to late nineteenth century in Europe and America as linguists began to study many of the world's languages. They recognized the inadequacies of imposing a traditional Latin-based grammar on other languages, especially those outside the Indo-European family, and sought instead to describe language structures they observed in actual use. They made no evaluative judgments on the various kinds of grammar found in a culture and so did not privilege one set of grammar rules over all others.

Descriptive linguists constructed their grammars based upon users' knowledge of their language. So, for instance, as part of their methodology they tested phrases and sentences on native speakers, asking them to judge their acceptability. Those structures deemed

> Danish linguist Otto Jespersen (1860–1943) was one of the earliest practitioners of descriptive linguistic approaches. His rejection of traditional evaluations of languages, the rating of some as "better" than others because of their complexity or because of other factors, as well as his notions that individual languages had their own unique systems of rules, revolutionized the ways in which linguists studied languages.

acceptable to native speakers the linguists called *grammatical*; those that were unacceptable structures were called *ungrammatical*.

Let's see how this type of analysis works by looking at the following English sentences:

1. *Me and him went out last night.*
2. *He and I went out last night.*
3. **Last out I night he and went.*

Examining the structures of the language, we would say that sentences 1 and 2 are grammatical because they are commonly used by native speakers; sentence 3 is clearly not grammatical because it is unacceptable to native speakers. Sentence 1 is a variety of nonstandard English. Note that a **nonstandard variety** does not mean a "substandard" variety; for linguists, the term "nonstandard" solely means that it is not one of the standard varieties of American English. Thus, even though prescriptivists would judge this sentence ungrammatical because it breaks the rules of a standard English, descriptive linguists judge it grammatical because native speakers find it acceptable. In the case of sentence 3, no one accepts this sentence, and so it is ungrammatical from both points of view.

As you can see, this descriptive approach to language study followed accepted scientific practice: linguists collected data from the speakers of a language, analyzed it, and, then, based on the objective evidence alone, drew conclusions about the grammar structures of the language. These objective approaches to analyzing language would profoundly affect the study of different American English dialects, some of which previously had been considered inferior or flawed.

More recently, since the development of data processing, linguists have been helped in the descriptive analysis of language by the creation of language *corpora*, or collections of large language data samples. A *corpus* is usually a whole text or sections of a text that faithfully represent the language as it is being used at a particular time. Corpora generally include as many variations of language use as possible, so typically contain both speech and writing examples, as well as varieties from a wide range of language users and contexts. From examining corpora, linguists can determine a range of information about a language, including its linguistic features, their frequency of use, the differences among varieties, and other data.

> The *Longman Grammar of Spoken and Written English* by Biber *et al.* is a corpus-based description of the form and function of grammar in both British and American English. The book looks at the grammar features of four different aspects of language: conversation, news, academic prose, and fiction. Containing over 40 million words, the Biber grammar reveals important information about how actual speakers and writers use English.

Syntax

In addition to word formation, a descriptive grammar also contains the rules for ordering the words that make up phrases and sentences, traditionally called **syntax** rules. For example, one syntax rule that every English speaker intuitively knows is that English sentences have a linear word order, that is, words must appear in a certain order in sentences to convey the desired meaning. For instance, while you might say to a friend, "Emily bought the latest CD," you would never say, "The latest CD bought Emily," even though the words used are exactly the same. In response to the first statement, your friend might ask a question about Emily or about the CD, while the second statement will probably cause her to be very confused. Word order is essential for the conveyance of meaning in English.

Exercise 5.5

Read the groupings below. Then, for each grouping, explain how and why the meaning of the second statement differs from the meaning of the first statement.

1.   The end of the beginning/The beginning of the end.
2.   Harry sees only Jane/Only Harry sees Jane.
3.   The dog followed me behind the tree/The dog behind the tree followed me.
4.   They sat at the table in the back/They sat in the back at the table.

Although linear word order in English is essential to create meaning, sentences are not just strings of individual words that we read, one by one, for meaning. Instead, when we look at sentences we intuitively group certain words together, words that seem to belong together because their meanings go together. Linguists call these groupings **constituents** of a sentence. Looking at one of the sample sentences from the exercise above, *The dog followed me behind the tree*, we can analyze it for its constituents. Most native English speakers would probably break the sentence into these constituents:

> *The dog   followed me   behind the tree.*

What causes us to group these words this way? Why do the words *followed* and *me* seem to have a closer relationship than, say, *me* and *behind*, for most people? Linguists have theorized that native speakers intuitively group words that make up meaningful units in a sentence. The verb phrase *followed me*, for instance, is a group of words that has a meaning of its own and that, when joined to other words, contributes to a larger meaning: *Something* followed me *behind the tree*. In contrast, although each word, *me* and *behind*, has its own individual meaning, when grouped together, they do not form a meaningful unit. Identifying constituent groups is part of a descriptive analysis of language that shows how elements of a sentence interact and depend on one another.

We can further describe sentence constituents by assigning them to **syntactic categories**, groups of words that share similar morphological and syntactic properties and thus act in similar ways. Linguists name these categories by using abbreviations of grammatical terms borrowed from traditional grammar, such as S for Sentence, NP for Noun Phrase, VP for Verb Phrase, PP for Prepositional Phrase, and others. Syntactic categories are part of native speakers' mental grammar: Although they might have never heard of the technical names,

Table 5.1 *Common syntactic categories*

NP	Noun Phrase
VP	Verb Phrase
Aux	Auxiliary
Adj	Adjective
Adv	Adverb
Det	Determiner
PP	Prepositional Phrase

they intuitively know which words comprise the NP category, the VP category, and so on. Table 5.1 lists some common syntactic categories.

Generally, sentences have two main constituents, the NP and VP. The NP contains a noun (N) or pronoun (Pro). NPs may also contain a determiner (Det), the article *a*, *an*, or *the*, or an adjective (Adj). The words and phrases listed below are all possible NPs:

Humans
The woman
A young child
Mr. Miller
They

NPs can also be identified by the function that they fulfill in a sentence, either subjects or objects. The following sentences with underlined NPs demonstrate four different functions that they serve:

The baby played quietly. (subject)
The mother sang to the baby. (object of the prepositional phrase)
She picked up the baby. (direct object)
She gave the baby a block. (indirect object)

Verb phrases (VPs) must contain a verb and may contain other categories as well, such as NPs, prepositional phrases (PPs), Adverbial phrases (AdvPs), and others. In English sentences, VPs typically come after subject NPs. Any of the VPs listed below could complete the following sentence, *"The man _____."*

1. *ordered his dinner at the restaurant*
2. *watched the game*
3. *woke up at 7:00 a.m.*
4. *carefully stirred the spaghetti sauce.*

One way to visually represent the constituents of sentences and their functions is to put them into tree diagrams. You may remember doing this kind of exercise in your English classes as you learned the names of different parts of speech and their functions within sentences. In tree diagrams, which actually

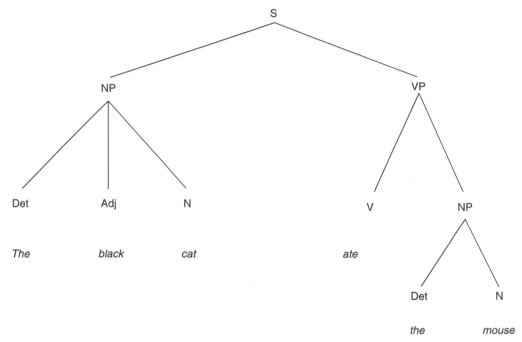

Figure 5.6 *Tree diagrams graphically represent the structure of a sentence*

appear as though they're growing from the top down, we see the different levels of constituent categories: at the top, an S consists of a NP followed by a VP; further down, a VP consists of a V that may be followed by an Adv or PP, and so on. Figure 5.6 shows how tree structures graphically represent the structure of a sentence: As we move down the tree, the categories are expanded at each level until there are no more constituents to be analyzed.

Tree diagrams are attempts to describe the syntactic grammar of a language, that is, the rules for constructing and arranging phrases within sentences. They help us to see the linear order of words and phrases in a sentence, the functions of words and phrases, and the levels at which they occur.

Exercise 5.6

On a separate piece of paper, draw tree diagrams for the following sentences.

1. The athletes trained in Colorado for the Olympics.
2. The new museum exhibit quickly broke attendance records.
3. The lady in the red jacket is my aunt.

Phrase structure rules

In addition to employing tree diagrams, we can analyze sentence grammar by using **phrase structure rules**. Phrase structure rules are written in

linear fashion. The phrase structure rule for a simple sentence in English is S →
NP + (Aux) + VP. The arrow in this case means "can consist of," so the rule
states that a sentence can consist of a noun phrase, an optional (indicated by
parentheses) auxiliary, and a verb phrase. The phrase structure rule for NP is
NP → (Det) + (Adj) + N, where a determiner or an adjective is optional, and
the noun is a requirement. The following is a list of common English phrase
structure rules:

S → NP + (Aux) + VP
NP → (Det) + (Adj) + N
NP → Pro
NP → NP + PP
PP → P + NP
VP → (Aux) + V + (NP) + (PP)

If we wished to use phrase structure rules to describe one of our sample
sentences above, we would write it thus:

S →   NP   +   VP
      The dog   *followed me behind the tree.*

We could then break down the sentence constituents even more, into their
respective parts:

NP → Det + N   *the dog*
Det → *the*
N → *dog*
VP → V + NP + PP   *followed me behind the tree*
V → *followed*
NP → Pro   *me*
PP → P + NP   *behind the tree*
P → *behind*
NP → Det + N   *the tree*
Det → *the*
N → *tree*

Exercise 5.7

A. Write a phrase illustrating each of the following phrase structure rules. We've completed the
first rule for you:

1.   VP → Aux + V + NP + PP *has jumped the curb on the street*
2.   PP → P + Det + Adj + N
3.   S → NP + Aux + VP
4.   NP → Det + N + PP

B. Write a phrase structure rule for the following sentence:

The frightened mouse ran up the clock.

Generative grammar

Drawing on theories of language innateness, linguists have hypothesized that the set of phrase structure rules not only describes actual sentence structures, but generates all potential sentences as well. Because of this potential, linguists call this set of rules a **generative grammar**, a finite set of grammar rules from which all possible sentences of a language could be produced.

A generative grammar rests on the idea that two sets of rules reflect every language user's mental grammar: the knowledge of the language rules needed to construct individual sentences, that is, phrase structure rules, which we have discussed above; and **transformation rules**, rules about changes that can be performed on basic structures to produce an infinite number of sentences. Let's examine a few examples of basic sentence structures and their transformations to see how a generative grammar might work.

In our earlier set of sample phrase structure rules, we saw that a sentence (S) always has the constituent order NP + (Aux) + VP But what happens when we see a sentence type like that shown in sentence 2 below?

1   *The baby is crying.*
2   *Is the baby crying?*

We see that the word order has changed from sentence 1 to sentence 2, and the latter now has the structure Aux + NP + VP. The auxiliary (Aux) in the first sentence has moved before the NP of the second. Linguists account for this structure by suggesting that a *transformational* rule has been applied to basic structure Sentence 1, which results in the new structure of Sentence 2. You will recognize the transformation here as one that allows speakers to create yes/no questions: the auxiliary verb has been moved to the left of the noun phrase. The transformation rule for creating these types of questions can be formulated thus: NP + Aux + VP → Aux + NP + VP. We can apply this transformation rule to other sentences having auxiliaries as well:

He can swim one hundred yards./Can he swim one hundred yards?
The teacher will give out the test./Will the teacher give out the test?

and so on. Notice that transformation rules act on structures and not on words: the rule for creating yes/no questions can be applied to any basic sentence containing a NP + Aux + VP.

This is just one example of a transformational rule in English. There are many others, including rules about adverb and prepositional phrase movements, question formation using wh-words, such as "Which" and "What," and passive verb constructions. We have introduced you to the notion of phrase structure rules and their transformations to show you yet another type of syntactic analysis. Drawing upon their observations of language use, linguists theorized about an internal set of rules that users unconsciously employ to construct an infinite number of sentences.

Table 5.2 *Differing approaches to grammar study*

	Prescriptive grammar	Descriptive grammar	Generative grammar
Purpose	Teaches speakers and writers to be "correct"	Identifies usages acceptable and unacceptable to language community	Identifies rules that would generate all meaningful potential utterances in a language
Methodology	Analyzes parts of language and their functions	Analyzes language usage of individual language communities	Reveals native speakers' intuitive knowledge of language rules
Theoretical Approach	Privileges Latin	Describes actual language usage	Generates phrase structure and transformational rules

Generative grammar is one of several approaches to studying grammar and syntax that we have covered in this chapter. Table 5.2 summarizes their differences. Other approaches exist as well, based on other theoretical models. Even though we can't explore every approach here, we hope you now recognize that grammars and methods of grammar study are complex and dynamic, rather than the static set of rules and lessons most often associated with the subject. Because any study of grammar asks the fundamental and intriguing questions, what do humans know about their language structures and how do they know it?, we can be assured that linguists will continue searching for answers in the future. In the next chapter you will learn more methods of language analysis as we move on to examine the sound system of English.

Chapter summary

In this chapter we've stressed that a grammar is not a fixed, timeless system, but a constantly changing paradigm that is influenced by many factors. We've seen how the privileging of Latin shaped the early study of English and is still an influence today. **Prescriptive grammar** developed from this privileging in an attempt to improve English, based upon the belief that some grammars are more "correct" than others. The prescriptive approach is now termed **traditional grammar**. Adopting the approach of scientific inquiry, linguists began using nonevaluative methods of grammar analysis and thus became more **descriptive** than prescriptive in their grammars. Linguists have developed theories about the rules regarding the **syntax** of English, which include naming **constituents**, identifying **syntactic categories**, and constructing **phrase structure rules**. In an attempt to describe users' inherent knowledge of their language syntax, or their **mental grammars**, linguists hypothesized a **generative grammar**, a small set of rules that could theoretically generate an infinite number of **grammatical** sentences.

Critical Thinking exercises

1.   What is a sentence? In *The Cambridge Encyclopedia of the English Language*, David Crystal (1995) questions traditional definitions of a sentence, pointing out that none of them is completely accurate. One common definition, "the complete expression of a single thought," means that a phrase like "Good Morning!" would be a sentence, but most people would not identify it as such. Another frequent definition, sentences are "units of meaning which 'make sense' by themselves," falls short as well because conversational English frequently begins with conjunctions and includes incomplete references. Consider the following line of dialogue: "So we'd been to town and then back very quickly to meet before we went there." You'd have no trouble understanding this line of dialogue in a conversation, but when it stands alone on a written page it is confusing. Does this example suggest that a sentence is differently defined for written English and for spoken English? (Crystal 1995, pp. 214–215). Working as a descriptive linguist, attempt to write one definition that fits written texts, spoken dialogue, and electronic communication. Then exchange definitions with someone else in the class to test this definition. Can the two of you write a definition of *sentence* that can be applied to the language of American English? If so, why? If not, why not?

2.   Consider the following two remarks: 1) The eighteenth-century poet John Dryden explained that his writing process required translating his English into Latin to determine the best possible expression for English. 2) You might have heard friends or even teachers say that learning a foreign language will teach you about English grammar. Consider the validity of these two statements, given what you have learned in this chapter. Then write a rationale supporting your opinion as to their accuracy or inaccuracy.

3.   Apparently, there are many people, besides linguists and teachers, who think about English grammar and even worry about their usage. For people interested in grammar, there are numerous resources, such as journals, advice columns, online newsletters, telephone hotlines, and other venues that discuss and often answer questions about grammar. Go to one of the sites listed below and read some of the discussions. Report back to your class about how grammar is presented; for instance, decide whether the author(s) are prescriptivists or descriptivists. Examine how the writers defend their rules. What authorities are invoked when making their arguments?

http://owl.english.purdue.edu/handouts/grammar/
www.protrainco.com/info/grammar.htm
www.dailygrammar.com

Hot Topic: Is Instant Messaging ruining our kids?

You've undoubtedly heard criticism of electronic discourse in a variety of contexts. Many people believe that the use of Instant Messaging (IM) and Text Messaging teaches users incorrect word and sentence structures, and, as a result, students today no longer know how to write English correctly. We would like you to explore this claim by first analyzing, and then drawing conclusions about, IM and texting.

Form a group and have each group member print out a typical IM dialogue, or, if you can re-create a text dialogue, bring that in. The dialogue should consist of a number of exchanges to give a true perspective of language use, so use one that continues for several screens. Then let group members exchange print-outs and begin to construct a grammar of the IM or text exchange. To do this, look for repeated word forms and/or usage patterns. For example, do you notice particular prefixes or suffixes being repeated? Or particular types of sentences that rely on a certain word order? Do you see sentences at all? Once you've identified patterns and structures, write down a list of grammar rules regarding IM or Text Messaging use. After completing the list, decide as a group whether IM and Text Messaging are indeed ungrammatical. Let the principles you've learned about language in this textbook guide you in your decision.

Now, place your analysis within the context of the larger debate. Do you believe users are failing to learn "correct" word and sentence structure because they use these electronic discourses? To complicate your thoughts on this, you should be aware that IM is an important tool in the corporate world, where it has been embraced for speeding communication and connecting people across vast geographical expanses. In fact, it's reported that more than 80 percent of corporations use IM in their professional communications (Strom 2006). Should we worry about our culture's use of IM? Or about its effect on SAE? As a group, write a short essay (two or three pages) responding to this controversy using your knowledge of linguistics and your group's analysis of IM texts.

Learn more about it

Historical perspectives on the study of grammar

Bagley, A. 2004, *Grammar as teacher*, The University of Minnesota College of Education and Human Development, http://iconics.cehd.umn.edu/lecture_hall/grammar.htm

The author examines the iconic imagery of Grammar from the past, explaining its significance to the study of grammar in schools.

Baron, D. 1982, *Grammar and good taste: Reforming the American language*,
    New Haven, CT: Yale University Press.
The author traces efforts to shape American English from its origins to the
present in a well-researched and reader-friendly text.

Crystal, D. 1995, *The Cambridge encyclopedia of the English language*, Cambridge:
    Cambridge University Press.
As the title suggests, this is an encyclopedic survey of the English language that
is both thorough and interesting.

Contemporary perspectives on the study of grammar

Patterson, N. G. 1999, *The role of grammar in the language arts curriculum*, www.msu.
    edu/user/patter90/grammar.htm
In this essay, Patterson summarizes the major theories of grammar and grammar
instruction that have developed since the 1960s.

Radford, A. 2004, *English syntax: An introduction*, Cambridge: Cambridge University
    Press.
This volume is a concise, accessible introduction to current syntactic theory,
suitable for the student with little or no prior grammatical knowledge.

6   American English sounds and spelling

Overview

This chapter adds to your knowledge of descriptive linguistics by teaching you the basics of the American English sound system. You'll learn how linguists classify sounds and then record them visually in order to analyze them. You'll also understand why the standard American English spelling system fails to accurately represent the language's sounds. Because of this failure, many Americans have proposed reforms to the alphabet and/or the spelling system currently in use. Finally, the Hot Topic asks you to research the methodology of different dictionaries to discover whether or not they are legitimate language authorities.

Introduction

Every year in the United States and in other English-speaking countries, school-aged children participate in spelling bees, competitions in which contestants hear a word pronounced and then must spell that word out loud. Because competition is stiff, contestants prepare months ahead of time, memorizing the spelling of lists of words and their origins. What makes these spelling competitions so difficult? Read out loud some of the following words from a study guide for spelling bee contestants, and see if they give you a clue:

occa<u>si</u>on	*peti<u>tion</u>*
exis<u>tence</u>	*resis<u>tance</u>*
s<u>ie</u>ve	*braz<u>ie</u>r*
pan<u>ache</u>	*head<u>ache</u>*

You probably quickly realized from these examples that no one-to-one correspondence between sound and spelling exists in American English. In other words, users can't always determine pronunciation from spelling and, vice versa, determine spelling from pronunciation. Over the years, various groups, including that pictured in Figure 6.1, have complained about English spellings.

Figure 6.1 *Spelling reformers protesting at a spelling bee*
(Credit: Simplified Spelling Society)

This lack of correspondence presents problems for all users, not just those competing in spelling bees, because it creates difficulties moving between the spoken and written forms of the language. For example, think about the word *salmon*, which many American English speakers pronounce without the *l* sound. Even someone who hears this word spoken regularly might have trouble recognizing its written form, and someone who's only read it might not understand the word when spoken. You can undoubtedly think of many more words illustrating this lack of correspondence between spelling and pronunciation: *knife*, *unique*, *fuchsia*, *gauche*, and on and on.

The word *salmon* illustrates another important issue in the relationship between spoken and written language: Although some speakers pronounce this word without the *l*, other speakers distinctly articulate this sound. This fact reveals that American English speakers vary in their pronunciation of words. Such variation occurs frequently: Do you pronounce the word *government* so that the root *govern* is clearly audible, or do you say *goverment*? Do you use three or four syllables when saying the word *poinsettia*? *Nuclear* or *nucular*? No matter which of these variations you choose to use in your own speech, chances are quite good that you'd be easily understood. But the same flexibility doesn't exist in the written word. If you wrote a sentence with the words *goverment*, *poinsetta*, and *nucular*, you'd probably create confusion rather than understanding. For these three words, and many others, pronunciations differ based on an individual's speech patterns, but spellings don't.

This inconsistent relationship between spelling and pronunciation is found in English, and in other languages as well, making it difficult not only for those learning to read and write but also for those who study how language is communicated through its sound and spelling systems. How does one analyze a language's sound system without being able to preserve it in a consistent, unambiguous manner?

The following chapter explains how linguists resolve this problem through **phonology**, or the study of the unique set of sounds and sound patterns of a language. And since writing came into existence as a means to preserve speech sounds, the chapter will also examine American English **orthography**, the study of how these sounds are represented in writing, in order to understand why there are discrepancies between the ways in which American English words are pronounced and spelled.

The phonology of American English

Linguists who study the distinctive speech sounds of a language and the rules and patterns of language sound systems are called phonologists. Phonologists examine individual languages to identify their unique sets of sounds or, in other words, to identify the distinctive sounds that create meaning when brought together in certain patterns. This is no small task because, as you know, people often produce sounds in their speech that have no apparent meaning: consider for instance those "ums and uhs" that sometimes appear in our conversations. Have you ever heard someone say something like this:

> "Iumthoughtuhthatwecouldgooutsometimehmm?"

The word *phonology* combines two lexical morphemes that originated in Greek: *phono*, meaning *sound*, and *logy*, meaning *the study of*. With the addition of the derivational suffix *-ist*, the noun shifts from describing an intellectual activity to describing an individual with a particular specialization.

Was it difficult for you to understand? Now think about someone who does not know English. He or she would have a hard time distinguishing the meaningful from the meaningless sounds in this sort of sentence.

In addition to voicing meaningless sounds while speaking, speakers also pronounce meaningful sounds in slightly different ways. Think of a Southern speaker saying *bahn* instead of *barn*, for example. Speakers familiar with American English sounds understand that these two different pronunciations don't affect the meaning of the word; they both mean *a building used to store hay*. But in another word, a change in pronunciation like this might completely change the meaning. Try saying *bit* and *boat* to yourself. In this instance, the middle sounds are not interchangeable: *bit* and *boat* mean two different things. In addition to identifying meaningful sounds, phonologists must identify the patterns of usage when variation in sound makes a distinction in meaning.

In the field of linguistics, speech sounds are called **phonemes**, the smallest distinct units of sound within a particular language's sound system that carry meaning when combined with other sounds. Consider the English word *pot*, for example. This word contains three phonemes: the *p*-sound, the short *o*-sound, and the *t*-sound. Individually, these sounds have no meaning, but when combined with other sounds, they produce a meaningful word.

How do phonologists go about identifying a language's set of phonemes? One method they use is to write lists of words they hear and then to ask native speakers the meanings of these words. For example, if a phonologist unfamiliar with American English were to study this language, he might come up with a list of words like the following:

pot	lot	dot
rot	got	not

From asking native speakers, the phonologist would learn that these English words differ in meaning. And since the words differ from each other by only one sound, in the initial position, he would conclude that each initial sound is a phoneme, that is, each initial sound distinguishes meaning. We can test this theory that *p*, *l*, *d*, are indeed phonemes with other words as well. For example, the words *peer*, *deer*, and *leer* have distinct meanings and only differ from each other by one sound, again the initial one. This kind of testing can be done with any number of examples where the words differ by only one speech sound: the words *bug*, *but*, and *bun* reveal that *g*, *t*, and *n* are phonemes; *sit*, *set*, and *sat* show that *i*, *e*, and *a* are phonemes, and so on.

Phonologists have identified a total of about forty phonemes in English, which is fairly average for the world's languages. Remember that other languages may have a different phonemic system, though. For example, if you've studied Spanish, you know that Spanish speakers use some phonemes not found in English. One of these is indicated by the Spanish spelling *r*, whose pronunciation requires a single touch of the tongue to the roof of the mouth, and a second is indicated by the Spanish spelling *rr*, which requires a trilling between the tongue and the roof of the mouth. Neither of these phonemes is the same sound spelled with the American English *r*, which doesn't require the tongue to touch the roof of the mouth at all. Some languages have many more phonemes than American English does – over 100 – and others have far fewer – some as few as 8–10.

Transcribing phonemes

To analyze a language's sound system, phonologists need to be able to **transcribe** its phonemes, that is, transfer them from the oral medium to a written one by using a single symbol to represent each significant sound in a particular language. As you've already seen, some spelling systems, such as that of American English, are not very reliable in indicating precise pronunciations, so instead phonologists use a **phonetic transcription system**, most commonly the International Phonetic Alphabet (IPA). The IPA is an important linguistic tool because it provides a unique symbol for every sound uttered in all of the world's languages. This means that a linguist can go into any culture and, using the IPA, transcribe the language she hears in order to discover the rules and conventions for that particular sound system.

Note that the IPA can represent not only every sound in the world's languages but every variation of a sound as well, variations that do not create a distinct, or contrastive meaning. Here's an illustration of what we mean by this. Say the words *pin* and *top* while holding your hand in front of your lips. Did you feel the puff of air, the aspiration, made when you pronounced the initial consonant sound in *pin*? This doesn't occur when pronouncing the *p* in *top*, so technically these two sounds are not exactly the same. Yet to English speakers, pronouncing the *p* with or without aspiration doesn't affect the meaning that it carries. So when we use the term *phoneme* we're really talking about a class of sounds comprising all the variations of a phoneme. The *p* phoneme class in English, then, would contain two sounds: the aspirated and unaspirated *p*'s. The IPA is precise enough to represent all the variations of sounds in one phoneme class, but for our purposes here we'll use the IPA to represent only those sounds that do contrast in meaning, the phoneme classes, and not the variations. And to help you distinguish IPA symbols from American English alphabet letters, we'll indicate IPA transcriptions by using brackets.

Table 6.1 *IPA symbols for American English consonants*

IPA symbol	Example
p	pet
b	bed
m	man
t	tea
d	dog
n	noon
k	kite
g	goat
ŋ	sing
f	foot
v	vinyl
s	sun
z	zoo
θ	think
ð	this
ʃ	shop
ʒ	vision
ʧ	church
ʤ	judge
l	line
r	rock
j	yes
w	wild
h	high

For ease in linguistic description, American English sounds are divided into **consonants**, produced when the speaker constricts or completely stops the airflow, and **vowels**, produced with relatively little or no constriction of airflow. Table 6.1 lists the IPA symbols for many of the consonant sounds used in common American English dialects alongside an example for each of a common spelling correspondence.

Table 6.2 lists the IPA symbols representing many of the vowel sounds used in many American English dialects and an example for each of a common spelling correspondence.

> For a complete list of international IPA symbols, see www.langsci.ucl.ac.uk/ipa/ipachart.html

Because the IPA allows phonologists to represent all the sounds of a language, it enables them to examine the differences between *accents*, or the way that individuals pronounce words based on their own, unique, background. We'll examine variations in American English in more depth in Chapter 8, but here we want to emphasize that phonologists analyze pronunciation as it actually occurs. The following exercise asks you to practice using the IPA.

Table 6.2 *IPA symbols for American English vowels*

IPA symbol	Example
i	m<u>ea</u>t
I	m<u>i</u>tt
e	m<u>a</u>te
ɛ	m<u>e</u>t
æ	m<u>a</u>t
u	b<u>oo</u>t
ʊ	b<u>oo</u>k
ʌ	m<u>u</u>tt
o	m<u>oa</u>t
ɔ	c<u>au</u>ght
a	m<u>o</u>m
ə	<u>o</u>f
aj	r<u>i</u>de
oj	b<u>oy</u>
au	l<u>ou</u>d

Exercise 6.1

Working with a small group of classmates, take turns reading the following list of words out loud to one another. What variation do you hear in pronunciation among the members of your group? Once you have discussed the variations in your pronunciations, work individually to transcribe these words into their phonetic symbol correspondences, using Tables 6.1 and 6.2 as your guides. Compare your answers with those of the other people in your group, and discover the hometowns of your group members. Can you identify any features of pronunciation that seem to be tied to a particular geographical location?

1.   might
2.   thought
3.   rot
4.   Mary
5.   merry
6.   talk
7.   near
8.   greasy
9.   sang
10.   witch
11.   which
12.   aunt

Classifying phonemes

To help themselves describe the phonemes of a language, phono-logists group sounds into classes based upon **distinctive features**, or the unique characteristics of phonemes that create differences in meaning. Such features include the **place of articulation**, the place in the mouth where the speech sound is produced, and the **manner of articulation**, the way in which the airstream is modified as it travels up from a person's lungs and through his mouth as he speaks.

Places and manners of articulation

Consonants Consonants are produced by stopping or constricting the flow of air as it moves from the lungs through the mouth. The three major places of articulation in the mouth are the lips, the alveolar ridge (directly behind the front teeth), and the soft palate.

The following list indicates the manner of articulation of American English consonants:

Stops: produced from the surge of air released after the lips have completely stopped the air's movement. [p], [b], [t], [d], [k], [g]

Fricatives: produced when the air "rubs" through a constricted opening. [f], [v], [θ], [ð], [s], [z], [ʃ], [ʒ], [h]

Affricates: produced when a surge of air is released after being completely stopped but then "rubs" through a constricted opening rather than being released. An affricate is thus a combination of stop and fricative. [tʃ], [dʒ]

Liquids: produced from a loose constriction of the airflow, enabling it to be sustained indefinitely. [l], [r]

Nasals: produced by forcing the flow of air into the nasal cavity rather than letting it escape through the mouth. [m], [n], [ŋ]

Glides: produced with very little constriction of the airflow, similar to that of a vowel. [j], [w]

Another distinctive feature of American English consonant articulation is the presence or lack of **voicing**, which is created by a speaker's use of her vocal cords. When a person's vocal cords are together, the air must force its way through them, causing the vocal cords to vibrate, thus creating *voiced* sounds. Put your hand on your throat, over your Adam's apple, and say the *th* sound in *though*. The vibration that you feel comes from your vocal cords. When a person's vocal cords are apart, however, the air stream passes freely through the mouth, and the sounds that are created are called *voiceless* sounds. Put your hand on your throat and say the *th* sound in *through*. Feel the difference between this voiceless sound and the voiced sound you made earlier? There are about nine voiceless consonant sounds in English and fifteen voiced consonant sounds; all vowels in English are voiced sounds. The distinctive feature of voiced/voiceless is important in English phonology because it often is the only feature that distinguishes phonemes. Box 6.1 presents pairs of words where voicing creates a difference in meaning. Table 6.3 illustrates the voicing, and places and manners of articulation for American English consonants.

Box 6.1 Voicing contrasts

Pronounce each word of the following pairs out loud to hear the contrasting sounds:

path/bath	safer/saver	mace/maze	back/bag
[pæθ]/[bæθ]	[sefr]/[sevr]	[mes]/[mez]	[bæk]/[bæg]

Table 6.3 *Voicing, and places and manners of articulation for American English consonants*

MANNER OF ARTICULATION	PLACE OF ARTICULATION							
	Bilabial (two lips)	Labio-dental (lip-teeth)	Inter-dental (teeth)	Alveolar (behind upper teeth)	Alveolo-palatal (before palate)	Palatal (palate)	Velar (back of mouth)	Glottal (vocal cords)
Stop (voiceless)	p			t		k		
Stop (voiced)	b			d		g		
Fricative (voiceless)		f	θ	s	ʃ			h
Fricative (voiced)		v	ð	z	ʒ			
Affricate (voiceless)					tʃ			
Affricate (voiced)					dʒ			
Liquid (voiced lateral)				l				
Liquid (voiced retroflex)				r				
Nasal (voiced)	m			n		ŋ		
Glide (voiced)	w					j		

Table 6.4 *Places and manners of articulation for American English vowels*

	Front of mouth	**Center of mouth**	**Back of mouth**
High	i (m<u>ea</u>t)		u (b<u>oo</u>t)
	I (m<u>i</u>tt)	ə (<u>o</u>f)	ʊ (b<u>oo</u>k)
Mid	e (m<u>a</u>te)	ʌ (m<u>u</u>tt)	o (m<u>oa</u>t)
	ɛ (m<u>e</u>t)		ɔ (c<u>au</u>ght)
Low	æ (m<u>a</u>t)		a (m<u>o</u>m)

Vowels Vowel sounds are created by the tongue shaping the flow of air as it moves from the lungs through the mouth, a less precise physical movement than that required for creating consonants. So rather than exact physical locations, the places and manners of articulation of vowels are general descriptors, indicating the place of the tongue in the mouth (high, low, back, front) and the relative rounding of the lips. Table 6.4 indicates both the places and manners of articulation for American English vowels.

Sometimes American English vowel sounds include **diphthongs**, two sounds merged into one phoneme. Think about saying the word *time,* for instance. Articulation of the initial vowel sound begins toward the back of the mouth, and may be represented by the IPA symbol [a]. The place of articulation then glides forward toward the front of the mouth for the ending of the vowel sound, which is represented for most speakers by the symbol [j]. So a phonetic transcription of the word *time* is [tajm]. Other diphthongs in English include [oj] (**toy**) and [au] (**cow**).

Digital audio equipment used in data gathering and computerized data analysis have greatly aided the many dialect studies, both large and small, currently taking place in the United States. The following website, supported by the University of Iowa, illustrates the sounds of English with audio clips and video animations of the anatomical changes necessary to create each sound: http://www.uiowa.edu/~acadtech/phonetics/english/frameset.html

Exercise 6.2

Using Tables 6.3 and 6.4, give a three-part articulatory description (manner of articulation, place of articulation, and voicing) for each of the following speech sounds:

1. [z]
2. [k]
3. [I]
4. [o]
5. [j]
6. [tʃ]
7. [b]
8. [n]

Combining phonemes

You learned in previous chapters that all language users unconsciously follow certain morphological and syntactic rules when using their native languages. This occurs for phonological rules as well. In the following discussion, we'll give you a few examples of phonological rules in American English. Remember, just as in the morphological or syntactic systems, these "rules" come from listening to the language as it is actually used. They are descriptive rules, rules that describe the speech sound patterns of English speakers.

Native speakers of English do not learn phonological rules consciously but instead intuitively produce sounds and sound clusters that are "allowed" in English. For instance, these speakers know that certain groupings of sounds or sound clusters cannot occur at the beginning of English syllables and thus never produce words like *tvep or *pgor (note that we put an asterisk by words deemed unacceptable by native speakers). How would linguists, however, describe this unconscious knowledge as a phonological rule? Typically, linguists identify the features of a sound: its voicing, place of articulation and manner of articulation. Next, they examine the neighboring sounds in order to detect phonological patterns, or the rules about the distribution of sounds. By noting the features of the sounds and the environment in which they appear, and by determining from native speakers what is and is not permitted, linguists can then construct the phonological rules of a language. For instance, in the examples of *tvep and *pgor, after identifying the features of the first two consonant sounds of each word, linguists might hypothesize that a voiceless consonant followed by a voiced consonant at the beginning of English words is not allowed. Of course, they would need much more data – many more examples of both acceptable and unacceptable words in English – in order to prove their hypothesis.

> Other language systems follow different phonological conventions that English speakers may find particularly difficult. For instance, the phonology of the Xhosans in southern Africa includes clicks and pops that Americans may not even recognize as meaningful sounds. And of course other language speakers have difficulty with American phonological conventions. For example, Cantonese phonology has no consonant clusters, so Cantonese speakers learning English might have difficulty pronouncing these kinds of combinations. Such speakers commonly reduce the clusters at the ends of words, resulting in utterances like *mo'* instead of *most* or *ki'* instead of *kick*.

Changing rules

In addition to explaining the existence of phonological rules, we also need to recognize that these rules may change over time. As in morphological and syntactical changes, phonological change tends to be driven by the realities of everyday usage. Let's examine two specific reasons why phonological rules might change over time.

Assimilation occurs when the articulation of one sound within a word is influenced by a nearby or adjacent sound so that, together, the differences between the sounds are minimized. Just think about how many people pronounce the word *horseshoe* as [horʃu] rather than [horsʃu]. The [s] and the [ʃ] are difficult to distinguish from each other when they are pronounced side by side, so many speakers allow the [ʃ] to influence [s], merging the two sounds together into a single pronunciation. Examining the inflectional morpheme *-ed* provides other examples of assimilation. When it occurs after voiceless consonants, as in *trapped*, the final consonant is articulated as a voiceless [t], so that the word is pronounced [træpt]. But when *-ed* follows a voiced consonant, as in *bagged*, the final consonant remains a voiced [d]: [bægd]. In each case, the pronunciation of the past tense inflection has assimilated the voicing of the consonantal sound before it.

Exercise 6.3

In English several morphemes indicate negation, including *non-*, *dis-*, *anti-*, *in-*, and *im-*. Have you ever wondered why some words take *in-* and some take *im-*? You'll know the answer if you consider the phonological patterns of the words in which they appear. Examine the list of words below, noting each word's phonological features. Construct a rule for using *in-* and *im-* in English.

incorrect	impossible
incarcerated	impermeable
intangible	imperceptible
inhospitable	impersonal

Another change in the "rules" of pronunciation occurs when speakers have to distinguish between similar sounds in a sequence. In this case, they frequently use **dissimulation**, making nearby sounds less similar or even omitting one so that the sequence of sounds is easier to articulate. For instance, think about the pronunciation of *surprise*. The consonant *-r* at the end of the first syllable is frequently omitted in conversation, leaving the word pronounced as [sʌprajz]. *Library*, pronounced [lajbəri], and *governor*, pronounced [gʌvənər], are other examples of this phonological convention, which frequently creates spelling problems.

Over time, as more and more speakers use these pronunciations, they might eventually completely replace the original sound patterns. Sound changes like these explain one of the reasons why the pronunciation and spelling of a word might differ. After all, when a spelling system first originates, words are usually spelled to indicate how they are pronounced. Look at *knife* for an example. When it first entered Old English, the word was pronounced [knIf]. Over time the initial consonant became silent, and the vowel sound became a dipthong. But even though we now pronounce this word [najf], the spelling still reflects its earlier pronunciation. Let's now examine the history of the American English spelling system to understand some of the other reasons for spelling changes. As you'll see, American English spelling tends to reflect historical, rather than contemporary, pronunciations.

The spelling system of American English

An **alphabet** is a writing system for a single language that links each meaningful sound to a written symbol. The contemporary American English spelling system uses the Latin alphabet adapted to represent the sounds of the English language. The Latin alphabet was first used in England in 597 CE, when Roman Catholic missionaries began arriving to convert the Anglo-Saxons to Christianity. Because the Old English sound system was similar to that of Latin, Christian scribes were able to use the Latin alphabet with only a few additions, such as the rune þ (*thorn*), for sounds used in Old English but not in Latin. Over the next few centuries, though, runes disappeared from use.

The earliest types of writing systems in England were alphabets, used by both the Celts and the Germanic tribes who began invading in the fifth century CE. Although they were related, each group had its own language and its own writing system. These Germanic peoples carved their alphabet letters, called **runes**, on wood or stone. Runes were composed primarily of straight lines, which were much easier to carve into hard surfaces than curved lines.

Early changes in English spelling

After the Norman Conquest in 1066, the French brought their own writing system into England. Although they also used the Roman alphabet, the French did not always represent a sound with the same alphabet letter that the Anglo-Saxons did. In some instances, they would use a **digraph**, or two alphabet letters used together to represent a single sound. Instead of using either the Anglo-Saxon letters thorn (þ) or eth (ð), for instance, the French writing system used the digraph *th*. So the Anglo-Saxon words *boð* or *wiðer* might have been written in Middle English as *both* or *wither*. And gradually, over the next few centuries, this digraph completely replaced thorn and eth. Modern American English users are also familiar with another French digraph: the doubled vowel that indicates a long vowel sound in contemporary pronunciation also came from the French writing system, giving us *beet* instead of the Anglo-Saxon *bete*, for example.

The Ruthwell Cross (ca. 700 CE) is of particular interest to both linguists and language scholars today because it contains runic and Latin alphabet transcriptions of the same passage. The words inscribed on the Cross are the beginning of the Old English poem *The Dream of the Rood*, a poem in which the narrator relates a dream about the cross on which Christ was crucified. The Ruthwell Cross is a work of art produced during a time when two different cultures, languages, and writing systems were merging: the Germanic pagan past represented by runes and the Christian future represented by the Latin alphabet.

In addition to these variations, the French introduced alphabet letters not used by the Anglo-Saxons at all. For example, our contemporary word *queen* was spelled *cwēn* in Old English; the letter *q* was not used in English until after the Norman Conquest. Neither were the letters *v* and *j*. Box 6.2 explains some of the other spelling changes brought by the French.

As you can see from the examples below, many contemporary American English spellings follow the French writing conventions introduced after the

---

Box 6.2 English spelling changes after the Norman Conquest

	Old English spelling	French spelling
c → ch	cild, ceorl, cirice	child, churl, church
sc → sh	sceal, fisc, sceaft	shall, fish, shaft
u → ou	mūs, hūs, sūþ	mouse, house, south
e → ee	bēte, dēme	beet, deem
o → oo	gōd	good
cw → qu	cwēn, cwell	queen, quell

Norman Conquest rather than continuing the Anglo-Saxon practices. The mixing of the Old English, Latin, and French languages – and their separate writing conventions – early in the history of the English language is another reason why American English spelling today is not completely based on phonic representations. And finally we have to recognize how attempts to standardize English spelling have also played a role in shaping spelling practices.

The standardization of written English

For many centuries the concept of a standard English didn't exist at all. During the Old English (ca. 500–1100) and Middle English (ca. 1100–1450) eras, the majority of the public was illiterate, so most writing was done by scribes and clerks. These writers spelled words as they personally pronounced them. And the technology didn't exist to make exactly the same language available to everyone, such as happens today through radio, television, and electronic communication. Then new technology appeared that revolutionized the English writing system.

William Caxton and the printing press

In 1476, English readers and writers saw the introduction of the printing press, a new technology that would change their writing system, their literacy rate, their language, and ultimately their culture. The Englishman William Caxton established in London, near the court, a printing press similar to the one first created by Johannes Gutenberg earlier in the

The Chancery clerks in London played a significant role in the standardization process. The Chancery was part of the royal administration of the country, responsible for keeping public records, and the clerks recorded documents in London English. These scribes made an effort to standardize the spelling in documents they produced, particularly by revising highly individual or local spellings to a version that would be more widely understood. And since these documents carried the authority of the court, the spelling choices were influential in shaping the written dialect of London English. For example, the word we recognize today as *such* might have appeared in early Middle English as *sich, seche, sych, swiche* or some other variant. Chancery clerks consistently spelled the word *such* and so gave birth to this particular standardized spelling.

Figure 6.2 *Opening page of "The Knight's Tale" from Caxton's 1483 printing of Geoffrey Chaucer's* The Canterbury Tales *©The British Library Board. All Rights Reserved 16/06/2008, G.11586*

century. Caxton printed works in English, ultimately producing a total of almost eighty books in all, including some of his own translations, as well as the works of English writers such as Geoffrey Chaucer (see Figure 6.2) and Sir Thomas Malory.

Caxton's introduction of the printing press provided the technology for a national standard of written English to develop. Mass copies of a single text meant, first of all, that more people had access to texts, and so more people could learn to read and write. It also meant that people in different regions of the country would have access to the same text, with the same spelling, punctuation, and syntax.

The language choices made by Caxton and his fellow printers also encouraged standardization. Because they wanted to run successful businesses, selling as many books as possible, they needed to use spellings that would be understood by as many people as possible.

In the middle of the fifteenth century, Johannes Gutenberg, a German metalworker, founded a commercial printing company. His innovative presses used moveable type, joining together small blocks with individual letters on them to create a page rather than creating a single carved woodblock for the whole page. Gutenberg's improvement to printing technology meant that more texts were available at lower costs than had previously been possible. For example, copying a Bible manuscript by hand might have taken a scribe as long as twenty years, while Gutenberg probably produced a printed Bible in fewer than three years. The following link will take you to the British Library's Gutenberg Bible Homepage, where you can learn more about this important work and compare two different versions of the Gutenberg Bible through the Library's digitalization project: www.bl.uk/treasures/gutenberg/homepage.html

Even though the printing press created the possibility of standardizing both the English lexicon and the English spelling system, standardization didn't immediately occur. It took time for the concept to develop and then be accepted into everyday practice.

As the ability and desire to standardize spelling increased, writers and scholars began articulating concerns about "correct" spellings, trying to control which ones would be accepted. This led to re-spellings based on etymologies rather than on pronunciation and use. Some words had letters inserted into their spellings in an effort to make them correspond to their Latin counterpart. For example, the *b* in *debt* comes from the Latin spelling *debitum* rather than from an archaic English pronunciation. Other spellings were altered in an effort to create consistency. *Delight* was originally spelled *delite*; it became *delight* to make the spelling parallel with *light*, since the two words rhymed. But the *(gh)* in *light* originally represented a distinct sound that had disappeared over time. To make the spelling and pronunciation truly parallel, the *gh* should have been dropped from *light* rather than added to *delight*. The following exercise asks you to explore some of the other reasons why spellings have been intentionally altered.

Some of the prologues to Caxton's texts discuss these concerns about the lack of a standardized English. For example, in the "Prologue" to Virgil's *Booke of Eneydos*, Caxton illustrates the lexical problem created by the lack of a national standard when he narrates a story about a sailor from the north of England visiting the southern region. When the sailor asked for *egges* (*eggs*) he wasn't understood because the southern word was *eyren*.

Even the alphabet didn't become fixed in the form we know today until the early seventeenth century. Until this period, the letters *u* and *v* did not represent specific phonemes. They had first been used interchangeably in Anglo-Saxon manuscripts. Then, under Norman influence in the Middle Ages, *v* appeared at the beginning of a word and *u* appeared in the middle. In the first decades of the seventeenth century, each letter became tied to a specific phoneme. The *v* represented a consonant sound, and the *u* represented a vowel, the same practice we follow today. This change, which took place almost 400 years ago, was the last change in the English alphabet system.

Exercise 6.4

The contemporary spellings for the following words have been influenced by etymology rather than by pronunciation. Use an etymological dictionary to identify 1) the earliest English spelling of the word, 2) the date of the earliest use of the modern spelling, and 3) the rationale for the change.

	Earliest spelling	Date of modern usage	Rationale
Arctic			
Island			
Throne			
Fault			
Whole			
Judge			

Another reason for the lack of correspondence between spelling and pronunciation is that pronunciation changes over time as well. One of the most significant of these changes, the **Great Vowel Shift**, took place during the end of the Middle Ages just as spelling was becoming standardized. Although

Figure 6.3 *Noah Webster (Credit: The Library of Congress, LC-USZC4-1586)*

linguists aren't sure why it occurred, during this period of time the places of articulation for the long vowels in Middle English shifted, moving more toward the front and top of the mouth. For example, the word *boot* was pronounced [bot] during the Middle Ages, but as a result of the Great Vowel Shift became the modern-day [but]. The Middle English *feet* [fet] became the modern [fit], and so on. But as you can see just from these two examples, even though the vowel sounds themselves had changed, the spellings remained the same.

In the sixteenth century, the early colonizers brought these English spelling and pronunciation practices with them to North America, where, as you know from Chapter 2, the language began to change and develop as American English.

American English spelling

Some of the standardized spellings and pronunciations that American English users learn today differ from their British English origins because of the widespread sense of nationalism in the country after the American Revolution. In 1828, Noah Webster published *An American Dictionary of the English Language*, describing the way that Americans actually used their language. Webster also consciously marked American English as being different from British English by prescribing changes to the standardized spellings of the time, changes that would more consistently represent American pronunciations (see Figure 6.3).

The following are some of the spelling revisions Webster suggested that later became Standard American English:

A number of Americans have also linked spelling reform with political idealism. In 1768, Benjamin Franklin revealed his own interests in tightening the correspondence between American English spelling and its pronunciation when he produced *A Scheme for a New Alphabet and a Reformed Mode of Spelling*. Franklin designed six new letters and reassigned the Latin alphabet already in use so that, in his writing system, American English

- change -*our* to -*or* in words like *honour* >*honor* and *favour* >*favor*
- change -*re* to -*er* in words like *theatre* >*theater* and *fibre* >*fiber*
- drop the final, silent -*k* in words like *publick* >*public* and *musick* >*music*

Some of Webster's other suggestions were not accepted. We still maintain the final, silent -*e* in words like *envelope* and *medicine* rather than dropping it to get *envelop* and *medicin*, and we still maintain the double -*ff* at the end of words like *pontiff* rather than reducing it to get *pontif*.

Webster's desire to mark American English's difference from British English specifically encouraged other would-be American reformers. The end of the nineteenth century saw more proposed spelling reforms, but rather than suggesting general spelling rules like Webster had, these were specific spellings for problematic words. For example, the American Philological Association wanted to see *ar* replace *are* and *giv* replace *give*, while the National Education Association wanted Americans to use *thoroly* rather than *thoroughly* and *prolog* rather than *prologue*. Perhaps one reason for the lack of success of these proposals was their lack of agreement on what to change. Yet even if reforms have not yet been successful, American English spelling has changed over the years and will undoubtedly continue to change in the future.

would have only one sound per letter. In 1854, Brigham Young supported the development of the Deseret Alphabet, also intended to represent the sounds of English with a more complete system of graphic symbols. And, in 1906, President Theodore Roosevelt ordered the Government Printing Office to use Simplified Spelling, a list of 300 words spelled phonetically that had been created by the Carnegie Spelling Reform Committee. But the House of Representatives voted against this change, and Roosevelt withdrew his order.

In 1934, the *Chicago Tribune* announced its intention to introduce and then consistently use reformed spellings, a practice that continued until 1955. Some words readers accepted, like *hiccup* for *hiccough*; others, though, such as *sofomore* for *sophomore*, were immediately rejected. And the *Tribune* didn't completely give up its attempt to shape the nation's language until an editorial in 1975 announced the paper's withdrawal from spelling reform. Eric Zorn's 1997 article explaining this history of the *Tribune*'s efforts ends by pointing out that the elevators in the *Tribune*'s building are still labeled *Frate*.

Exercise 6.5

Consider some of the following spelling changes that have taken place within the last thirty years or so: *light* to *lite*, *night* to *nite*, *through* to *thru*, *love* to *luv*, and so on. Then see if you can come up with examples of more recent English spelling changes, say within the last five to ten years. To help you with this, think of aspects of popular culture, like advertising, music, and literature, where spelling changes often occur first. Once you've identified at least four or five spelling changes, consider why these alternatives have come about. Who originally changed these spellings, and for what purposes?

Chapter summary

This chapter has examined the systems of **phonology** and **orthography** in American English in order to understand how both work, as well as why they are not in alignment with each other. You've learned how linguists analyze speech sounds by identifying their **distinctive features**, such as **voicing** and **places** and **manners of articulation**, and then by transcribing each sound with an **IPA** symbol. You also now understand why the American English spelling system is varied and often inconsistent, and you have learned some of the ways in which people and institutions have attempted to standardize the language through the years.

Critical Thinking exercises

1. The English inflection for making a noun plural is -*s*, but it is pronounced in three different ways: [s], [z], and [əz]. The pronunciation used depends upon the phonological environment in which the -*s* appears. So, [s] ends nouns such as *wasp*, *tack*, *pit*, and *laugh*; [z] ends nouns such as *pad*, *can*, *leg*, and *song*; and [əz] ends nouns such as *craze*, *bench*, *ledge*, and *mass*. Using this information and Tables 6.1, 6.2, 6.3, and 6.4, identify the sounds preceding the *plural inflection* in each word that determine its pronunciation. Then classify these sounds by their manner and place of articulation, and by their voicing, in order to create a general phonological rule predicting when each ending will be used. (Hint: transcribe each of the words above into the IPA to help you analyze the phonology.)

2. As noted in this chapter, many people over the years have attempted to improve upon the American English spelling system. Below are listed six websites for spelling reform. Go to one site and evaluate its plan for reform. Would the plan work? How difficult would it be to initiate? What potential problems can you identify with the plan? Be prepared to report on your research and analysis in class.
   - The Unifon Alphabet: www.unifon.org/
   - E–speec.com: www.e-speec.com/
   - New English Writing: www.new-english-writing.info/
   - Cut Spelng: http://victorian.fortunecity.com/vangogh/555/ Spell/cut-spl.html
   - Fanetik: www.fanetik.org/
   - Rite Spelling: www.ritespel.org/

3. Although this chapter has discussed arguments for spelling reforms, you also should be aware that many reasons exist for maintaining American English spelling just as it is. Choose a position, either for reform or against it, and then write a position paper supporting your choice. You can easily find information about spelling reform in journals and newspapers, and by searching online.

Hot Topic: How valid is a dictionary?

Have you ever had someone correct your pronunciation of a particular word? Or wondered how to pronounce a word you only knew through reading? Do standard pronunciations for American English words exist? You've undoubtedly turned to a dictionary to answer questions like these, but you've probably never wondered how a dictionary editor determines the content for each entry. And you may not have realized that the numerous dictionaries of American English do not all agree on pronunciations or spellings or definitions or etymologies, because no single American English language authority exists. Yet our culture tends to view any sort of dictionary as an authority on language use. How much authority do dictionaries really have?

For this assignment, work with two or three of your classmates to research the specific dictionaries listed below assigned by your instructor. Find out the following information about your dictionary:

1. Objectives, or goals
    a. Type of information in entries
    b. Range of entries
    c. Format of entries
2. Intended users
3. Methodology
    a. Identifying content – How are new words identified? Are words ever deleted?
    b. Gathering content – How is information about words gathered?
    c. Evaluating content – What sort of categories and usage labels are used in individual entries? How are these judgments made?
    d. Updating content – What is the process for updating information about new usages, such as new definitions, new connotations, or new historical discoveries?
    e. Resolving difficulties – How are conflicts over precise definitions, new words, and so on resolved?
4. Authorities – Who makes final decisions on spelling, pronunciation, meaning, usage? (Advisory Board? Editor? Usage Panel? Other?)

As you gather this information, you may wish to compare/contrast it with that of another dictionary, say one of the dictionaries that you use for your own studies (paperback, abridged, whatever), to give yourselves a larger perspective.

As a group, prepare an oral report for the class on your dictionaries, and present a written version of the report to your instructor. Your report should contain a comparative analysis. How effective did you find these dictionaries for their intended audiences and purposes? Should users be aware of any limitations? How do the usage labels help you to understand these dictionaries?

1.   Am*erican heritage*, 4th edition, 2000 and *Merriam–Webster's third new international dictionary, unabridged*. Merriam–Webster's. 2002 (or the most recent editions in your library).

2.   *Oxford English dictionary* ("About the *OED*" explains background information; "Writing the dictionary" includes collecting evidence, writing definitions, etc.): www.oed.com/ and a dictionary of American English in your library, such as the *Cambridge dictionary of American English*.

3.   *Longman dictionary of contemporary English online*: www.ldoceon line.com (Be sure to read about the *Longman corpus network*: www.longman.com/dictionaries/corpus/index.html) and *Wordsmythe dictionary-thesaurus*: www.wordsmyth.net/

4.   *Urban dictionary*: www.urbandictionary.com and *The jargon file*: http://catb.org/~esr/jargon

5.   The *PseudoDictionary.com*: www.pseudodictionary.com/ and *The rap dictionary*: www.rapdict.org/Main_Page (Be sure to explore the "About Rap Dictionary" link at bottom right of page).

Learn more about it

American English phonology

Callary, E. 1998, Phonetics, in V. P. Clark, P. A. Eschholz, and A. F. Rosa (eds.), *Language: Readings in language and culture,* New York: St. Martin's Press, pp. 113–133.
In this essay, Callary explains articulatory and acoustic phonetics. He then investigates English phonetic conventions, the "permissible" sound sequences that allow meaning to be clearly communicated.

Ladefoged, P. 2004, *Vowels and consonants: An introduction to the sounds of languages*, 2nd edition, Oxford: Blackwell Publications.
In this text Ladefoged provides an accessible introduction to the study of phonology, using recent technological advancements to show the relevance of the field.

Phonetics: The sounds of American English, The University of Iowa, www.uiowa.edu/ ~acadtech/phonetics/english/frameset.html
This animated website from the University of Iowa provides both visual and audio illustrations for each American English phoneme, accompanied by the appropriate IPA transcription.

American English orthography

Ager, S. 2007, *Omniglot: Writing systems and languages of the world*, www.omniglot.com/
Even though Ager is not a linguist, he has collected and explained information about the writing systems of many different languages, including examples and helpful links to other sites.

Bailey, R. W. 1991, *Images of English: A cultural history of the language*, Ann Arbor, Michigan: University of Michigan Press.

Bailey explores the connection between language and culture by tracing the history of English, including a discussion of attempts to reform the English writing system.

Crystal, D. 1995, *The Cambridge encyclopedia of the English language*, Cambridge: Cambridge University Press.

As the title suggests, this is an encyclopedic survey of the English language that is both thorough and interesting.

7 Meaning and usage in American English

Overview

In earlier chapters, you've learned about the words, sentences, and sounds of English. Now you'll consider a fourth element of language, the meanings attached to words and sentences. You'll find out about some of the various linguistic approaches to the study of meaning, including the analysis of word relationships, categories, and non-literal meanings. In addition, you'll see how meaning is crucially tied to context, rather than being exclusively communicated by words. Finally, the Hot Topic asks you to analyze a political speech for its meanings and effects.

Introduction

Here's a question for you: What do the phrases *melting pot*, *salad bowl*, *symphony*, and *mosaic* have in common? Got the answer? If you're at all familiar with American society, you probably recognized that these terms have all been used to describe the pluralistic culture of the United States. Each phrase expresses a different view of the manner in which immigrant cultures have assimilated in America. Given that we don't normally equate a country with a dish of vegetables or a musical composition or an art work, how is it that we understand a phrase such as "America is a salad bowl?" For that matter, what about other phrases that have been used to describe or represent the United States: *Mom and apple pie*, *Uncle Sam*, *the Stars and Stripes*, and so on? How do we know, in other words, that we shouldn't read these phrases literally but instead should understand them on another level of meaning? To begin to answer this question, we turn to the study of **semantics**, the subfield of linguistics that explores how people make meaning of their language. In the following pages, we'll introduce you to some approaches to this linguistic study.

Word meanings

A principle focus of the study in semantics has been on the meaning of words and their relationships with other words, or the **lexical semantics** of language. Probably the most obvious place to start thinking about the lexical semantics of American English is with its lexicon, the vocabulary or wordbank of a particular language community. The term *lexicon* refers directly to the meanings that individual words carry and so is a more precise term than *vocabulary*, which refers only to the set of words used by a community. A lexicon is made up of **lexemes**, the smallest units of lexical meaning, while **words** are individual units of language that contain lexical and/or grammatical meaning. We are all familiar with the concept of lexemes because it underlies our use of dictionaries. For instance, if you were going to look up the word *jumping* in the dictionary, you'd look for the headword *jump* because you'd know that the suffix didn't affect the lexical meaning of the word. Box 7.1 further illustrates the difference between lexemes and words.

Lexemes may also consist of several words together that convey a single unit of meaning, different from the meanings conveyed by each individual word. Consider, for instance, the phrase *hold the line*. Together, these words create a lexeme that means *maintain the current position or situation*. Notice, however, that the meaning changes if we consider the words *hold*, *the*, and *line* separately.

> **Box 7.1 Contrasting lexemes and words**
>
> To identify lexemes one should focus exclusively on the lexical meaning being conveyed by a specific passage of language and then recognize the minimal units in that specific passage. A *lexeme* may be a word, but the two are not necessarily the same thing. If you look at the following list, you'll see four words but only one lexeme:
>
> <u>jump</u>ing   <u>jump</u>   <u>jump</u>ed   <u>jump</u>s
>
> The morphological principles you learned in Chapter 3 will help you in this analysis. Each of the words *jumping*, *jumped*, and *jumps* contains both the root morpheme and an inflectional suffix, while the lexeme *jump* consists of the root alone. Morphological analysis shows us how we understand the meaning of words in two different ways, both lexically and grammatically. The root, *jump*, in all of these words is the lexeme because it carries identifiable meaning: It refers to or represents something. In contrast, the inflectional suffixes give grammatical meaning, which is primarily functional: They typically express relationships between morphemes.

Because their individual meanings differ, the number of lexemes in the phrase changes from one to three. Other examples of this type of lexeme are *back up*, *under the weather*, and *sit a spell*; the meanings of each phrase, and thus the lexemes they contain, change if the words are individually considered.

In differentiating between lexemes and words, we've shown you that lexemes are part of the semantic structure of language, a complex web of meaning relationships. This is why we can't think about lexemes solely as separate words with definitions that one might find in a dictionary. In fact, we associate a variety of meanings with each individual lexeme we hear or read. Consider the word *dog*, for instance. When we think of *dog*, we may think of the dictionary definition, *a domestic animal closely related to the common wolf*, but we also think of many other meanings as well. We might think of things we associate with a *dog*, a cat, for instance, since dogs and cats are often linked in our culture. Or maybe we think about cultural definitions of *dog*, such as the description of a dog as "man's best friend." We also might attach a personal meaning to *dog* (my dog, Maddie), or perhaps we think of literary or entertainment uses of *dog*: Clifford, the big, red dog in the book series of the same name, or Lassie, the dog star of television and movies.

We see from this discussion that lexemes are part of an intricate interplay of meaning and meaning relationships, meanings that can't be contained in a dictionary because they are infinite in number. And describing the rules or processes involved in making linguistic meaning challenges linguists because meaning works on several different levels, including the referential (the actual thing being referred to), the cognitive (individual mental associations and meanings), and the social (meanings in context). Despite this challenge, linguists have been able to formulate some theories about how people make sense of their language.

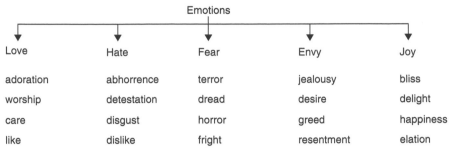

Figure 7.1 *A semantic field shares a common feature*

Semantic fields

One approach linguists use to study lexical meanings has been to group words into specific categories of meaning called **semantic fields**. They do this by identifying the features of words that comprise their meanings. For instance, the words *bird*, *dog*, *horse*, and *cat* would belong to a semantic field that has the common feature ANIMAL. Another field might include the words *blue*, *green*, *yellow*, and *red*, whose common semantic feature is COLOR. See Figure 7.1 for other examples of semantic fields.

The idea of semantic fields is intriguing because it offers a suggestion for how we order our lexicon by using the features of words to classify them. In addition, the notion of semantic fields also explains some of the cognitive associations we make between words. Going back to our example above, we all understand that the words *bird*, *dog*, *horse*, and *cat* contained in a semantic field have more related meanings than, say, *fish*, *bottle*, *bicycle*, and *flag*, for which there may be no common semantic feature.

Although a useful means of analysis, the notion of semantic features also has its problems. Sometimes it's difficult to identify semantic features of words and thus to categorize them: How would we define the meaning of *what*, *but*, or *drat*, for instance? And other words, while seeming to be part of a group, still contain subtle meaning differences that aren't clearly distinguishable, at least in a semantic field: *scheme*, *plan*, *plot*, and *strategy*; or *miserly*, *stingy*, *parsimonious*, and *sparing*, for example. Many lexemes also seem to belong to more than one field. Where do we put the lexeme *soda*, for instance – is it a kind of sweet drink or a chemical compound? Finally, what's the best way to define a *field*? Is a *computer* part of the field of "technological equipment" or part of the field of "communication systems"? Does a *poster* belong to the field of "art," "information media," or "graphics"?

Many standardized mental aptitude tests for children in the United States assess reasoning by presenting groups of words (semantic fields) for analysis. Typically, a sample group contains one member that clearly doesn't belong because it has different semantic features from the other words. Presented with the grouping of *bottle*, *can*, *fork*, and *glass*, for instance, a responder should identify *fork* as the odd word because its meaning does not contain the semantic feature of "container."

Semantic relationships

The grouping of lexemes into semantic fields also reveals relationships between words and their classes. If we consider that semantic fields are really sets of meanings, we can identify subsets within them. Take for instance the category ANIMAL above. Contained within this set are the subsets of *bird*, *dog*, *horse*, etc. This kind of relation between words, when a more general term contains a more specific one, is called **hyponymy**. In this case, all of the subsets are hyponyms of the more general word *animal*. The meaning of the more general term is always contained within the hyponym: for example, *bird* contains the meaning *animal*. *Bird* itself is another semantic field and can be broken down further into the subsets *sparrow*, *robin*, *ostrich*, *turkey*, and so on. All of these latter terms are hyponyms of the word *bird*.

Exercise 7.1

For each of the following word groups, identify the distinguishing semantic feature(s). Then find a semantic feature that the two groups share.

1.   a. princess, actress, nun, lady, queen _____
              b. ewe, goose, mare, cow _____
   Shared feature:
2.   a. table, desk, counter, buffet _____
              b. chair, sofa, recliner, stool _____
   Shared feature:
3.   a. many, some, few, much _____
              b. two, red, round, soft _____
   Shared feature:
4.   a. talk, sing, scream, murmur _____
              b. write, row, knit, golf _____
   Shared feature:

Most people are familiar with another semantic relation between words, **synonymy**, because they often define words by giving their synonyms. If someone asks you, for instance, what an *automobile* is, you might say that it's a *car*, thus giving the synonym for the word. As you learned in Chapter 4, over time the American English lexicon has gained many words borrowed from other languages, creating a variety of synonyms such as the following:

alibi (Latin)	*excuse* (Middle English)
silent (Latin)	*mute* (French)
forbid (Old English)	*prohibit* (Latin)
noodle (Dutch)	*pasta* (Italian)
folk (Old English)	*people* (Old French)

Looking at these examples, though, raises the question of whether two words can really mean exactly the same thing; certainly the example of a car and an automobile comes quite close, but other words traditionally regarded as synonyms may not be able to replace each other without a slight change in the meaning conveyed. For instance, in the list above the words *folk* and *people* may mean slightly different things. Some people believe *folk* is a reference to the common people of a community, while they understand *people* as a more general term.

When a word has multiple meanings that are related, that is, when their word histories, or etymologies, are the same, then we can say they are polysemes. An example of **polysemy** is found in the term *honey*, which has several senses. An Old English word originally used to name the sweet yellow fluid made by honeybees, the meaning of *honey* became extended in the Middle English period when people began to use it to describe someone's sweetheart or lover. Today, of course, we use both meanings: we might put *honey* on a piece of toast or look forward to seeing our *honey* this weekend. Another example of polysemy is seen in the word *raw*: originally from Old English and meaning "not cooked" or "in a natural state," today *raw* has the additional meanings of "vulgar," "coarse," "naked," and "inexperienced." We're sure you can see how the later senses, although not exactly the same, are related to the original Old English meaning.

When a lexeme has two or more unrelated meanings, it is an example of **homonymy**. The word *bark* is a homonym because its two meanings (the outer layer of a tree and the sound a dog makes) cannot be traced to a common source. When two or more different words sound alike, they are called **homophones**. The following homophones also have completely unrelated meanings: *by*, *bye*, and *buy*; *through* and *threw*; *there*, *they're*, and *their*. In cases such as homonyms and homophones, where word meaning is ambiguous, users must consider word relationships in sentences to create meaning.

Exercise 7.2

For each set below, note the meaning of each word and decide whether polysemy or homonymy is present. You may need to use a dictionary to confirm your answers.

1. pig (*noun*)/pig (*noun*)
2. needle (*noun*)/needle (*verb*)
3. blue (*adj*)/blue (*adj*)
4. red (*noun*)/read (*verb*)
5. down (*prep.*)/down (*noun*)
6. stern (*adj.*)/stern (*noun*)
7. milk (*verb*)/milk (*noun*)
8. quarter (*noun*)/quarter (*noun*)

Another way that we classify lexemes is by the semantic relation of opposing meaning or **antonymy**. Two words may be *binary* antonyms if their meanings directly oppose each other, such as in the following pairs: *fake/real*, *dead/alive*, *true/false*, and so on. Other antonyms are *gradable*, in the sense that they are not absolute opposites but that their meaning falls along a scale or grade. Thus the meaning of gradable antonyms, such as *poor/rich*, *young/old*, *cold/hot*, and so on, depends upon the objects they modify. The meaning of *poor* in some circles might mean a person can't buy the latest model car every year; in others, being *poor* might be defined by not being able to afford food. Finally, antonyms may also be pairs of words that are *relational* opposites. This means that they are not opposed to one another but, rather, have a symmetrical relation. The pair *parent/child*, for instance, describes the identity of each noun in terms of its relationship to the other. Other examples include *above/below*, *right/left*, *teacher/pupil*, and so on.

Other word relationships appear in the sentence level where we see that some lexemes set up certain expectations for others. Consider the sentence *The girl licked the ice cream cone*. In this case, the lexeme *lick* creates specific expectations for what is contained in the rest of the sentence. We have preconceived notions about who or what does the action of licking and what one licks. Sentences like *The television licked the ice cream cone* or *The girl licked the calculator* would seem nonsensical to us. We expect that the performer of the action will be human, or perhaps animal, and we expect the receiver of the action to be something soft, perhaps cool, liquid, etc. We see from these examples that meaning drives the sequencing of words because certain lexemes set up expectations for others.

> That we expect certain words to go with others is borne out by research on language usage. By employing computers to analyze large sets of spoken and written texts, linguists can determine how frequently words occur and which words usually appear near one another. This type of analysis, called *collocation*, may be useful not only for what it tells us about word relationships but for more practical purposes as well, such as designing teaching materials for second language learners.

Our intuitions and expectations about meaning also allow us to appropriately substitute some words for others in sentences. So, for instance, we can substitute the performer of the action in the sentence above, *girl*, with *man* or *child*, and the verb *licked* with *ate* or *bought*, and, finally, the receiver of the action, *ice cream cone*, with *frosting* or *stamp* and still have sentences that make sense. The fact that we can do this reveals that lexemes fulfill certain **semantic roles** in sentences. Some perform actions in certain sequences, others receive action, and so on. Semantic roles may seem very similar to the grammar functions that you studied in Chapter 5, but remember that we're speaking here about elements of *meaning* and not elements of structure. Because of this, different terms are used to describe these roles: *agent* (the performer of the action), *theme* (the thing involved in or affected by the action), and so on. Table 7.1 lists some of the many semantic roles words can fulfill.

So far, we've discussed some of the observations that linguists have made about how we understand and use word meanings. The creation of meaning, however, goes much beyond understanding lexemes. The following discussion explores other aspects of meaning.

Denotation and connotation

We typically can assign the lexemes of a language two types of meanings: denotative and connotative. **Denotations** are the referential meanings

Table 7.1 *Common semantic roles*

Semantic roles	Definition
Experiencer	a person experiencing a feeling or perception
Agent	the doer of an action
Theme	the entity affected by the action
Source	where the action originates
Location	the place of an entity
Goal	the end or objective

Sample sentences

The police officer	started	his siren	at the intersection.
Agent		*theme*	*location*
He	stopped	Elizabeth's car.	
Agent		*theme*	
Elizabeth	felt	a sinking feeling.	
Experiencer		*theme*	
She	got	her driver's license	from her purse.
Agent		*theme*	*source*
The officer	gave	Elizabeth	a ticket.
Agent		*goal*	*theme*

of words, that is, they are the things, persons, objects, ideas, etc. to which words refer. Denotations are the standard dictionary definitions for words, the meanings usually agreed upon by the largest language community. For example, some American English speakers might use the word *homey* to refer to a neighbor or a fellow member of a group of friends, but most speakers would probably use the term to refer to something that is home-like, or comfortable and familiar. Because a larger group of people uses the latter definition of *homey*, it is the primary definition listed in standard American English dictionaries.

Connotations are the additional meanings that accompany denotations when emotional shadings, attitudes, and opinions enter into the construction of meaning. Connotations are not universal meanings, that is, the same connotations do not exist for all people. Instead, they can be very personal. For instance, the phrase *insurance company* would have very different connotations depending on whether you are an insurance agent who sells policies (a positive connotation) or a homeowner who just found out that her policy does not cover the flooding in her basement (a negative connotation). Connotations are difficult

The term *feminist* is a good example of one term's dramatically different denotative and connotative meanings. Most dictionaries define *feminist* as *someone who supports the political, economic, and social equality of the sexes.* What the dictionary entries do not indicate, however, are the connotative meanings of this word, which have appeared during the recent history of the women's liberation movement in the United States. In fact, today, *feminist* has become a loaded term, a word that evokes strong emotional reactions. For some people, the term *feminist* may imply a person who is a militant, man-hating social radical.

for the non-native speaker to learn. How would a non-native speaker know, for instance, that applying for a bank loan for his business *scheme* might not get him the money, but that his business *plan* would probably inspire more confidence? Or how does the non-native speaker addressing a roomful of parents know that she'll probably anger her audience if she calls their offspring *urchins* instead of *children*? In the dictionary the words *scheme* and *urchin* are defined as *plan* and *child*, respectively, yet most native speakers of English know they are typically used to convey a pejorative meaning.

Exercise 7.3

Look at the following words and decide whether they have connotations and, if they do, whether they are negative or positive. Discuss possible reasons for these connotations with your classmates.

1. whistleblower
2. informant
3. house
4. mansion
5. maid
6. cleaning lady
7. instructor
8. teacher
9. therapist
10. counselor

Lexical change

In addition to connotations, which complicate word definitions, another potential problem when trying to attach a specific meaning to an individual word is that meanings may change over time. For example, popular usage has caused words to *broaden* in meaning, resulting in a word's meaning becoming much more general than the sense it originally possessed. Consider the verb *to ship*, for instance. At one time this only meant to send something by boat, but today it means to send something by any means of transportation. Another broadening has occurred with the word *tool*. Originally a tool referred only to a hammer or an awl. Nowadays, we use *tool* to mean any device that helps us get a job done. For example, knowledge of a variety of ways to begin a sentence can be considered a writing tool, while a scalpel is a surgeon's tool.

Word meanings also *narrow* over time, referring to the process when a word's meaning becomes much more specific than the one it originally held. Today

One of the reasons many students have difficulty reading classical pieces of literature lies in the fact that a word's meaning changes over time. And the older the piece of literature, the more possibility there is that meanings have changed from what the author originally intended. In the medieval classic *Sir Gawain and the Green Knight* a green girdle plays a significant role in the plot, yet the

Figure 7.2 Hound *has narrowed in meaning from* a dog *to* a hunting dog

the word *deer* signifies just one type of four-legged mammal, but earlier, *deer* referred to any four-legged animal living in the woods. Another narrowing has occurred with the word *igloo*. An Eskimo word, *igloo* means any house. But now in English, *igloo* primarily means a dwelling made of ice blocks. In another example, genealogy guides often warn readers that words referring to familial relations have undergone a narrowing of meaning. For instance, in the past, the words *junior* and *senior* could have referred to a nephew and an uncle, or even to two people who weren't related but had the same name, a fact that could confuse a beginning genealogist today (see Figure 7.2).

author certainly didn't mean the elasticized undergarment we refer to today with the word *girdle*. Without knowing that *girdle* meant *sash* or *belt* in the fourteenth century, modern readers miss the entire point of the work.

Over time, words can even undergo reversals in meaning. In the United States, up until the 1960s, the word *bad* carried only negative meanings. After that time, however, in some American slang the word began to mean just the opposite: Something bad now meant something good. Finally, some words have undergone lexical change as they have acquired new, unrelated meanings. The word *gay* now refers to a person's sexual orientation and no longer just his disposition; a *cell* today is a type of telephone and not only a room in a prison or a unit of an organism (see Figure 7.3).

The word *cool* has had a long and varied history of usage. It's been in use since around the twelfth century, when it first referred only to temperature. Later, in the United States, it gained other meanings: In 1825, the phrase *to lose one's cool*, meaning to become explosively angry, was coined. In the 1930s, Black Americans used *cool* to mean *trendy* or *fashionable*. And by the 1980s, *cool* had started to mean *very good* or *great*, as in *Wanna hear a cool new band?*

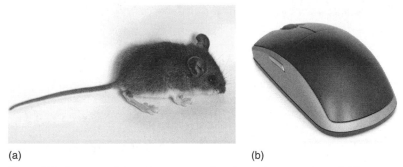

(a)   (b)

Figure 7.3 *Some words acquire new, unrelated meanings over time (field mouse* ©iStockphoto.com/Stacy Brogan, *computer mouse* ©iStockphoto.com/Alina Solovyova-Vincent)

Exercise 7.4

We've mentioned above some words that have changed meaning through narrowing, broadening, or reversal, or through the addition of new meanings. See if you can add to these examples by coming up with five more words that have undergone change. Choose words from a variety of fields, such as medicine, information technology, cinema, news reporting, politics, etc. Then trace each word's etymology. Can you identify any sort of overall pattern? Finally, report to the rest of the class what you have discovered.

Language in context: pragmatics

As you've probably realized by now, the process of making meaning is significantly tied to the context in which something is said or written. This means that to understand meaning, we also need to investigate the circumstances in which language is used – an enormous task, given the number of situations in our lives when spoken or written language appears. Researchers from a number of fields, such as sociolinguistics, philosophy, literature, and others, employ a variety of approaches to studying the creation of meaning in context. In the following discussion we will briefly review some of the linguistic research in this area.

Typically, linguists consider two kinds of contexts that produce meaning. The first is *linguistic context*, which is the relational meanings of words or phrases to other words or phrases. You've already learned some of these relationships in our discussion above on synonyms, homonyms, polysemes, and so on.

The second type of context is the *situational context*, which refers to all the nonlinguistic factors of a situation that affect meaning. **Pragmatics** is the linguistic subfield that concerns how meaning is created in situational contexts. Just as linguists are able to theorize a set of principles regarding linguistic meaning, so too have they been able to theorize a system of language use based upon their observations of how people make meaning in context.

Table 7.2 *Speech acts occur when speakers perform actions through their words*

Speech act	Examples	Type of action
Representatives	descriptions, claims, assertions, statements, notifications	utterances used to describe the state of something
Commissives	promises, threats, vows, pledges, oaths	utterances that commit a speaker to something
Expressives	apologies, condolences, congratulations	utterances that convey an emotional state
Directives	orders, commands, suggestions, recommendations, requests	utterances intended to produce a certain action
Declarations	firing, hiring, marrying, blessing, honoring	utterances that bring about a change

Speech acts

Some of the work in pragmatics has centered on describing not only what speakers mean when they say something, but also what they *do* when they use language. Researchers have shown that certain of our utterances actually perform actions, in addition to conveying meaning. For example, if you say to someone, *You're fired*, you're both saying something (conveying meaning with your words) and doing the "action" of letting someone go. These "actions" performed by speakers when they say something are called **speech acts**. We can use language to perform a number of speech acts, including making requests, giving orders, making promises, declaring information, and so on. Table 7.2 lists some common speech acts and their functions.

Speech acts can be both direct and indirect. When we communicate directly, we perform one speech act. For example, we might give an order such as *Give me the screwdriver* or make a request such as *Will you give me a ride?* In contrast, when we speak indirectly, we perform more than one speech act at a time. If we say to an auto glass technician, *My windshield has a crack in it* (a statement), we really mean *Can you fix it?* (an indirect request). If a housemate comes into a room and says, *This room is a mess*, she's not only describing the room, but she's also indirectly suggesting that someone had better clean it up.

To understand indirect speech acts, both speaker and listener must consider the context of the utterance. If they don't, then miscommunication will arise. Consider, for example, if the windshield technician were to respond to the statement, *My windshield has a crack in it*, by saying, *I'm sorry*. His response would indicate that he understood the statement only as a direct speech act instead of an indirect one, a request that he fix the windshield. Because the meaning of indirect speech acts depends upon the context in which they're spoken, speech act theory is a part of pragmatics.

The theory of speech acts reveals the often complex ways in which speakers communicate, forcing hearers to rely on both linguistic and situational clues to achieve meaning. We rely on these clues as well when we encounter nonliteral speech, such as when someone is using figurative or idiomatic language. Let's see how meaning is constructed in these situations.

Nonliteral speech

When we communicate literally, our words express what we mean. For example, in response to a question about what time it is, we state *"It's ten o'clock."* In contrast, when we communicate nonliterally, we don't actually mean what our words express. If we say, *"She's a twig,"* we don't mean she's really part of a tree, but that she resembles a twig because of her slenderness. Consider other examples of nonliteral speech:

1.   *A man responding to someone's comment that it's going to rain on the day for the picnic: "Oh, that's just great."*
2.   *A television announcer: "The White House has decided to attend the conference on trade agreements."*
3.   *One person to another: "I was sidetracked for a moment."*

In Sentence #1 above, presumably the man is speaking nonliterally when he says, *Oh, that's just great*. In fact, he probably means just the opposite of what he says. He is being *ironic*, or calling attention to the situation by saying the opposite of what he means, when he responds to the comment about the weather. To be able to understand that the man speaks ironically, we would have to draw upon many situational clues, such as our knowledge that picnics take place outside, that they are meant to be entertainments and so people aren't typically averse to attending them, that they are events to be planned for, etc. Note, however, that we can't know for sure the man's feelings about the weather just by reading on the page what he says: We would have to use other extra-linguistic clues, such as his tone of voice and body language, to accurately interpret his meaning.

Sentence #2 is also an example of nonliteral speech. The White House, the building, cannot literally make a decision or attend a meeting, of course. Because we know this, we understand that the White House in this sentence represents the President or perhaps members of the President's staff who have performed these actions. We see here an example of **metonymy**, or the naming of one thing to indirectly represent another (see Figure 7.4). Metonyms are common in English and, like all other nonliteral speech, must be understood from context. Here are a few more examples of metonyms, with their meanings in parentheses: *The chair of the committee* (the person in charge) *is displeased by the vote*; *A couple of suits from the IRS* (two workers, typically bureaucrats) *came and audited my business yesterday*; *The audience gave the performer a hand* (clapped).

Figure 7.4 *"Wall Street suffered another loss today"*
(©iStockphoto.com/Christopher Steer)

Finally, Sentence #3 illustrates the use of a metaphor, another example of nonliteral meaning. A **metaphor** is a way of describing one thing in terms of another that is similar enough to it to make a comparison. When the person says she was *sidetracked*, she means that she was distracted or diverted from her purpose. The expression, of course, comes from the image of a train that is sidetracked, or diverted to a secondary track. Once sidetracked, the train can no longer move forward and complete its original journey. In a similar way, a person who is sidetracked cannot complete the action or thought originally undertaken until she comes back *on track* (see Figure 7.5).

You'll remember that we used a metaphor at the beginning of this chapter in the phrase, *America is a salad bowl*. Taken literally, the meaning of the sentence is odd, and so we must understand that the speaker is speaking figuratively, or metaphorically. In this case, we probably understand the sentence to mean something like *America is like a salad bowl*: It contains a variety of disparate cultures, which when brought together make a harmonious whole. Perhaps you think that a salad bowl seems too different from a country for comparison, but if we extend the metaphor it becomes more apt: *America is a mix of cultures that when tossed together make up a savory, harmonious whole.*

Metaphors are interesting for what they may reveal about the content of a culture, or for what is given emphasis in a culture. Box 7.2 discusses two examples of metaphorical language found in American English and what they may say about American life.

Two other examples of nonliteral language are also common in English: euphemisms and idioms. **Euphemisms** are words or phrases that we employ when we want to avoid the use of a blunt, harsh, or unpleasant word and so

Figure 7.5 *"May you always have smooth sailing in your life"*
(©iStockphoto.com/technotr)

Box 7.2 American English metaphors

Consider the following sentences containing metaphors commonly found in
American English:

1.   *You're going to have to earn my trust.*
2.   *Our company insists you be a team player.*

If metaphors may express cultural characteristics, as we've suggested, then what
might the sentences above suggest about English and its speakers? The metaphorical
expression in Sentence #1, which can also be seen in other, particularly western,
languages, may reveal what is of importance or emphasized in American culture.
In America, people value money and treasure their material goods, and often these
sentiments are expressed with metaphors of wealth. (Note the example of these
metaphors in just this last sentence in our use of *value* and *treasure*.) Indeed,
American English contains many common expressions grounded in the language of
finance: *I wouldn't bank on it. What is the worth of complaining now? It's money
in the bank! The area is rich in history. Here's a wealth of ideas. These coupons are
as good as gold!* and so on.

In Sentence #2, *be a team player* is a phrase taken from the world of sports and is
now applied to any situation where cooperation and collaboration among people is
encouraged. Many other sports terms have become common metaphors in American

English and are used in a variety of contexts: *play to win* (engage in something seriously), *play by the rules* (do something according to accepted standards), *level the playing field* (allow all those involved an equal chance), and so on. That Americans frequently use sports terms in all kinds of situations suggests that they believe the attitudes and lessons learned in sports carry over well into other sectors of American life. These lessons may include working hard, persisting, staying positive, being fair, and so on.

replace it with a milder or less offensive word. Euphemisms reflect the usage of the time in which they appear. For instance, in nineteenth-century America, when there was considerable public furor over the existence of houses of prostitution, persons in polite circles referred to them as *assignation houses* or *sporting houses*. Later terms coined in the twentieth century included *cat house*, *call house*, and *house of ill fame*, all terms designed to avoid mention of their real purpose. Today in the western state of Nevada, the only US state where some forms of prostitution are legal, a prostitution house is often called a *ranch*, a name given probably as a nod to its western location but, of course, still a euphemism.

Another type of nonliteral language is the idiom. **Idioms** are phrases common to a particular language community that have acquired meanings different from the literal ones. Let's say that you go to Nevada, which is famous for its gambling casinos, and you *bet the ranch*. Here *ranch* means something different from that conveyed by the euphemism above. *Bet the ranch* is an idiomatic phrase, which contains one lexeme and means *to bet all your assets*. If you then go and lose your bet, thus losing every asset you own, you will have *lost your shirt*, another idiom, which means that you've suffered a total financial loss.

Idioms create special trouble for learners of English who must memorize idioms rather than expect to find clues to the meaning of the phrase in the words themselves. Think for instance of the idiomatic lexemes in the sentences *Emily bit the dust* or *Emily went down in flames*. Both sentences mean that Emily lost the competition or failed to achieve something, but the individual words being used don't directly convey this meaning. Instead, one has to be familiar with American English usage to understand their significance.

Exercise 7.5

In English, war and battle words are often used to describe other, totally unrelated, actions. Consider expressions like *I fought to get my credit rating improved*, *The company's going on the defensive*, *He was gunning for me on that new contract*, or *The administration is on the frontlines in this war against hunger*. Think of other expressions commonly used in English that employ similar words, and then consider why they are used. What in American culture prompts people to *wage war*, as it were, in the interactions of daily life? Can you identify other areas of human activity (consider entertainment, politics, art, law, etc.) that have also spawned metaphors used in a variety of contexts? Work with a partner and create a list you can share with the class.

Until now our discussion of how meaning is conveyed has been focused at the level of the word, phrase, and sentence. But we know that meaning is generated as well beyond these structural elements of language. M. A. K. Halliday (1985) recognized this when he theorized about the nonstructural aspects of discourse, or all those additional relations within a text that are not limited by the rules of specific grammar structures. For instance, he identifies several ways in which meaning is conveyed across texts, for example through *reference*, such as when speakers use a pronoun to refer to a noun preceding it (sometimes even at great distance), or through the use of *ellipsis*, the conscious omission of language. Ellipsis occurs when we answer questions such as *Would you like to go now?* with the answer *Yes*. The questioner understands our meaning because the rest of our answer is implied: *Yes. (I would like to go now)*. Notice that examining this kind of meaning making takes us to a level of analysis that goes beyond the clause or sentence: We're examining language as a system, identifying those relations in a discourse that create meaning. Let's now explore some of the ways in which linguists analyze discourse.

> M. A. K. Halliday's theory of *systemic functional grammar*, which interprets language as a network of relations, reveals yet another approach to describing the *grammar* of a language. The theory has been employed for a variety of purposes, including the analysis of spoken and written texts and in educational applications such as the teaching of children's initial literacy and of foreign languages. For a very brief introduction to systemic functional grammar and links to other resources on Halliday, go to http://language.la.psu.edu/tifle2002/halliday.html

Discourse analysis – conversations

When linguists study the pragmatics of language within large pieces of discourse, such as conversations, legal testimonies, or meeting transcripts, they're performing **discourse analysis**, or what has been defined as the analysis of a multisentence text. In studying conversations in English in particular, linguists have shown that there are principles that govern these discourses, including "rules" about participating, taking turns, making contributions that are relevant to the topic, and so on. They've also studied some of the features that are commonly found in conversations, such as greetings, closings, shifts in direction, etc. Researchers have suggested that when we engage in conversation with someone, we're constantly negotiating meaning, that is, we have to agree with that person on what meanings our language contains. Usually we're not conscious of this negotiation because we naturally follow the discourse conventions of a particular situation. For instance, when you're in the cafeteria line at school and a server looks at you and asks, *whole wheat or white?* you understand the server's meaning, given the setting, purpose, participants, and other aspects of the discourse context. This context requires that you respond by only telling what your choice is. In a different situation, say when you're arriving at a party and are greeted at the door by the hosts, there will be different discourse expectations: You will engage in much more conversation, including greeting your hosts and making other small talk, because these are the conventions of that particular situation. As we gain experience in the world, we learn to negotiate diverse discourse contexts. Consider now one type of discourse, a conversation, which illustrates some of the many ways in which meaning is communicated:

> JENNIFER, ENTERING THE KITCHEN: *"Hi Adrienne, I'm back."*
> ADRIENNE: *"Hi. Did you get . . .?"*
> JENNIFER: *"Can I open a window in here?"*
> ADRIENNE: *"It's 35 degrees outside! The baking's almost finished. Where's the sugar?"*
> JENNIFER: *"The store was out. Big strike or something. Maybe I can get some from the Smiths."*

In the conversation above, when Jennifer enters, she uses a greeting convention, *Hi*, commonly found at the beginning of casual conversations. Next we see the first of many indirect speech acts: Jennifer makes a request to open a window, and at the same time indirectly declares that it's too hot in the room. Notice that Adrienne infers this second meaning when she in turn notes the temperature outside. Although not a direct answer to Jennifer's question, Adrienne's response is entirely appropriate. Jennifer makes meaning of Adrienne's comment by drawing on her knowledge that 35 degrees F is a cold temperature and that normally people don't open their windows in the winter.

Adrienne's second comment about the baking being almost finished also recognizes Jennifer's indirect statement that it's hot in the room. Like her comment on the temperature, it seems unconnected, but in fact Adrienne is appropriately responding to Jennifer's concerns by indirectly saying the source of the heat will soon be turned off. These indirect comments create dramatic shifts in the direction of the conversation, a common feature of conversations in general. Other common features of conversations include references to something said before, subtly related utterances, and inferred meanings, as well as more conventionalized forms of discourse, such as greetings. For mutual understanding to take place, the participants must follow the discourse conventions and use their experience and knowledge to make meaning.

We have shown you here in the analysis of a casual conversation just one context where discourse analysis may be applied. There exist many, many other contexts, of course. In Chapter 8, we will show you another area when we discuss the use of discourse analysis in the study of gender and language.

Chapter summary

This chapter has introduced you to the linguistic subfield of **semantics**, the study of linguistic meaning. Through the study of **lexical semantics**, which examines word meanings and relationships, linguists have suggested several ways in which people order and understand meaning. In addition to linguistic context, the creation of meaning also depends upon situational context. The study of **pragmatics** examines the situational context to discover speaker intention and purpose. Because a speaker's meaning can be indirect and non-literal, people must be aware of extra-linguistic factors to make meaning of a speaker's utterance. Finally, the chapter describes **discourse analysis** by examining some meaning conventions found in conversations.

Critical Thinking exercises

1. Using the following websites as resources, find five examples each of euphemisms, metaphors, and idioms. Record how the expressions came into the English language, if given; if not, consider for yourself what their histories might be. Can you make any overall generalizations?
Websites:
"'Nyms & such" www.yourdictionary.com/library
"Metaphor Examples" http://knowgramming.com/metaphors/metaphor_chapters/examples.htm
"Euphemism" http://en.wikipedia.org/wiki/Euphemism
"Euphemism" www.reference.com/browse/wiki/Euphemism

2. You are probably familiar with the rhetoric of advertising, that is, the language used in advertisements to sell products. This specialized language contains what many rhetoricians have called "weasel words," words and phrases that imply certain product benefits or that lead the consumer to believe the product has particular attributes that actually aren't there. For instance, when a dishwashing liquid is advertised as making dishes "virtually spotless," we note the weasel word, *virtually*, meaning *existing in essence but not in actual fact*. Apparently, the advertisers are hoping that the use of this qualifier will be ignored when read by the intended audience.

   Watch an hour of television and pay close attention to the advertisements that come on, or read the advertisements found in two or three popular magazines. Do these advertisements employ weasel words? What are they, and what are their effects on the viewer/reader?

3. War is another topic that, because of its horrors, is written about euphemistically and metaphorically. Think of how the US government described the second US–Iraq war as *Operation Iraqi Freedom*, a name that emphasized the United States' purpose for going to war and downplayed the actualities of war. We're sure it comes as no surprise to you that in speaking of this same war the Iraqi government and press used a very different metaphorical language from that used by the Americans, including calling the war an *invasion*, a *genocide*, a *return to imperial colonialism*, and other names.

We see from these examples that each language has been manipulated to produce a specific effect in its intended audience. Do some further research into the language used on both sides in the US–Iraqi conflict. How are battles, technical aspects, civilians, soldiers, and other aspects of war described?

Hot Topic: The rhetoric of American speeches

A field closely related to semantics is **rhetoric**, which is concerned with the effects of language on its hearers or readers. Oftentimes, users will manipulate language to produce particular understandings, or effects, in their audiences. You are probably familiar with this notion of manipulating language to create effect since it occurs in almost every spoken or written communication we produce; indeed, most speech and writing courses teach us how to manipulate our language to produce a desired effect in our target audience.

Perhaps one of the most common areas of our lives where we see the manipulation of language is in politics. From stumping for passage of a bill to campaigning for elected office, politicians use language in a variety of ways to convince us of their ideas. Just think about recent political campaigns, with the differences between John McCain's and Barack Obama's speeches. The meanings conveyed by such political language depend upon both linguistic and situational contexts. When a politician comes out on a stage in Texas and begins his speech by saying *Howdy, folks. How y'all doin' tonight?* his greeting not only welcomes his listeners but also suggests that he's a regular guy, just like they are, and perhaps their friend. This latter meaning is implicit in the greeting, whether his audience is convinced of its truth or not. In another example, if a politician addresses residents of the Bible Belt, you can be sure that words typically found in religious texts will creep into her speech. Again, the rhetorical purpose for such inclusion may be to encourage audience members to identify with or approve of the politician. In both of these examples, the politicians know that their language creates layers of meaning, all of which, they hope, will be understood by their audiences.

Of course, much of a politician's speechmaking is persuasive in nature – he or she speaks to convince the audience of something: to fund a project, support a cause, elect a candidate, and so on. Speakers create effective persuasive arguments by appealing to their audiences in one or more of the following ways:

- by fostering trust and confidence in themselves, the deliverers of the message;
- by presenting arguments based upon logic and reason;
- by playing on the emotions of the audience;

The following assignment asks you to do a rhetorical analysis of a speech, for which you will consider how the speaker appeals to the audience in one or more of these three ways. As you begin your analysis, consider what you have learned in this chapter about how meanings are conveyed and identify the ways in which the speaker produces meaning in his or her text. Questions below will help you analyze the language of the speech.

A rhetorical analysis is a description of both the linguistic and situational contexts of a text, so, in addition to analyzing the language and its effects, in your analysis describe the extra-linguistic factors as well: speaker, setting (in this case, where the speech was delivered), audience, political and social context, and so on. Then decide how these factors, combined with the language and its meanings, produce an effective text.

Go to the website "American Rhetoric," www.americanrhetoric.com/top100 speechesall.html, which features 100 of the most significant political speeches of the twentieth century, and select one of the four speeches listed below to analyze. Use the questions following to guide you in your analysis.

Ronald Reagan, "The Evil Empire"
Shirley Chisholm, "For the Equal Rights Amendment"
Malcolm X, "The Ballot or the Bullet"
John F. Kennedy, "Ich bin ein Berliner"

Guided questions

Linguistic context:

1.   Are there specific word connotations that the speaker seeks to make the audience understand?
2.   What speech acts does the speaker engage in while speaking? Does he or she promise? Threaten? Cajole? etc.?
3.   What kind of nonliteral language does the speaker use, and what is its effect?
4.   What is the tone of the speaker's language, and what contextual clues must the audience pick up on to gain understanding of the speaker's position or feelings on the topic?

Situational context:

1.   What is the topic of the speech?
2.   What purpose does the speaker have for speaking on this topic?
3.   What is the context for this speech? When and where was it given? What was the political and social climate of the time?
4.   Who is the intended audience of the speech? How much do they know, and what are their ideas about the subject of the speech?
5.   Who is the speaker, and how might he or she come across to the audience?
6.   How does the speaker maintain credibility and show that he or she is an authority on the subject?

Learn more about it

Understanding semantics

Fromkin, V., Rodman, R., and Hyams, N. 2007, *An introduction to language*, 8th edition, Boston: Thompson Wadsworth.
In this introductory linguistics text, the authors present two chapters on semantics and pragmatics, introducing major concepts in the two fields.

Lobner, S. 2002, *Understanding semantics*, New York: Oxford University Press.
This volume is a thorough introduction to semantics, going beyond the current chapter's overview to explain compositional semantics and other aspects of the field.

Negotiating meaning

Hickerson, N. P. 2000, *Linguistic anthropology*, 2nd edition, New York: Harcourt.
A useful introduction to linguistic anthropology, the study of how language is used in various social contexts, this text covers many topics, including discussion of the social variables that affect language.

Lakoff, G. and Johnson, M. 1980, *Metaphors we live by*, Chicago: University of Chicago Press.
Lakoff and Johnson's text is one of the first to explain theories about the centrality of metaphor in human language and the importance it has in interpreting cultures.

Pragmatics

Cutting, J. 2002, *Pragmatics and discourse: A resource book for students*, London: Routledge.
This is a comprehensive introduction to pragmatics and discourse that employs a range of real texts for analysis.

Yule, G. and Widdowson, H. G. 1996, *Pragmatics*, New York: Oxford University Press.
The authors write a useful introduction to pragmatics that lays a solid foundation for further study in the field.

Discourse analysis

Gee, J. P. 2005, *An Introduction to discourse analysis: Theory and method*, 2nd edition, New York: Routledge.
Gee writes a highly accessible introduction to discourse analysis, using a wide range of contemporary oral and written texts for analysis.

Schriffin, D., Tannen, D., and Hamilton, H. E. (eds.) 2003, *The handbook of discourse analysis* (Blackwell Handbooks in Linguistics), London: Blackwell.
This book is a collection of contemporary essays that present a variety of research in discourse analysis. Included is an overview of the field written by the authors.

8   Variations in American English

Key terms

Accent
Dialect
Chain shift
Chicano English (CE)
Learner language
African American English (AAE)
Pidgin
Creole
Ebonics debate

Overview

This chapter asks you to continue your work as descriptive linguists by focusing on American English dialects. You will learn why so many different varieties of American English exist, and you'll read about some of the most commonly discussed dialects spoken today in the United States. Finally, the Hot Topic asks you to consider the linguistic implications of self-improvement courses intended to help speakers modify their particular dialects.

Introduction

On your first day at college you probably heard many different varieties of American English, especially if the users were from other regions of the United States. Perhaps a classmate confused you by asking where the "bubbler" was, or maybe you couldn't easily understand the New Yorkese of someone in your dorm. When your roommate commented that the window "needs washed," you knew you had entered a new language community, one in which speakers varied in their vocabulary use, their pronunciation of certain words, and even in their syntax. In this chapter we are

> An individual's **accent**, the way that person pronounces certain sounds, may indicate his regional and social identity. Some of the most commonly identified accents in the United States today include the Southern drawl, the Texas twang, the urban rap, and the redneck tone of voice.

145

interested in exploring some of the language varieties of American English, tracing their histories, as well as describing their characteristics.

Because vocabulary, pronunciation, and syntax differences are all markers of particular American language communities, we can discuss them as characteristics of particular dialects. A **dialect** is a variety of a language spoken by people of a particular region (regional dialect) or social group (social dialect) that varies in systematic ways from other varieties of the same language. Linguists seek to identify language differences among dialects. But remember that any discussion of dialects is about generalizations. You may be from the South but not have a drawl, or you may live in the city but not have an urban accent.

In fact, our individual idiolects are shaped by our personal characteristics, including our educational level, socioeconomic class, gender, upbringing, and all the other factors that make us who we are. Because a person's idiolect is affected by many aspects of his individuality, people who live in the same area, or who are the same age, gender, or race, may still speak very differently from one another.

To further complicate our discussion of language variation, remember that the language we use is always changing. So we need to remember that when linguists identify a certain pattern in language usage, they are not identifying a concrete aspect that will always be present. Instead, they are indicating a particular usage common to a certain place, a certain situation, and a certain type of speaker. These language generalizations are formed by gathering specific, detailed data about language usage and then abstracting general concepts from the data.

We want to be very clear in distinguishing between linguistic generalizations and language stereotypes. Both deal with broad observations, but stereotypes arise from cultural attitudes rather than from concrete facts. For example, Ted Bundy, a notorious serial murderer who eventually confessed to twenty-eight brutal killings in the 1970s, at first was passed over by police searching for him because he was articulate and confident in his language. Bundy appeared "squeaky clean" both to the young women he lured to their deaths and to initial investigators because American culture holds a particular stereotype about the kind of people who commit violent murders: They will be unattractive in appearance and ungrammatical/uneducated in speech. You are probably familiar with other kinds of stereotypes about the language of certain regions or certain people, stereotypes that link language usage with personality and character traits: Anyone who uses "bad" grammar with the cashier in the grocery store will pay with food stamps, or anyone who uses academic language outside a school setting is a snob. Stereotypes are not supported by facts; instead, they are linked to emotion and to cultural values.

In this chapter you'll learn about the scientific study of language variation, including how linguists gather information and hypothesize about dialect differences.

Exercise 8.1

A.   Choose one of your own language communities, such as one connected to a sport, a hobby, a geographical region, or even a gender, and identify stereotypes that speakers outside your community may hold about your chosen community. Explain why these opinions are stereotypes rather than linguistic generalizations.

B.   Identify a language community outside your own and identify stereotypes your community holds about these other speakers. Explain why these opinions are stereotypes rather than linguistic generalizations.

Studying dialects

Since SAE is the privileged dialect within the United States, many Americans have the idea that it is "correct" and so stigmatize all American English dialects that depart from SAE conventions. People not familiar with the study of language frequently misunderstand the study of dialects, thinking that the purpose is to identify and then eliminate all the nonstandard "errors." As you know, though, linguists conduct language research in as objective a manner as possible, with the purpose of identifying the language that's actually in use. Through the data they've gathered, researchers have demonstrated that all dialects, regional ones such as Southern American English and ethnic ones such as Chicano English and African American English, are just as systematic and rule-governed as SAE.

In addition to identifying the language itself, linguists interested in regional dialects also link that particular language usage to a specific location. In this process, data is gathered as objectively as possible by having field workers either record people's speech or ask people about their use of particular words or phrases. The data is then correlated by its geographical location, or "mapped," as Figure 8.1 illustrates. Using this method, linguists can generalize about the ways in which dialects have migrated and changed over time, and they can project future changes. To help you understand how dialect mapping works, as well as to give you some practice in objectively "collecting" language data and drawing generalizations, the following exercise asks you to discover the various lexicons at work in your classmates' language.

As you undoubtedly know, using double negatives within one sentence is not acceptable according to the conventions of SAE. Yet this usage is frequently heard throughout the United States in a variety of different dialects. Speakers will double a negative to add strong emphasis: "I don't want no more complainin'" leaves you in no doubt about how the speaker feels about whiners. You may not know, though, that the double negative has a long tradition dating back hundreds of years. Chaucer (1899) even uses four negatives when describing the Knight in "The General Prologue" to *The Canterbury Tales*: "He nevere yet no vileynye ne sayde/ In all his lyf unto no maner wight" (lines 70–71) [He never yet said anything offensive to any type of person in his entire life]. Even though Chaucer doesn't use SAE in this line, we easily understand Chaucer's point that the Knight was a model of courtesy.

Various mapping projects of American English dialects are currently going on in the United States. The following websites of the TELSUR Project, http://ling.upenn.edu/phono_atlas/home.html, and the Dictionary of American Regional English, http://polyglot.lss.wisc.edu/dare/dare.html, give more information about these studies.

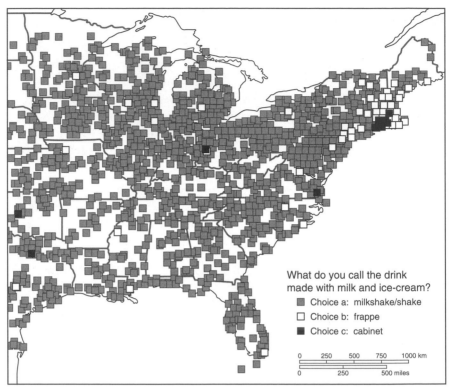

Figure 8.1 *Example of mapping a dialect (After B. A. Vaux and S. A. Golder 2003,* Dialect Survey, http://www4.uwm.edu/FLL/linguistics/dialect/staticmaps/q_63.html)

Exercise 8.2

Look at the following list of words and circle the one that is part of your lexicon. Then ask your classmates what part of the country they are from and note which words they use. If you discover terms from your classmates that are not listed below, include them too. Based on their answers, can you sketch some generalizations about regional usage of some of these terms? Try creating a map that shows the location where each term is used.

1.	dragonfly	mosquito hawk	darning needle	ear sewer	snake feeder
2.	soda	pop	tonic	soft drink	coke
3.	frosting	icing			
4.	run	kill	brook	branch	creek
5.	hoagie	sub hero	po'boy	grinder	torpedo
6.	lightning bug	firefly			
7.	green beans	string beans	snap beans		
8.	seesaw	teeter totter			
9.	hot dog	frank/frankfurter	wiener	link	
10.	sprinkles	jimmies			

The mini-study of your classmates' dialects in Exercise 8.2 might have made you realize the extent to which language varies in the United States. Now let's consider why there are so many diverse dialects. Why do people in one country speak in a myriad different ways? The answer to this question is complex, since differences can be attributed to physical, social, and linguistic factors. The following discussion examines variation in both regional and social dialects so that you can understand the interaction of these diverse factors.

Regional dialects

Regional dialects of American English can be traced back to the diverse English dialects spoken in Britain. Early settlers from England brought their dialect varieties with them, thus immediately creating regional differences in colonial America as they settled across the eastern seaboard. Once early settlements were established, migratory routes extending out from these population centers would usually follow, and each settlement's dialects would be disseminated along these routes. Looking at the dialect map in Figure 8.2, we can see that the dividing lines between dialect regions today are quite often the same routes of migration that settlers took.

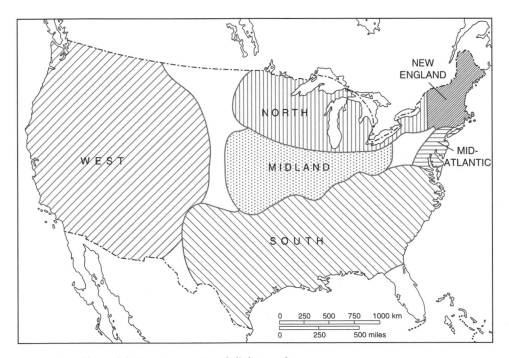

Figure 8.2 *American regional dialects today*

The lines dividing the Southern Region from the Midland and the Midland from the North East Region indicate typical east–to–west routes as first Europeans and, later, Americans moved into the western territories.

Exercise 8.3

Consider your hometown or the place where you spent most of your time growing up. Can you identify the first people who settled that area? If not, do some quick research and see if you can determine the ethnicity of those who founded your town. Then, think about your home dialect: What characteristics of the dialect might include traces of the original founders' language? Take into consideration all aspects of the language: words, accent, syntax, etc. Write up a summary of your research.

Today the terms *Northern*, *Midland*, and *Southern* describe diverse dialects of the Atlantic seaboard, although linguists also recognize regional differences within each classification. The Northern dialect shows distinct variation, for instance, between speakers in Eastern New England and New York, and those in the Inland North. If you listen to speakers from Boston and New York City, for example, you may notice the loss of [r] in words like *dark* [dak] and *bar* [ba], whereas speakers in other northern areas, such as western New York State, usually retain the [r].

The Midland dialect has been divided into Northern and Southern Midland, with various regional differences under each division. Some states contain several dialect communities: Pennsylvania, for instance, has three distinct Northern Midland dialects found in the Philadelphia, Susquehanna Valley, and Pittsburgh areas, respectively.

Variations of the Southern Midland are found in parts of Maryland, West Virginia, Kentucky, Carolina, and Tennessee. Finally, the Southern regional dialect also has variations, extending from the eastern shore of Maryland, down through portions of Virginia, North Carolina, and South Carolina. One characteristic distinguishing the Coastal Southern dialect from other Southern dialects is that Coastal Southerners tend to omit the -r, typically only pronouncing the preceding vowel. In this particular southern dialect, *door* becomes [do] and *par* becomes [pa].

Linguists seem to agree that the diversity of American English dialects is reduced the further West one travels in the United States. This is so because the English-speaking population of the West came in large part from the East, and therefore its dialects represent

Today, of course, American regional dialects continue to change, reflecting the people of each region. For example, the Northern Cities Shift is a twentieth-century change in vowel pronunciation that has taken place in the cities south of the Great Lakes, including Chicago, Detroit, Milwaukee, Cleveland, and Buffalo, and spreading from upstate New York westward to Minnesota. This particular change affects the six short vowels in *caught*, *cot*, *cat*, *bit*, *bet*, and *but* in what is called a **chain shift**, when a group of sounds seems to change their pronunciation at the same time. Such a change is triggered when one sound begins to shift. Then others change as well, in order to keep phonemes distinct in their pronunciations. You may recall the Great Vowel Shift discussed in Chapter 6, which is another example of a chain shift.

Figure 8.3 *Ethnic diversity in the United States*
(Credit: Lloyd Wolf/US Census Bureau)

a merger, to some extent, between the more distinct dialects of the North, the South, and the Midland. Western dialects may have some unique characteristics, though. For example, a more recent variation found in California in the 1980s was dubbed "Val-speak," after the language spoken by girls living in the San Fernando Valley area of Los Angeles. You may be familiar with Val-speak, since it has now spread to other parts of the country.

Geographical location and immigration history do not account for all of the dialect differences in American English. You may be aware that many dialects are also known by the social and ethnic characteristics of their speaker communities. In the following section we will discuss how these characteristics affect dialects.

Social language variation

Ethnic variation

Annual events held across the country celebrate the United States' diverse ethnic heritage: the Irish St. Patrick's Day Parade in New York City, the Cinco de Mayo celebration in San Antonio, the kielbasa-eating contest held every year in Milwaukee, the Cajun music fest in Louisiana, the African American Love Feast in Baltimore, and so on. What could be more natural than to be proud of one's cultural heritage? (See Figure 8.3.)

A person's cultural heritage, of course, includes his linguistic background. Whether someone was born somewhere else and is now an American citizen, is an immigrant living in the United States, or is a native-born American, he probably can trace his roots to a particular "foreign" culture and thus to a particular, non-American-English language community. While classifying people by their ethnic heritage might seem natural, though, in fact, many social factors create our individual ideolects. For instance, African American English is strongly associated with certain geographical regions, such as the southern United States and large urban centers, but it is also linked with a particular socioeconomic status. Likewise, the Italian English dialect is associated with particular areas (cities in the northeast, especially) and a certain type or class of people. Thus we can't consider only the "ethnic" aspect of a dialect; we must consider its users' other characteristics (Wolfram 2004).

Another difficulty of analyzing the ethnicity of dialects is trying to determine if the language is a true dialect of English or actually an example of transference from another language. Are the speakers using different forms of English because they are in the process of learning English and so still being influenced by their native tongue, or are these nonstandard forms a distinctive part of the dialect maintained through generations? In fact, the only way to determine whether a dialect is an actual dialect or merely a stage in the process of learning a language is to study the language over time, noting whether these different forms are retained or eventually discarded. Many English dialects in the United States today are often mistaken for learner languages, including the Chicano English (CE) dialect, which we will now examine in detail.

Dialect focus: Chicano English Perhaps you've overheard a customer in a Mexican restaurant ask a server who has a "Spanish" accent where she is from. The customer may assume that the server is a non-native speaker of English whose language reflects that of a language learner, that is, that she speaks a language filled with forms transferred from her native tongue. In fact, when they hear an accent that seems foreign to them, most Americans think the same thing. They might be surprised to find out that not all Spanish-influenced Englishes are learner languages but that many are fully rule-governed dialects of American English.

Figures from the US Census Bureau (2007) on ethnic populations reveal that, in 2006, approximately 44.3 million Hispanics, or people of Spanish or Latino origin, are now living in the United States. The presence of Hispanics in the United States has expanded the group of American Englishes to include a wide variety of Spanish-influenced dialects, including Cuban English, Columbian English, Puerto Rican English, and others. Belonging to this group is Chicano English (CE), perhaps the most widely spoken of these dialects because it is the language of choice for many Mexican-Americans, one of the largest ethnic minorities in the United States. Just like the Southern

> Hispanic or Latino? Although you've probably seen the terms used interchangeably, either one can carry distinctly negative connotations. To some, *Hispanic* carries historical overtones, referring to Spain's colonial conquests, and so *Latino* is the preferable term because it indicates ties to Latin America and its indigenous cultures. Cubans and Puerto Ricans, on the other hand, may prefer *Hispanic* precisely for that reason; their identity isn't linked to Latin America but to Spain. Mexicans may have yet another perspective on the word *Hispanic*. Because they see it as a name used by the US government, which has practiced discrimination in the past, some Mexicans prefer the term *Chicano* because it indicates a specific cultural, as well as ethnic, heritage. Such concern over terminology reveals once again how closely language and identity are interconnected.

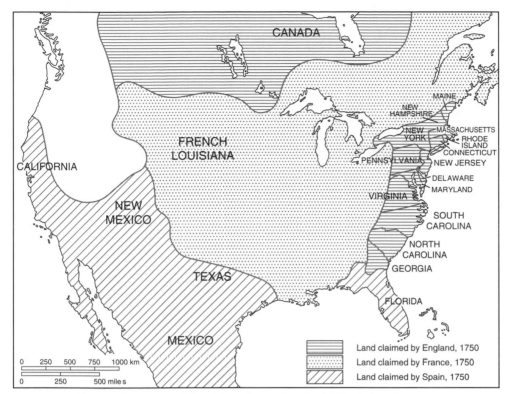

Figure 8.4 *Regions of Spanish settlement in colonial North America*

dialect, the "Valley Girl" dialect, the Boston dialect, and so on, **Chicano English (CE)** is a specific variety of American English with systematic usage features, such as pronunciation, lexicon, syntax, and morphology, that are shared by the entire language community. And just like these other dialects, CE usages can be traced over time, so it is not a learner language, as some Americans wrongly assume.

CE emerged from a historical language contact situation between Spanish and English speakers in the southwestern territories of the United States. Figure 8.4 illustrates the extent of Spanish holdings during colonial times. These lands were first settled by the Spanish and, later, when British colonists and then Americans began moving into these areas, a language contact zone between the two language communities formed. The boundaries of this zone would shift, of course, as the border shifted, for example after 1848 when California, parts of Arizona and New Mexico, and Texas became part of the United States. In addition, language contact became more frequent as Mexican immigration to the United States increased. During the process of learning English as a second language, these immigrants, like all second language learners, used a **learner language**, that is, a non-native variety of the target language (in this case, English) that was influenced by their first language (in this case, Spanish). As linguist Carmen Fought (2003) notes, this learner language was the precursor to the more established and enduring dialect of CE, which the children and successive generations of these immigrants would speak.

Even though it began as a learner language generations ago, CE is now a recognizable dialect, spoken only by native speakers of English, persons who were born in the United States. CE speakers are distinguished, then, from Mexican immigrants who have come here and learned English as a second language and so may use a learner language. Many CE speakers do not know any Spanish, and some do not live within Mexican or Mexican-American families. CE is a form of English that has been influenced by contact with Spanish; it is not a form of Spanish that's been influenced by English.

Table 8.1 identifies a few commonly recognized rules of Chicano English.

Table 8.1 *Commonly recognized rules of Chicano English*

	Rule	Example
Phonology	Reduction of consonant clusters at the end of words	*last* and *board* pronounced as [læs'] and [bor'] respectively.
	Devoicing of [z] in all positions	*easy* = [isi]
	Devoicing of [v] in final position	[lʌv] = [lʌf]
Morphology	Deletion of the -*s*/-*es* endings on the third person singular verb form	"She don't want to hear that" or "The dog come when I call"
	Use of simple past tense forms as participles	"I had went there before" or "She had wrote that down"
Syntax	Use of multiple negatives in one sentence	"I don't have no classes" or "We can't get no help"

Exercise 8.4

Nonlinguists sometimes refer to combinations of Spanish and English as *Spanglish*, a general term that doesn't describe a specific dialect or even a specific type of usage. Discuss the following questions with a partner, and then be prepared to share your ideas with the class. First, why might a Chicano English user find such a reference to her language insulting? Then consider the semantics of using the term *Spanglish*. Would the meaning change if the user was non-Spanish speaking? Non-American-English speaking? Finally, based on your own observations or research, give some examples of Spanglish and explain in what situations it might be used.

Dialect focus: African American English The general term **African American English (AAE)** refers to a group of related dialects spoken primarily by a large population of Americans of African descent. Note that not all African Americans speak AAE, and that not all those who speak AAE are African Americans. As is true for any language, people learn the dialect of their community, and for most, this is the dialect they grow up with. Skin color does not determine the dialect one speaks, but one's culture or environment does. As linguist Salikoko S. Mufwene (2001) reminds us, the term AAE covers a broad span of diverse varieties, just as Southern American English does, for example. People in coastal Mississippi speak very differently from people in Appalachia, but the elements they share in common make them both "Southern." Region also has an impact on AAE: An AAE speaker in the southern United States will sound different from an AAE speaker in the north. An urban AAE speaker might sound different from an AAE speaker in a more rural area. But they all share certain elements of their language that mark AAE as a distinct dialect.

> People sometimes confuse AAE with the language of rappers and other members of hip-hop culture. The two are not the same, though. Users of hip-hop language tend to be members of certain social groups, while AAE users spread across all demographic groups throughout the United States. Hip-hop has only been in existence for a few decades, and AAE has been in use for centuries. Hip-hop language has roots in AAE, but since hip-hop culture is tied specifically to the arts and innovation – dance, art, and music – rather than to a particular history and ethnic background, it has grown in a different direction.

As the name indicates, the earliest speakers of AAE were African Americans, or, to be more direct, Africans brought to the United States as slaves. Obviously, newly arrived slaves wouldn't have known much, if any, American English. However, their language difficulties began before arriving in an American port. Even though each group of slaves on board a trading ship came from the same continent, they would probably not have shared the same native language. Slave traders bought slaves from a variety of locations, so each shipload would have contained individuals from a number of different tribes and of different places. Some slave traders may even have intentionally increased the communication difficulties by separating groups of Africans who spoke the same language as a way to maintain control and prevent uprisings while at sea. So how did AAE develop from this mesh of different languages?

Linguists have several different theories about the development of AAE that focus on the influence of prolonged language contact between the slaves' native tongues and American English, as well as on the preservation of older language forms that geographical isolation creates. Proving these theories is difficult because we have few factual records of oral language from earlier periods.

AAE may have developed as a **pidgin** language, a language that arises when people who do not speak the same language come into contact. In this case, the native languages of the slaves came into contact with English, Spanish, Dutch, and Portuguese, the languages of the slave traders. In order to communicate, slaves may have developed a common language, combining elements of their traders' various languages and including terms from their native African dialects. Most pidgins are developed only enough for rudimentary communication and so typically do not include function words, like articles and prepositions, or extended vocabularies. This changes when the children of those who speak a pidgin are born. The language of these second-generation speakers is called a **creole**, which means that it develops more language features and a more complete grammar. Some creoles remain languages unto themselves, that is,

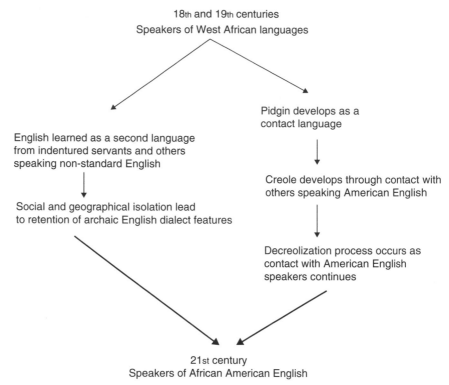

Figure 8.5 *Theories about the development of AAE*

they exist alongside other languages and do not slowly blend with others over time. The fact that AAE shares some words and grammar structures with some of the Caribbean creole languages may be evidence that AAE began as a pidgin language.

Today, though, AAE resembles SAE much more closely than it resembles any other language. Doesn't this contradict the creole theory? Not necessarily. In some situations, a creole may become dominated by another language, so much so that it becomes decreolized, meaning that it loses so many elements of its originating mix of languages that it becomes a dialect of that dominant language rather than a separate language in its own right. In the case of AAE, even if it began as a creole, it certainly has had prolonged contact over several hundred years with SAE. Over time it could have gradually absorbed more and more English, losing elements of the other parent tongues.

Other linguists have theorized that the newly arrived slaves would only have had contact with a very few native English speakers. So, rather than being forced to develop a pidgin for communication, they would have had to learn English because it was required to communicate with those in power. And rather than interacting with the most articulate SAE speakers of that time, the slaves probably only spoke to those who used nonstandard English dialects of their own. The English that the slaves learned, then, would not have been the SAE of that era. Supporters of this theory point out that some of the distinctive features of AAE today also existed in older varieties of English used in earlier time periods and with other nonstandard dialects such as Appalachian English. If it developed in this way, AAE then originated as a dialect of American English and not as a separate language. Figure 8.5 contrasts these two theories.

Notice that these different theories for the development of AAE could also have worked together. Slaves could very well have developed a pidgin to communicate with speakers of a variety of American English dialects, a history that would support both of these theories. Where linguists do seem to agree is that the development of AAE happened over a period of time and was produced by its speakers coming into continual contact with other languages – perhaps languages other than English, or perhaps earlier forms of English alone. And no matter how AAE came into being, today it is a distinct dialect with its own usage conventions.

Until linguists began studying AAE in the 1970s, most Americans believed that this dialect was simply an abbreviated or shortened form of SAE. And because it was considered a partial form of English, most people thought AAE was ungrammatical, that is, that it lacked a systematic set of grammar rules by which it was governed. The contrary proved to be true, however, after linguist William Labov (1972) analyzed AAE and found that its grammar was just as complex as that of other dialects of English, including SAE. Table 8.2 examines some of the most commonly recognized rules of AAE.

After reading the linguistic description of AAE, you now know that it is a structured, rule-governed dialect of American English. Many Americans however, do not share this view and still regard it as a broken form of English, much as they might consider Chicano English a broken dialect as well. This general attitude toward AAE became very apparent in what became a national discussion in the late 1990s on its possible use in one public school system. The discussion is important for what it reveals about the role of language variation within a particular language community, as well as American attitudes about nonstandard dialects. Box 8.1 examines the origins of the national controversy over African American English.

William Labov is an influential American scholar working in the fields of sociolinguistics and dialectology. Labov introduced a more objective methodology for gathering language data, helping transform the field of linguistics into a quantitative science. His early work studying social groups in Harlem relied on objective observation of real-life language use, which was then subjected to mathematical analysis. So when Labov articulated the grammar rules of AAE within the language community he'd been studying, he was able to prove their existence rather than merely assert an opinion that they might exist. You can read Labov's essay, "How I Got into Linguistics, and What I Got Out of It," on the PBS website *Do You Speak American* www.pbs.org/speak/speech/sociolinguistics/labov/

Gender variation

Another area of study within social variation examines gender and language. For centuries stereotypes have existed about the ways in which men and women use language. Do women really talk more than men? Do men really interrupt more than women? Questions like these have made researchers wonder if a relationship exists between a speaker's

Table 8.2 *Commonly recognized rules of AAE*

	Rule	Example
Phonology	Reduction of consonant clusters at the end of words when the following word begins with a consonant	*desk top* [destp]
	Reduction of consonant clusters when past tense ending *-ed* added to verbs ending in consonants	*dropped* [drp] *missed* [mIs]
	b, *d*, and *g* at the ends of words become [p], [t], and [k], respectively	*bad* [bæt] *gag* [gæk]
Morphology	Express habitual actions or states in the present by using the uninflected *be*	*He be tired. She be happy.*
	Deletion of the *-s/-es* endings on the third person singular verb form	"She don't want to hear that" or "The dog come when I call"
Syntax	Use of multiple negatives in one sentence	"I don't have no classes" or "We can't get no help"

Box 8.1 Controversy over the Oakland School Board resolution

In 1996, the Oakland, California School Board passed a resolution intended to improve the academic performance of African American students in its district. The resolution focused on two main points: first, that some African American speakers use a language that is historically different from other American English dialects, including Standard American English (SAE), because of its roots in West African languages; second, teachers would be trained to use African American English (AAE) in the classroom as a bridge leading to students' acquisition of SAE proficiency. Due to the incomplete reporting of the resolution by the media, the general public came to believe that the Oakland School Board viewed AAE as a language distinct from English, and that teachers would be instructing students in both AAE and SAE in the Oakland schools. The resulting controversy began a national discussion about using AAE in schools, known as the **Ebonics debate**. Even later, after the board clarified its position, stating that it would only use AAE as a transitional tool and that it would not be taught as a language itself, the public could not accept the notion that an "inferior" language would actually be used in the classroom. Linguists joined the debate to educate the public that AAE was a dialect with a fully developed grammar rule system, just like SAE, and therefore no less "correct" than SAE, but today, over ten years later, many Americans still don't recognize AAE as a distinct dialect. You can read the Oakland School District resolutions, linguists' responses, and comments on the need for teacher training in American English dialects at http://linguistlist.org/topics/ebonics/

language and gender, and, if so, how this might affect social relations. Before we discuss the results of some of this research, however, we should first define what we mean by the term *gender*. Most scholars use *gender* to refer to a practice, or a set of behaviors, that expresses what *a culture* defines as masculine or feminine nature. Note that we stress that these behaviors are denoted masculine or feminine by a culture, different from sex characteristics, which are biologically determined. Gender differences are usually those seen between male and female, created when people carry out different activities thought to express either male or female natures. And these gender differences vary from one culture to another because the concepts of masculine and feminine vary from one culture to another. As a significant human activity, language communication has also been identified as gendered.

In the early years of gender and language research, scholars conducted studies that catalogued phonological, morphological, and syntactic traits of male and female speakers. In later studies, linguists used discourse analysis to examine gender and language, primarily focusing upon conversations and their contexts. Let's now look at the findings of some of these studies.

Differences in speech of males and females Studies have revealed some differences in the ways that English-speaking men and women use language within western cultures, from the words that they employ to the ways in which they hold conversations: how they contribute, what part they take, what they talk about, and so on. Table 8.3 illustrates some of these potential differences.

What causes these observed variations in the ways men and women speak? The answers to this question have been varied, but most can be grouped into essentially two positions: those that attribute these differences to power differentials between men and women, and those that attribute them to the different natures of men's and women's lives.

Explanations for gender speech variation As you have seen throughout this text, a person's language is shaped by the culture in which he resides. Researchers engaged in gender discourse analysis have noticed that a participant's language very much depends upon the nature of power within a discourse or exchange. These researchers suggest that in cultures where the masculine is privileged and males typically retain more power as a result, men will tend to hold the power in conversations as well, and so exhibit any or all of the characteristics noted in Table 8.3.

More recent studies have refined this thesis. They have found that not only men but also women whose power status is high engage in the discourse characteristics listed in the table, and that this use occurs in discoursal situations with both female and male subordinates. These findings suggest that the discourse of power, then, is not just the language of men or women but the

Table 8.3 *Differences in the speech of males and females within western cultures*

	Men's language	Women's language
Phonological differences	Lower pitch	Higher pitch
	Smaller range of intonation; more monotone	Greater range of intonation
	Stronger, louder voices	Softer, possibly breathier, voices
Morphological differences	Lexical terms reflecting cultural norms: in the west, perhaps a larger wordbank of sports, building construction, and other terms	Lexical terms reflecting cultural norms: in the west, perhaps a larger wordbank of color, fashion, and other terms
	Greater use of nonstandard terms, such as vulgarities	Greater use of prestige word forms
Discoursal differences	More interrupting in some conversations	More facilitative feedback in some conversations, such as use of tag questions

discourse of the more or the less powerful (Cameron 1998; Eckert and McConnell-Ginet 2003). While we might accept the idea that in almost all cultural contexts power differentials exist, does this fact explain all of these differences in gendered conversation? Some researchers have suggested that the dissimilarities stem from broader cultural experiences that are different for men and women. For instance, linguist Deborah Tannen (1993) argues that men and women use language differently because they are sexually segregated at various stages in their lives. This segregation into same-sex groups creates a group culture, or a group norm of behavior, which includes norms in the ways of speaking. Tannen believes that men and women learn different communication skills according to their respective group's purposes for creating relationships. For instance, women often seek intimacy, understanding, and reassurance from their relationships with other women, while men, who tend to favor more independence, are less concerned with forming close or equal relationships with other men. Those who favor the culture difference explanation propose that when men and women do come together, they often do not communicate well because they are using different communication skills.

> Research on gender differences in language has broadened our understanding of boys' and girls' learning styles in the classroom, which in turn has influenced pedagogical methods. Teachers today are very aware of their students' potentially different discoursal behaviors and may employ teaching approaches that complement these diverse styles.

Both of these positions attempting to explain the differences in male and female discourse have been criticized by other sociolinguists for their reliance on stereotypical views about men's and women's characters and for their neglect of other factors that influence discourse. As you've seen, many other variables come into play when a person uses language, including ethnicity, purposes of engagement, setting, and so on. Linguists clearly need to be aware of the consequences of excluding some factors and including others when they study discourse. While the research into the connections between gender and language use continues, for now we will recognize that gender is one factor among many that influences the ways in which we speak with others.

Exercise 8.5

Get into a group of two or three people and discuss the characteristics of language that you might hear in one or two of the single-gender groups listed below. Consider all aspects of language: what sounds, pitch, words, sentence constructions, and meanings (direct or implied) might you hear? Then think about these characteristics. Are they based upon societal expectations of the ways in which males and females talk or on your own experience of these groups? Or on both? Once your group has identified some of these characteristics, write a short dialogue that you imagine could take place among some of the members of the group you've chosen to analyze. Once it has been written, share the dialogue with your other classmates.

1.   a senior women's luncheon club
2.   a middle-aged men's bowling league
3.   a group of girls in a kindergarten class
4.   twenty-something male friends in a bar
5.   twenty-something female friends in their dorm room

Chapter summary

This chapter has introduced you to the notion of regional and social varieties of American English, as well as the methodology linguists use to study **dialects**. You have learned about the historical link between the development of regional American English dialects and the early migration routes of English-speaking settlers in this country. In addition, you now know about the history and some of the linguistic structures of both **Chicano English** and **African American English**, two of the most commonly spoken social dialects in the United States today. And finally the chapter explored the relationship between gender and language.

Critical Thinking exercises

1.   Go to the website of the International Dialects of English Archive (IDEA), a repository of source recordings of both English language dialects and English spoken in the accents of other languages,

downloadable at IDEA at web.ku.edu/~idea/ Listen to two or more American English dialects of your choice, jotting down some examples of the pronunciation, words, and syntax of each that you hear. Then, write up a descriptive analysis of each dialect, noting differences that you observe in phonology, morphology/syntax, and lexicon. Speculate on how these differences might have arisen.

2.   Pick a contemporary dialect to analyze from media portrayals in popular culture. For example, you might look at a music video or a movie or a TV show – anything that portrays speakers with two or more dialects interacting with each other. How are dialects and language variations used to create individual characters in this portrayal? Do they shape one's attitude toward a particular speaker, or comment on a particular language community in American society? You might also think about the reactions of other people to this particular portrayal. Are they the same as your own reactions?

3.   Sociolinguists (linguists who study language in social contexts) have found that people who might not take offense to a regional dialect do take exception to other kinds of dialects, often stemming more from their notions about the people who speak these dialects than from the dialects themselves. Think of some American dialects that have particular connotations attached to them. You can start off with the Southern and Northern, but then branch out and consider other dialects – class, ethnic, gender, etc. – as well. Speculate about why the dialects you have chosen have more connotations attached to them than other dialects. Write up your observations in a short essay.

Hot Topic: Change your life! Get a new accent today!

You may have seen advertisements in newspapers and online for companies that claim to be "accent reduction specialists," or "dialect modification experts." Their services aren't just for non-native speakers seeking to reduce their foreign accents but extend as well to American English speakers who wish to minimize their regional accents (suggested accents that need improvement include those of New York City, the American South, Boston, Chicago, Detroit, and the Midwest farmland). To help individuals seeking to change their regional accents, one company offers a special "articulation tape," which can be used to furnish the user with "elevated/classical, American diction."

The services provided by these companies bring up some interesting questions, especially in relation to the notion of "good" or "bad" accents. Think about these services and consider the following questions, in a group or by yourself. Jot down your ideas as you discuss or ponder, and then write them up in a short response. Note: If you wish to see some of these advertisements, you may seek out these companies by typing into your search engine "accent reduction" or "dialect modification."

1.   Who is the intended target audience of these ads? Consider which occupations might require people to think about and perhaps change their accents.
2.   Which American English accent do you think these companies might have selected as a goal for their customers to learn? One company mentions students learning "elevated/classical American diction." How might you define this? See if you can write down a list of words that might be included in its lexicon.
3.   What are some of the implications of these ads? Why might the existence of these programs be at the same time both characteristic-ally and uncharacteristically American? Hint: Consider some of the traditional values that are associated with Americans.
4.   How might linguists view these programs, given what you know about how linguists work? Finally, what are your own feelings about the services these companies offer?

Learn more about it

Studying dialects

Finnegan, E. and Rickford, J. R. (eds.) 2004, *Language in the USA*, Cambridge: Cambridge University Press.
The editors offer a comprehensive examination of American English, including essays discussing regional and social varieties.

Wolfram, W. 1991, *Dialects and American English*, Englewood Cliffs, NJ: Prentice Hall.
In prose meant for the reader unfamiliar with technical linguistic terminology, Wolfram introduces students to the subject of American dialect variation through discussions of the nature of dialects, descriptive detail of dialects, and the application of dialect information.

Dialect focus: Chicano English

Fought, C. 2003, *Chicano English in context*, New York: Palgrave Macmillan.
Fought provides an excellent study of Chicano English within the context of East Los Angeles, with a thorough description of the phonological, morpho-logical, and syntactic characteristics of CE.

Penfield, J. and Ornstein-Galicia, J. L. 1985, *Chicano English: An ethnic contact dialect*, Amsterdam: John Benjamins.
This early study of Chicano English gives a useful and detailed linguistic description.

Dialect focus: African American English

Green, L. J. 2002, *African American English: A linguistic description*, Cambridge: Cambridge University Press.

Green gives an authoritative introduction to the dialect of African American English (AAE). In addition to descriptions of AAE grammar, the book includes discussions of AAE in literature, contemporary media, and education.

Mufwene, S. S., Rickford, J. R., Bailey, G., and Baugh, J. (eds.) 1998, *African American English: Structure, history and use*, New York: Routledge.

This complete reference work describes AAE's structural features, its history and lexicon, its use in discourse, and its relevance to the educational problems of African American children.

Gender and language

Cameron, D. 1998, *The feminist critique of language: A reader*, London: Routledge.

This textbook provides extracts of primary source material from the leading scholars studying gender and language, giving readers an introduction to the range and depth of the field.

Eckert, P. and McConnell-Ginet, S. 2003, *Language and gender*, Cambridge: Cambridge University Press.

This introductory textbook explores the relationship between gender and language use.

Tannen, D. 1991, *You just don't understand: Women and men in conversation*, London: Virago.

One of the early researchers in this field, Tannen investigates the ways in which men and women communicate differently. She also examines how argument and interruption function within different discoursal contexts.

9   Language, community, and American policy

Key terms

Language policy
Sociolinguistics
Overt prestige
Covert prestige
Slang
Taboo
Jargon
Official language

Overview

In this chapter you'll learn how the interconnection of language, power, and identity can affect entire language communities, as well as the individuals within those communities. Those with power within a community are able to control the language, and thus the identity, of those without power. After explaining basic concepts, the chapter focuses on the complex language community of the United States, discussing a few of the laws implemented in the past that have directly affected language usage. You'll explore some of the historical conflicts over language usage, such as that between American English speakers and Native Americans, as well as examine the debate over "Official English." Finally, the Hot Topic asks you to reflect on the position of endangered languages in the world today and the policies that have been enacted to save them.

Introduction

Do you remember the 2006 public furor over a recording of "The Star-Spangled Banner" with Spanish lyrics? It made its debut on April 28, just before the US Congress began debating the topic of immigration reform, and immediately received a great deal of media attention, primarily negative. Adam Kidron, president of the song's recording company, explained that "Nuestro

The fact that some Latinos have felt a need to take the National Anthem, a sacred, symbolic and historical piece of music, and create their OWN version, one in Spanish, with different words, proves beyond the shadow of a doubt that they have NO desire to be Americans, no desire to assimilate. *Comment by Peggy D.–* *April 28, 2006 @ 8:16 a.m.*	What is America? One country or one continent? For Latin Americans America is all the continent from Alaska to Tierra del Fuego... Some of the singers [of *Nuestro Himno*] are Americans from Puerto Rico. Being part of the US I think they have the right of having the Anthem in Spanish. There is not an official language in the US. *Comment by Kathi S.–* *April 28, 2006 @ 1:16 p.m.*

Figure 9.1 *Representative comments about* Nuestro Himno *posted on the blog* About.com: Latin Music *(T. Ilich. April 24, 2006, Nuestro Himno: National Anthem in Spanish,* Tijana's Latin Music Blog, http://latinmusic.about.com/b/2006/04/24/ nuestro-himno-national-anthem-in-spanish.htm#gB3)

Himno" or "Our Anthem" was motivated by a desire to honor immigrants in America. Some newspaper columnists and bloggers, though, felt that using Spanish lyrics for the American national anthem expressed the opposite attitude, that immigrants have no respect for America and no intention of learning American English or American values. Even the title "Our Anthem" provoked controversy, meaning solidarity among all those living on American soil to some, while meaning the theft of American identity to others. Figure 9.1 illustrates this controversy.

You're probably not surprised to see that the same lyrics carry different meanings to different people because you're familiar with semantic relationships, and you know that languages are intertwined with the identity of particular language communities. But this debate over the lyrics to "The Star-Spangled Banner" introduces a new topic for our study because it illustrates the movement from attitudes about language to the creation of **language policy**. A *policy* is a plan of action intended to control future decisions and actions; a *language policy* is a policy directly about language usage and indirectly about the people who use that language. Language policies can be formal or informal, private or public, but in every situation, formulation of a specific policy defining appropriate language usage reflects concerns about defining a particular language community's identity.

The furor over "Nuestro Himno" seems particularly striking because "The Star-Spangled Banner" has been translated into other languages, such as German, Yiddish, and Samoan, many times since it was composed. In 1919 the US government even commissioned a Spanish version to use in its education programs. But in 2006, less than two weeks after "Nuestro Himno" was first introduced, public controversy was so widespread that the US Senate unanimously approved a nonbinding resolution (S. Res. 458) affirming "that statements or songs that symbolize the unity of the Nation, including the National Anthem, the Oath of Allegiance sworn by new United States citizens, and the Pledge of

Allegiance to the Flag of the United States, should be recited or sung in English, the common language of the United States" (US Senate 2006).

Why did this particular translation of "The Star-Spangled Banner" spur such an action by a branch of the federal government? Many suggest that "Nuestro Himno" was seen as an anthem for illegal Spanish immigrants during a time when the general public's emotions were stirred by the immigration reform debate. The public's resentment of illegal immigrants may have fueled their hostility toward a Spanish version of the national anthem. This public controversy then evolved into a government institution's action. With this resolution, the Senate was voicing its support for the use of English as the common language of the United States and politically privileging English over Spanish. And privileging the use of English also meant privileging English users. In this particular situation, the language policy created wasn't official, but in other scenarios the policies can be legally binding and are enforced.

The national anthem case is one example of how language reveals community beliefs and practices. The study of the ways in which language usage reflects both social identity and the social relationships between language communities is known as **sociolinguistics** because of the way that it combines the study of people with that of language. In this chapter we'll focus on the ways that language communities use language to identify their members. We'll begin by considering the links between individuals and their own language communities to understand how language reflects shared knowledge, experience, and beliefs. Then we'll examine how communities create language policies in attempts to enforce their own distinct value systems.

Individuals and their communities

You've probably already identified some of your own language communities, such as your own regional dialect, and maybe even language usages particular to your own family. But have you ever thought about your social groups in terms of language? Individuals belong to more than one language community at a time because we all have many facets to our identities. This means that we are constantly changing our language to fit the values of each distinct community. The language one learns at home and speaks with close family members may be very different from the language one speaks at work (see Figure 9.2). And both of these may differ from the language of a particular hobby community, such as that of a football fan or a choir member. When we use the language of a particular community, we mark ourselves as members both for other members and for outsiders. Those within the community use the appropriate language, while those without do not.

Just think about how other members of a particular community you belong to would react if you failed to use the appropriate language. Let's say that you talk to your history professor in the same way that you talk to your best friend.

Figure 9.2 *One type of language community*

The reaction probably wouldn't be a positive one. You might be labeled ignorant or rude; in some situations you might even be excluded from class discussions. Being able to use the appropriate language for a particular language community is similar to having a key to the front door of your home. Without the key, and without the language, you can't enter. All of those within the language community in some sense, then, are gatekeepers: They can keep people out who do not know the appropriate language. And since the community controls the language, it is also able to control, at least to some extent, the language that its members use.

Communities don't just exert power over their own members, though. Society as a whole may recognize one community as being more valuable than others and thus give one group power over others. This judgment carries over to their languages as well. The languages of those communities with more social power will be privileged over the languages of those communities with less power. Not only will the more powerful communities privilege their own language, they may also determine language policy for the other communities.

Exercise 9.1

Make a list of all the language communities with which you interact over the course of a day. For example, your list might include roommates, family members, particular classes, club members, and so on. Then identify the hierarchy among these communities. Which one has the most power over all the others? And so on down the line. Which one has the least power? Then write about how you determined the hierarchy. What clues did you seek for distinguishing the most powerful from the least powerful?

You probably discovered in Exercise 9.1 that a typical range of communities might span one's immediate family, best friends, acquaintances, teachers, other students, boss, coworkers, customers, grocery store or gas station cashiers, news anchors, radio announcers, and maybe even more. Was the most powerful community in your list identified as such because the other communities used its language, or recognized its language as being significant? In other words, was its language the most privileged?

Most people are unaware of the more subtle ways in which our language becomes a tool in power negotiations in our society. Because language is closely allied with social attitudes, speakers with social power also become speakers with language power, that is, the power to control how others express themselves. Their language is privileged, just as they themselves are privileged. And individuals or communities that accept the language choices of others have accepted a subordinate position because they have acknowledged the superior knowledge or experience or control of these others. Remember, though, that language and identity are interconnected. What happens when people don't want to identify with the privileged members of a particular community? The following discussion examines the tensions that sometimes develop among language, identity, and community.

> The sociolinguist James Paul Gee (1989) has coined the term *Discourse* with a capital *D* to discuss the concept of a community's language. For Gee, *Discourse* includes acting, speaking (or writing), believing, valuing, and social identity; it becomes, he says, an "identity kit" that enables an individual to take on a particular role that others will recognize. For instance, you may be working toward earning accreditation as a high-school teacher. You will not join the Discourse of high-school teachers, though, until you are no longer studying it but are instead acting, thinking . . . living like a high-school teacher. And because we are all complex individuals – daughter, student, psychologist, mayor – we all engage in a variety of Discourses.

Language and prestige

Because all language communities privilege certain languages over others, sociolinguists observe the values attached to particular language use, as well as to the language itself. **Overt prestige** refers to the positive values associated with the perceived "better" way of language usage in a particular community. For example, when college students write required research papers for their classes, they tend to use SAE because, in American culture today, that's the language that educated individuals tend to use. *Positive value* in this context translates to receiving a good grade. And obviously, the language associated with overt prestige is going to be the language that the most powerful individuals within that particular community use.

However, sometimes individuals want to identify themselves with a community that is not the privileged one. For example, have you ever written or thought about writing rap music lyrics? If so, you'd probably choose to use the everyday slang of urban youth rather than SAE. In instances like these, rap lyrics, which employ a nonstandard language that would otherwise be stigmatized within the larger society, are given **covert prestige**. The rap community values real-life experiences common to the undereducated and unprivileged members of society. So speakers wanting to identify themselves with the covert prestige of the rap community use a nonstandard vocabulary and usage.

Exercise 9.2

Working with a partner, consider the following scenarios in terms of overt and covert prestige. Why might the speaker in each scenario choose to use this particular language? What sort of value might be associated with its use? Also consider any tensions that might exist within each community over language usage.

1.   As a man enters a clothing store, the sales clerk greets him by saying, "Yo, dude. Watcha lookin for?" The man responds by saying, "Excuse me?"
2.   The doctor advises a patient, "For temporary alleviation of these symptoms, take NSAIDs PRN."
3.   As they are entering their business together, Joe turns to Sam and says, "Did you see the game last night? I couldn't believe the calls that f****** referee made!"

As you no doubt discovered when you considered the scenarios in Exercise 9.2, each of the individuals portrayed uses a language variety associated with a particular identity, and with an accompanying level of power, within that specific context. As these examples reveal, the language expressing overt or covert prestige varies from one community to another because the values of each community differ from one another.

Two specific kinds of language usage associated with both forms of prestige, however, exist in all kinds of different communities because the basic human desire to belong to social groups motivates their use. We'll now look at the use of slang and jargon so that you can understand how they express some of the power dynamics within language communities.

Slang and jargon

Slang is a specialized, informal language used by a group within a larger language community. Its existence illustrates covert prestige. Members of this subgroup want to identify themselves to each other, and so their slang becomes an obvious marker of identity. Frequently slang repels those outside the subgroup, which of course may be one of the purposes for using it, to maintain the exclusivity of the group. Think, for instance, of street gang members, whose slang is often a complicated blend of newly coined words, plays on words, and vulgarities. The fact that few people outside the gang can understand this language helps to maintain the cohesiveness and unity of the group. To break into a street gang, then, one must not only learn the members' habits but also their language. Figure 9.3 contrasts two different American slangs.

American gangster slang
(1930–1940s)

Cheese it– Hide things
Cooler– jail
Gat– gun
Heeled– armed with a gun
Hinky– skeptical

American gangsta slang
(1990s–2000s)

Beef– to hold a grudge against someone
Busta– a wanna-be; a poser
G Ride– a stylish car
Mack– A person who is successful at flirting and seducing women
Thug– a person who survives and even overcomes social and economic hardships

Figure 9.3 *Slang belongs to a particular time and place*

Because slang is usually spoken rather than written, it's informal in use and so often departs from the SAE rules of grammar and usage. As a result, slang is frequently seen as a liberating language that people can use in creative ways, for instance in songs, art, graffiti, and other contexts. This creativity often appears in slang lexicons. For example, the contemporary term *bling*, referring to showy jewelry, originated as a reference to the supposed sound of that jewelry as it is being worn. The hip-hop community uses this slang rather than the more formal word, *jewelry*, at least for now. By the time you read this, though, *bling* may have been replaced by another slang term. Slang may also contain words considered **taboo**, or stigmatized, by the larger language community, such as obscenities or swear words. Its oral, informal nature means that slang changes quickly to accommodate the immediate concerns and interests of its users, leading those outside the particular slang community to see it as transient and so less meaningful.

> Slang plays an important role in works of literature because it quickly shows a character's personality and sets the mood of particular scenes. Just think about how Chaucer uses slang to help create the variety of individuals in *The Canterbury Tales*. His portrayal of the young lovers, Allison and Nicholas, in "The Miller's Tale" would lose much of its humor without the bawdy puns that slang provides. Shakespeare's lively interchanges between Falstaff and Prince Hal in *Henry IV, Part I* rely on slang to establish each character's inner nature. And who can imagine Mark Twain's rebel, Huck Finn, speaking Standard American English? (See Figure 9.4.)

Jargon is another kind of language usage that, like slang, evokes strong emotional responses, but rather than being an informal, oral language, jargon is a specialized, or technical, language unique to a particular profession or workplace. Whether one is working at McDonald's frying french fries or performing brain surgery in the operating room, a specific vocabulary and syntax are required. Using the jargon of a particular field of study enables users to express concepts unique to that particular discipline and so to communicate efficiently with others in that same field. Let's say, for example, that you're working in a medical office, and you're looking for a piece of equipment. You could ask a coworker for the location of the *long tubes with earpieces*

Figure 9.4 *Can you imagine Huckleberry Finn speaking standard American English? (Credit: E.W. Kemble/The Library of Congress, LC-USZ62-98767)*

that make a patient's heart-sounds audible, or you could ask for the *stethoscope.* The single word is obviously more efficient in communicating your meaning.

Unlike slang, though, jargon is known throughout a particular field of knowledge, no matter where it's being used. So a nurse in Hawai'i and a nurse in Maine are both going to use the word *stethoscope.* Slang tends to be limited to a particular geographical region; it also tends to be limited to age groups. All age groups use slang, but they don't all use the same slang. In contrast, jargon is known within a particular field, regardless of age. And while slang tends to be regarded negatively, jargon tends to receive overt prestige because it is associated with specialized knowledge and/or specialized jobs. Like slang, jargon allows users to identify themselves as belonging to a particular language community, while at the same time it excludes others who don't know the language. So just as you must learn the language of a street gang to become a member, so must you learn the language of a profession to become an associate.

Exercise 9.3

The following passage is taken from an application to rent an apartment. Analyze the passage for its use of jargon, or what has come to be known as "legalese." What "lay" terms could be substituted for the technical ones? Which words have been used that are common to everyday speech? After analyzing the text, consider the issues of power and prestige as you answer the following questions:

1. Given that people unfamiliar with legalese must still read legal documents, such as wills, contracts, and agreements, why does the legal community persist in using legalese?
2. Now translate this text into SAE and consider its effect. What happens when you "translate" the legalese into lay language?
3. And finally, translate this text into the slang you and your immediate friends use. Can you do this? How is this different from the SAE version or the original version? Think about individual words, but also think about the concepts being conveyed. Do they change when the language changes?

CONSENT TO OBTAIN CREDIT INFORMATION

As a material inducement to be considered as a tenant for Pine Acres Apartment Complex, I both consent to and authorize _____, or any agent of same, to contact all references I have named in this application below, and to conduct a credit review, including obtaining my credit report from any authorized credit reporting agency.

I declare under penalty of perjury that the information listed in this application is true and correct.

Executed on this _____ day of _____, 2010, in the city of _____, state of _____.

As you've seen, language enables communities as a whole to immediately identify insiders and outsiders. And the larger the community, the more complex the issues of language become because they involve power and identity too. Thus communities frequently enact language policies not only to identify members but also to control identities and power. Just think about receptionists who must answer the phone with a specific phrase so that callers receive an appropriate impression of the company. This is just one example of how language policy is enacted within a community.

Exercise 9.4

Make a list of language policies with which you're personally familiar. They might be unofficial, such as not swearing in church, or official, such as using particular language in a workplace.

Discuss your list with a classmate and determine together possible reasons for such policies. Do they exist to give certain impressions of the community? Are they there for the benefit of the public? Do the members of the community benefit from them?

As you've just seen, separate language communities may enact language policies both to identify their members and to exclude others. We'd now like to examine what happens when a very large community, such as the United States, with many languages being spoken within its borders, consciously wants to distinguish its identity from those it perceives to be outsiders. As we will discuss below, this is when official language planning and policies come into effect as those with power in the community attempt to enforce language use. When we consider this power play in light of what we have said about the connection between language and identity, we quickly see that controlling the language of others can mean controlling their identity, even the identity of an entire community. Let's now focus on the language community of the United States as a whole.

American language policies

The privileging of American English

Even before the founding of the United States, North America was filled with peoples speaking diverse languages, perhaps as many as 2,000 Native American tongues. The first European settlers to the lands that would later become the United States arrived from Spain in the late fifteenth century.

Then, during the sixteenth and seventeenth Centuries, European immigration from other countries increased, ultimately displacing the Native Americans. The Spanish, English, French, and Dutch languages began to dominate in America. A colonial American living in a big city like Boston or New Orleans might have heard as many as twenty different languages commonly spoken in daily life as a result of the interactions among European, African, and Native American inhabitants. But sometimes new immigrants chose to live near others who spoke the same language and so did not interact with speakers of other languages. For example, large numbers of Germans settled in Pennsylvania, and Dutch communities were established in the state of New York. Overall, though, the majority of settlers came from English-speaking countries, and so English became the dominant language of the New World.

Many Americans today are familiar with the history of their country in terms of the gradual spread of British colonies. If we think historically, though, Spanish speakers were the first Europeans in most of what is now the United States, not just the Southwest. For example, in 1526 a group of approximately 500 Spanish colonists built the town of San Miguel de Guadalupe along the coast of what is now South Carolina. In 1570, nine Jesuit missionaries founded Ajacan, a settlement located near the area that would later become known as Jamestown in 1607. Even though these colonies ultimately failed, they introduced the Spanish language to the New World before the British colonists began arriving.

Figure 9.5 *The Continental Congress never voted on an official language of the United States (Credit: The Library of Congress)*

Although American English was dominant by the time of the American Revolution, the founders of the United States never identified it as the nation's official language in spite of several different opportunities to do so. In 1780, John Adams proposed that the Continental Congress establish an official Academy to standardize American English and control language usage in the new United States (see Figure 9.5). The Congress rejected his proposal as being undemocratic. During this period language usage was judged to be a matter of personal choice rather than an issue for national policy. Recognizing this individual language usage, the government printed official documents in German and French, as well as in English.

During the eighteenth and nineteenth centuries, the federal government generally continued a policy of neutrality and acceptance toward a variety of European languages being used in the United States. Local schools used the native language appropriate to their local populations rather than being required to use English. States also met the

Although the story that German failed to become the official language of the United States by one vote is widespread, it is just a myth. The fact is that the Continental Congress never voted on an official language. The moment in history that apparently spawned this myth began in the late eighteenth century, when a group of German-speakers in Virginia petitioned Congress to publish federal laws in German as well as in English. During the discussion in the House of Representatives, it was a vote to adjourn that missed passing by a single vote rather than a vote on the issue itself. The House later rejected the proposal.

needs of their various constituents by printing official documents in a wide range of languages, such as Welsh, Czech, and Norwegian, in addition to the more widely used Spanish, French, and German. According to data from the 1890 US Census (2006c), 3.62 percent of the entire United States population didn't speak English, and in some geographical areas the percentage was much higher. In New Mexico, for example, non-English speakers comprised over 65 percent of the population.

Despite this widespread acceptance of diverse language communities, however, not all non-English speakers escaped criticism. Those populations who were markedly different from the majority populations found themselves and their languages being treated in negative ways. Sometimes English speakers found communities of non-English speakers threatening, and so we find instances of criticism, such as Benjamin Franklin's complaints about the German speakers in Pennsylvania whose large numbers he believed threatened the preservation of English.

Other populations suffered more severe consequences due to the western expansion and economic growth of the American, English-speaking population. You already know from our discussion in Chapter 8 about the large numbers of slaves who lost their native languages when they were transported to the United States. In addition, the Native American, Spanish, and Hawai'ian populations suffered a variety of hardships that, in turn, affected their languages. The following discussion focuses specifically on these three languages because the most sweeping language policies affected their speakers, but be aware that other language groups also faced discriminatory practices during this period.

Nineteenth-century policies toward minority languages

Native Americans After the American Revolution, in its pursuit to expand its holdings westward, the US government used various means to dislodge the Native Americans from their lands. As a common practice, wars were waged periodically from colonial times throughout the nineteenth century, until the final war in 1890 at Wounded Knee, South Dakota. Scholars of American history estimate that over 45,000 Native Americans died during these Indian Wars occurring over more than 200 years. In addition, diseases such as smallpox and measles killed a large percentage of the Native American population. The eradication of the tribes, of course, also obliterated their languages. Indeed, before European contact, it is estimated that 1,000–2,000 Native American languages existed. After contact, this number dropped through the years to around 250, in large part because so many of the native speakers had died.

> As an example of another type of "war," in California, during the Gold Rush years of 1848–1860, Americans who killed a Native American living on land appropriate for mining received a bounty. In her essay, "Saving California Languages," Katharine Whittemore (1998) reports that the federal government paid over $1 million in such bounties in just one year. This practice decimated the Native American population in California and, of course, their languages.

The American government also used forced relocation as a way to gain Indian lands. This policy helped to sound the death knell for many native languages, as many Indian populations were required to leave their lands entirely, resulting in dividing some tribes and forcing their settlement on reservations with other tribes whose languages were different from their own.

In addition, during the late nineteenth and early twentieth centuries, the government created boarding schools for Native American children in the hopes of fostering their assimilation, or their absorption by or conversion to the customs and practices of the dominant or privileged group, in this case white, English-speaking Americans. Most of the Indian boarding schools were established in the northeast, hundreds of miles from the reservations, so that children would not be influenced by their native cultures, which officials thought promoted "uncivilized" behavior. Parents could not easily visit, and the children were frequently kept from going home during their vacations. The school

The Carlisle Indian Industrial School, founded by US Army Captain Richard Henry Pratt in Carlisle, Pennsylvania, was the first and best-known of these boarding schools. In his own words, Pratt's goal was to "Kill the Indian and save the man" by employing a military-like regimen. The Native American children wore uniforms, practiced marching, and learned manual skills such as farming for the boys and sewing for the girls. Although the intention was that these youngsters would grow up and join white American culture, in fact, most of the children after graduation returned to their reservations to live, hampered by a lack of knowledge of their native languages and cultural practices. Figure 9.6 illustrates one of the few success stories among the Indian boarding-school graduates.

Figure 9.6 *Jim Thorpe, a famous athlete of the early twentieth century, was a graduate of the Carlisle Indian Industrial School (Credit: Cumberland County Historical Society, Carlisle, PA)*

curriculum was conducted solely in English, and use of native languages was strictly forbidden at all times. The children were even given English names in an effort to have them assimilate more easily into white culture.

Exercise 9.5

Depending on its context, the notion of assimilation can have neutral, positive, or negative connotations. We talk about the positive benefits, for instance, of having a child in a new school become assimilated into her class, or we talk neutrally about the assimilation that takes place when plants absorb nutrients from the ground. But what about those negative connotations? As you've seen in the discussion above, oftentimes the assimilation of *people* can be harmful. In hindsight, we now recognize the damage done by those who took Native American children from their parents and sent them to boarding schools far away. Although the officials carried out those actions as part of their overall plan for a stronger America, such draconian measures surely would never be accepted today. And yet, other governmental policies based upon assimilationist views were enacted throughout the twentieth century, and some continue to exist today. Get with several members of your class and see if you can brainstorm about American social policies of the past or present that express an assimilationist viewpoint. Why were these policies created, and what were their effects? What far-reaching consequences might they have engendered? Be prepared to report on your considerations to the rest of the class.

Spanish and Hawai'ian Like the Native American tribes, nineteenth-century Spanish speakers in the west and the Hawai'ian speakers in Hawai'i also faced conflicts with American English speakers colonizing their territories. And in dealing with both groups the federal government enacted policies intended to strip these speakers of their cultural heritage, including their language.

> You may be unfamiliar with the symbol that looks like an upside-down apostrophe between the last two vowels in the word *Hawai'i*. This is the *okina*, the Hawai'ian alphabet letter that represents the consonant sound called a *glottal stop*. This sound is made by closing the glottis at the back of the throat to stop air movement. Think, for example, about saying the sounds *uh-oh*. The sound that divides these two syllables is the glottal stop.

At the end of the Mexican–American War, the United States and Mexico signed the Treaty of Guadalupe Hidalgo in 1848. The United States received a vast amount of land, including what now makes up the states of California, Nevada, and Utah, in return for giving Mexico $15 million and a promise to protect the property rights of the Mexicans already living on this land. In 1851, though, only three years later, the federal California Land Act required all Californians to prove ownership of their land in an English-speaking court. As you can imagine, the Spanish-speaking families who may have been living in California for many generations at this point found meeting this requirement almost impossible. About 14 million acres of land passed into the control of English speakers. This example demonstrates once again how laws regarding language usage can serve those in power.

The westward expansion of the United States also had a significant impact on Hawai'i and Hawai'ian speakers. Rather than large numbers of individual Americans moving west to find gold, as happened in California, American businesses moved west to Hawai'i in search of business opportunities. They became involved in the growing sugar-cane industry in the Hawai'ian islands, and, because of their acute financial interests, began to concern themselves with Hawai'ian governance. Although the exact role these American growers played in ending the Hawai'ian monarchy is debated, historians agree that these businessmen acted to protect American interests, including encouraging native assimilation of American ways. By the time Hawai'i had become an official territory of the United States in 1900, the use of Hawai'ian in schools had already been outlawed. As intended by this language policy, native Hawai'ian speakers grew fewer and fewer with each successive generation. The Hawai'ian language had lost all its status and was heading toward extinction. Note that these events were occurring just as the United States was enforcing the last Native American relocations to the reservations. It would take a change in governmental policy to finally reverse the dire trends experienced by both the Native American and Hawai'ian languages.

Because Hawai'ian was originally a spoken language only, it had no means of being preserved in a fixed form. This was to change, though, when a teenaged Hawai'ian, Henry Obookiah (Opukaha'ia in Hawai'ian), traveled to America, learned English, and became a Christian (see Figure 9.7). Obookiah then wanted to share his new knowledge with his countrymen, so he began writing a Hawai'ian dictionary and grammar and also began translating the Bible into Hawai'ian. His life and work inspired the American Board of Commissioners for Foreign Missions in Boston to begin sending missionaries to Hawai'i, specifically charged with learning the Hawai'ian language and teaching the Hawai'ians to read the Bible. Without Obookiah, the Hawai'ian language would probably not have achieved a written form so soon after westerners began visiting the island and so might have been even more difficult to keep alive.

Figure 9.7 *Henry Obookiah*
(Courtesy of the Women's Board of Missions for the Pacific Islands)

Twentieth-century policies toward minority languages

Scholars have pointed out that federal language policies tend to follow public sentiment, and that, at any given time, people's negative attitudes concerning immigration in the United States increase and decrease as the number of immigrants increases and decreases. Since immigration rates were higher in the earlier twentieth century than ever before, the general American population's attitudes toward all languages other than American English grew increasingly negative, even though they had been widely accepted in earlier periods. Figure 9.8 illustrates awareness of this changing perspective. According to the 1910 US Census Bureau data (Gibson and Jung 2002), 14.7 percent of the total US population was made up of foreign-born immigrants. Compare that figure with the most recent US Census Bureau (2003) data, which reported that 10.4 percent of the population was foreign-born.

> As you may know, the largest part of the foreign-born population in the United States today consists of Spanish-speaking immigrants, bringing their own rich culture and traditions to their new country, along with their diverse dialects. In Chapter 10, we'll focus specifically on language issues tied to contemporary Spanish speakers in the United States.

Prior to the twentieth century, newly arrived Americans frequently had been seen as assets rather than as liabilities, but that perspective now changed. For example, in 1911, a Federal Immigration Commission reported that "the 'old' Scandinavian and German immigrants had assimilated quickly, while the 'new' Italian and Eastern European immigrants were inferior to their predecessors, less willing to learn English, and more prone to political subversion" (American

Figure 9.8 The Immigrant: Is He an Acquisition or a Detriment? – *A political cartoon from 1903 (Credit: G.F. Victor/The Library of Congress, LC-USZC4-3659)*

Civil Liberties Union 1996). In response to these negative attitudes, language diversity became seen as a threat to national unity rather than as a matter of individual freedom, and federal policies were gradually implemented to directly address this concern.

The 1924 National Origins Act established quotas for immigration, quotas based on data from the 1890 census. This older data was used rather than the figures from the more recent 1920 census as a way to eliminate the "less desirable" surge of immigrants from southern and eastern Europe which had taken place in the early 1900s. In addition, language policies were enacted requiring immigrants to possess some knowledge of English to become American citizens. The 1906 Naturalization Act demanded, for the first time, speaking ability in English; in 1950, the ability to read in English was added to the requirements. This language policy continues today. According to the current US Citizen and Immigration Services (2003), applicants "must be able to read, write, speak, and understand words in ordinary usage in the English language."

Although the Native American languages had already been negatively affected by federal policies intended to promote assimilation, by the early 1920s, some thinkers suggested that the maintenance of cultural heritage was an important objective. So the Federal Bureau of Indian Affairs began allowing some boarding schools, as well as schools on the reservations, to teach Native American languages. But after World War II the government returned to its assimilationist policies, allowing the use of native languages only to help children become fluent in American English, rather than supporting the teaching of these languages. This position changed once again in the late 1960s, when the federal government ceded authority of the reservations to the Indian tribes, ushering in the era of Indian self-determination that continues today. Part of this new approach was recognizing the importance of preserving indigenous languages. More recently, in 1990, Congress passed the Native American Languages Acts, grant programs designed to "ensure survival and continuing vitality of Native American languages." Grants have been awarded to establish and support community initiatives such as radio and television programs in Native American languages, recording and transcription of oral native testimonies, and the printing and dissemination of written materials in native languages.

Ironically, one of the Native American languages proved to be an asset to the Allies during World War II, when marine commanders used Navajo in their coded messages because they knew the code would be difficult to break. Navajo had no official written form, that is, no alphabet or symbols, and was spoken only by the Navajo people of the American Southwest. Two hundred Navajo soldier "code-talkers" were given the job of transmitting battlefield communications to other Navajo speakers. The receiver would first translate the Navajo word into English and then would take the first letter of each word and spell an English word. If the message contained the word *navy*, for example, the code-talkers might have used the following Navajo words: *tsah (needle) wol-la-chee (ant) ah-keh-di-glini (victor) tsah-ah-dzoh (yucca)*. Not all words had to be spelled out: about 450 military terms were assigned Navajo words, such as *besh-li (iron fish)* for *submarine* and *dah-he-tih-hi (hummingbird)* for *fighter plane* (Molnar 1997).

What is the status of Native American languages today? The US Census Bureau (2006a) reports that out of the 4.3 million American Indians and Native

Table 9.1 *Living Native American language communities with more than 1,000 speakers (after R.G. Gordon, Jr. (ed.) 2005,* Ethnologue: Languages of the world, *www.ethnologue.com/)*

Language	Number of speakers	General location
Apache, Western	12,693	east central Arizona
Arapahoe	1,038	Wyoming
Cherokee	15,000 to 22,500	Oklahoma, North Carolina
Cheyenne	1,721	southeastern Montana
Chippewa	5,000	northern Michigan to North Dakota
Choctaw	9,211	southeastern Oklahoma, east central Mississippi
Crow	4,280	southern Montana
Dakota	15,355	northern Nebraska, southern Minnesota, North and South Dakota, northeastern Montana
Hawai'ian	1,000	Hawai'ian Islands
Hopi	5,264	northeastern Arizona
Inupiatun, North Alaskan	8,000	northwestern Alaska
Keres, Eastern & Western	7,971	New Mexico
Kiowa	1,092	west central Oklahoma
Lakota	6,000	northern Nebraska, southern Minnesota, North and South Dakota, northeastern Montana
Micmac	1,200	Maine, Massachusetts
Mohawk	3,000	northern New York
Muskogee	4,300	southern Alabama, east central Oklahoma, Florida
Navajo	148,530	northeastern Arizona, northwestern New Mexico, southeastern Utah
Paiute, Northern	1,631	northern Nevada, northern California, southern Oregon, southern Idaho
Shoshoni	2,284	northeastern Nevada, southern Idaho
Yakima	3,000	south central Washington
Yupik	10,000	Alaska
Zuni	9,651	New Mexico

Alaskans living in the United States, only 18 percent report speaking a language other than English in the home. Although approximately 155 Native American languages are still spoken in America, only 20 or so of them are still vital, used by speakers of all ages (Gordon 2005). (See Table 9.1.) While tribal leaders,

Figure 9.9 *The Lumbee tribe of North Carolina has struggled to maintain its own linguistic identity (Credit: F. Daughtrey)*

educators, linguists, politicians, and others have joined together in the last decade to revitalize these languages, their work remains ongoing to stave off the potential demise of these native tongues. The Lumbee tribe (see Figure 9.9) of North Carolina has struggled to maintain its linguistic heritage, exemplifying the difficulties Native Americans and their languages face today.

Like the Native American languages, Hawai'ian also faces the danger of extinction but has many people working to preserve it as a living language (see Box 9.1).

Our discussion of the federal language policies of the past has focused on the conflicts between language communities, showing you how concerns about community identity have shaped attitudes toward a nation's language. Obviously, many other policies exist that we haven't addressed here. But we've intentionally focused on historical tensions that are still present in American society. Today, many Americans worry that

In addition to helping preserve American Indian culture, the promotion of indigenous languages also benefits general Native American societal health and well-being. Recent figures show that the Native American population has the highest drop-out rate of all American minorities, with 6.7 percent of students leaving school before their senior year (National Center for Education Statistics 2007). High drop-out rates often lead to high rates of unemployment, with its resultant damaging effects. Some studies have shown that schools offering instruction in tribal languages may produce students with better academic performance and higher rates of graduation than those that do not. Graduation leads in turn to better employment opportunities and thus increased individual and tribal self-sufficiency (Reyner 1992).

Box 9.1 Efforts to save the Hawai'ian language

In the late 1960s and 1970s, when federal policies began shifting away from strict assimilationist practices, the state of Hawai'i attempted to prevent the loss of its native language by initiating programs to reinstate its use in a few school systems. In 1978, Hawai'ian became the second official language in Hawai'i, alongside American English, meaning it could now be used at all levels of the government and judicial system. Of course, the Hawai'ian being used today is quite different from the pre-European-contact Hawai'ian. Almost two hundred years of contact with English, as well as with other languages, has had a profound impact, particularly on Hawai'ian syntax. Hawai'i is currently the only state with two official languages.

What is the status of Hawai'ian today? In spite of renewed support for saving it, Hawai'ian is still considered a language in danger of extinction. Gordon (2005) reports only 1,000 native speakers of Hawai'ian, and another 8,000 or so who understand it as a second language. But as the result of the Pūnana Leo movement begun in the 1980s to resurrect the use of Hawai'ian as a living language, eleven schools are now in operation where only Hawai'ian is spoken. In 1999 the first students who had been educated entirely in Hawai'ian graduated from high school. Every year since has seen larger and larger classes. Today other, nonimmersion schools offer classes in the medium of Hawai'ian, and in yet others, Hawai'ian is taught through the medium of English. According to the most recent data from 'Aha Pūnana Leo (2006), approximately 2,000 children were enrolled in these programs in the 2005–2006 school year. So Hawai'ians are cautiously optimistic as they continue to work against the extinction of their native language.

---

non-English languages, particularly Spanish, are being privileged over American English. They fear that American English will disappear from use and, with it, American culture and even the American nation. As you now know, concerns like these about language usage and identity have been present throughout American history. Let's now explore current concerns as reflected within the debate about an official, national language in the United States.

English and the complexities of a national language

Because language expresses identity, people frequently link it to a national identity as well as to ethnic, socioeconomic, cultural, and individual identities. A national identity is different, however, from these others, because it is a political entity, created exclusively through political agreements rather than developed on its own from a shared history or even a shared geography. So because of a nation's unique development, declaring a national or an **official language** – formally identified in a country's constitution and so given legal privilege – can be a complex issue. As you are undoubtedly aware, many people today have strong feelings about establishing an official language of the United States because of their perceptions about the link between language and national identity.

A number of political organizations in the United States now exist at both state and national levels that either support or oppose having English declared the "official language" of the United States. Supporters of legislation mandating English as the official language point out that sharing one language will promote a sense of national unity and civic responsibility. They fear that without legislation to mandate English use, new immigrants won't learn English because the United States currently accommodates speakers of other languages by providing translated materials.

Opponents of these "Official English" movements identify many problems inherent in legislating an "official language," not the least of which is their fear that this movement encourages discrimination rather than creates unity. They argue that the history of the United States supports the concept of accepting people from other places who speak other languages. Opponents also worry about practical matters, such as enforcing a strict language policy. For instance, the state of Utah declared English to be its official language in 2000, requiring all state government business to be conducted in English. Lawsuits immediately arose as exemptions to the law were demanded: Law enforcement, for instance, and promotions for tourist events such as the 2002 Winter Olympics eventually didn't have to conform to the "English only" requirement.

Those against making English the official language of the United States also point out the difficulties of enforcing such a law. They wonder how a legislative body could determine *which* English is the "official" language of the country, since the legislation proposed or already enacted doesn't identify a specific dialect as being the "official" one. Having read in this textbook of the many dialects of English in the United States, you'll recognize that this would be a very difficult question to decide. Many of these proposed or enacted policies don't even specify American English as the official language but instead just say "English." And to complicate the issue even further, neither the legislation at the federal nor at the state level addresses the concept of language change. Would laws written fifty years from now be invalid because they weren't written in the "official" 2008 English? This may seem like an irrelevant detail to supporters of such legislation, but opponents point out that even a single word is significant in legal issues.

Other nations have tried to eliminate conflict between language communities by mandating more than one official language. For example, in Switzerland, four national languages – German, French, Italian, and Romansh – reflect the major divisions within the nation. Originally, German, French, and Italian were the national languages, but the Swiss citizens felt that their national identity included the members of this fourth ethnic group and so, as a nation, granted them recognition. We can see the same sort of situation in Canada, where French speakers were not given the right to use French until the Official Languages Act was passed in 1969, legitimizing the use of both French and English. And you've just read about how Hawai'ian and English are both the official languages in Hawai'i. In each of these cases, a specific language became legally recognized when its speakers were recognized as full members of the nation.

See James Crawford's web pages on "Language Policy in the USA" for specific examples of written legislation concerning official English, such as the Wyoming statute passed in 1996 (http://ourworld.compuserve.com/homepages/JWCRAWFORD/wyo.htm), or the English Language Unity Act, proposed in the House of Representatives in 2003 (http://ourworld.compuserve.com/homepages/JWCRAWFORD/HR997.htm).

Over the last two decades the US Congress has been considering different bills to amend the Constitution by naming English as the national language, but none has yet been passed. And since some think that Congress has been slow to act, supporters of such "English only" legislation have turned their attention to proposals at the state and local level. To date, thirty states have passed "English only" laws, including Alaska, Arizona, California, North Carolina, and New Hampshire. Since immigration reform has become an increasingly politicized topic, the national "English only" discussion has been directly linked to it. In 2007, both the US House of Representatives and the US Senate considered proposing English as the "official language" of the United States.

The passage of such legislation at state and local levels, though, has created some unanticipated problems. Consider the following situations that were reported after "English only" laws were enacted:

Opponents of the national "English only" movement question why English needs to be promoted by casting the use of other languages in a negative light. After all, they remind us, human beings are capable of being fluent in more than one language. The "English Plus" movement promotes English and other languages together by guaranteeing language rights and supporting educational opportunities. Like the "English only" advocates, "English Plus" proponents also support an amendment to the Constitution defining specific language policy. And its supporters have also turned to state proposals because of their frustration with Congress' indecision. So far, four states – Oregon, Washington, New Mexico, and Rhode Island – have passed "English Plus" resolutions.

- A Mexican immigrant sued the state of Alabama as a result of its 1990 "English only" law because it denied her a Spanish translation of the driver's license test. She felt that the state was discriminating against minorities.
- A supervisor formally reprimanded healthcare workers in a San Rafael, California, nursing home for speaking Spanish to non-English-speaking residents.
- A casino in Colorado implemented a strict "English only" policy for its housekeeping staff, warning that anyone who spoke even a single word in Spanish could be fired. One of the housekeepers was so afraid of losing her job that she would only speak to her non-English-speaking husband, another employee at the casino, while hiding in a closet or after going outside.
- In November, 2000, the state of Arizona passed an "English only" law prohibiting teaching and teaching materials in any language but English, intended to help immigrant children become fluent in American English as quickly as possible. Now, though, rather than simply defining a new English vocabulary word by giving its counterpart in a student's native language, teachers must use pictures, charades, or find other props to help students understand the meaning of the new word. This is a time-consuming practice, but using other languages in the classroom is illegal.

As you can see, the consequences of "English only" policies are far-reaching and introduce a host of questions. Should non-English-speaking individuals expect governmental agencies to supply interpretations of official documents? What language rights do patients in a medical facility have? Should a privately owned business be allowed to control its employees to the extent of controlling their language? Who is responsible for helping children learn "Official English?" What are the language rights of people in this country?

Exercise 9.6

Jot down some of the things that you might normally do every day, such as going to class, studying in the library, having coffee with friends, watching TV, shopping, and so on. Now consider your typical day and how it might be affected by an "English only" policy that demands only English be used in all public settings, documents, etc. To help you think about this, look up some of the Official English websites that outline their proposed legislation.

Pro-English: www.proenglish.org/main/programs.htm

US English policy statements: www.us-english.org/

English First: www.englishfirst.org/

How might your life be affected by such a law? Would there be any changes to it? For example, would you have to use a different dialect in public from the one you use in private? Would the language of those around you have to change? Discuss with your classmates what possible effects might occur.

Chapter summary

In this chapter, you've considered the intersection of language, politics, and power within the context of large language communities. You've learned that the values of a community can be reflected in its language use when that language is tied to **overt** or **covert prestige**. You've also seen how communities use **language policies** to shape their own identity as well as identify members. You learned that the United States has a long history of national language conflicts. The American public's attitudes toward a language, and toward that language's users, quickly become reflected in national policy. And the chapter ended by asking you to consider the current conflict over creating "Official English" policies at the state and federal levels.

Critical Thinking exercises

1. Choose a position either supporting or opposing these "English only" mandates discussed earlier in the chapter; which do you think would best serve the American people as a whole? Reflect on some of the ideas you've learned in this textbook about language communities, language and identity, first and second language acquisition, language change, and so on. Come to class prepared to debate this topic with classmates who've taken the opposing view.

2.   First, make a list of all the languages that you think are spoken in the area where you are. Then, visit the MLA Language Map Data Center at www.mla.org/census_data to discover the languages most commonly spoken in this area, according to the US census. How accurate were your predictions? Any surprises? Record your reactions to learning about these languages and the populations of their speakers. Next, interview two people who also live in your geographical community and find out their perspectives on the range of languages spoken around you. (You may or may not choose to share the precise details of the MLA Language Map.) Be sure to record their comments and opinions, as well as more objective observations about these languages and language speakers. Finally, prepare a report explaining the results of your survey. You will want to include information about the language community as well as the questions asked in the survey. Can you make any recommendations about language policies in your area? If you want to gather more information about languages spoken, geographical location, and the US census, visit the Modern Language Association Language Map homepage: www.mla.org/map_main.

3.   Choose two of the communities you included in your response to Exercise 9.1. Then make a list of at least ten slang and/or jargon terms used in each one. Next, analyze each list separately. Do you have more slang terms for one community than the other? More jargon? Do the terms have anything in common with each other? Where do terms come from? How do you learn terms for each community? Finally, compare and contrast your analyses; what sort of similarities and/or differences do you see between these two language communities?

Hot Topic: Taking a position on endangered languages

According to Gordon (2005), 6,912 living languages currently exist in the world today. Six percent of the world's population speaks 95 percent of these languages or, put another way, 94 percent of the world's population speaks 5 percent of the world's languages. These statistics indicate that change in the world's languages is inevitable. Some of the lesser-spoken languages will soon become extinct when the culture that supports them dies, just as plants and animals become extinct when their ecosystems can no longer support them. Others will become endangered, doomed to die in the future, when their users die.

Many see this sort of change as an inevitable feature of human life. Cultures go through life cycles of birth and death, just as people themselves do. Attempting to artificially preserve a language without its culture is a meaningless exercise from this point of view. Others worry that the loss of a language means the loss of that culture's knowledge and perspective on the world. Each culture is unique, so no guarantee exists that the wisdom and learning carried within one language will also be held by another. As an example, think about the medicinal knowledge of local plants held by native peoples, knowledge that has been lost as native languages have been lost. Such loss of knowledge may affect the future of humanity; who knows what we will need to face upcoming challenges? And still others are anxious about the ethics of allowing languages to become extinct because of social justice. These individuals see the loss of a language as equivalent to violence against the users of that language because of the damage to their identity.

This chapter has articulated some of these concerns as they affect American languages. You've learned about the loss of Native American languages, as well as the more hopeful situation of Hawai'ian. And you've thought about the survival of American English itself. Based on what you've learned about linguistics and languages, think carefully about the topic of language loss, and then take a position. Should Americans engage actively in the fight to preserve the American languages still in use today? If so, who should take action, and how? If not, why not? What reasons would you give the last speakers of Yurok, for instance, a Native American tribe from the northwestern corner of California, for refusing to help them save their language? Would you give the same answer to those concerned about the survival of Hawai'ian, which is still endangered, even though its legal and social status has improved? What would you say to the native peoples in Alaska? Note that you can also consider endangered *dialects* of American English for this topic: For instance, should the Gullah dialect in the South Carolina sea islands be saved? What about the hybrid language of the Cajuns in southwest Louisiana? And should we be concerned that the Appalachian dialect is in danger of becoming extinct? Think through the issues involved by drafting a statement addressing a specific group of endangered-language users (you may need to do some reading about this specific culture). Then be prepared to take part in a class discussion on this topic.

Learn more about it

America's first languages

Crawford, J. 1995, "Endangered Native American languages: What is to be done, and why?" *Bilingual Research Journal* 19, available at http://ourworld.compuserve.com/homepages/JWCRAWFORD/brj.htm

In this essay, Crawford investigates the causes of language loss and why such loss matters.

Dwight, E.W. [1818] 1990, *Memoirs of Henry Obookiah, A native of Owhyhee, and a member of the Foreign Mission School; Who died at Cornwall, Connecticut February 17, 1818*, Honolulu, Hawai'i: Women's Board of Missions for the Pacific Islands.
Dwight, one of Obookiah's friends, composed this memoir from Obookiah's own letters and diary, as well as from recollected conversations and experiences.

Seay, E. 2003, *Searching for Lost City: On the trail of America's native American languages*, Guilford, CT: Lyons Press.
Journalist Seay travels to Lost City, Oklahoma, where the whole community still speaks a native language and explores the problem of preserving Native American languages, discussing the reasons why we should strive to keep them alive.

Spolsky, B. 2002, "Prospects for the survival of the Navajo language: A reconsideration," *Anthropology and Education Quarterly* 33 (2): 139–162.
Spolsky updates an earlier article that had blamed Navajos' increasing access to schools as the major cause of Navajo language loss, now suggesting that many factors contribute to the demise of Navajo, including improved communication, the breakdown of isolated living, and a general ideological acceptance of English among Navajos.

Language policy

Ricento, T. (ed.) 2005, *An introduction to language policy: Theory and method*, Malden, MA: Blackwell.
This introductory text brings together essays by experts in the field of language policy that explore a wide range of topics, theories, and methods.

Schmidt, R., 2000. *Language policy and identity politics in the United States.* Philadelphia: Temple University Press.
Schmidt explores the two conflicting approaches toward language policy – linguistic assimilation and linguistic pluralism – that are current in the United States today.

English and the complexities of a national language

Crawford, J. (ed.) 1992, *Language loyalties: A source book on the official English controversy*, Chicago: University of Chicago Press.
Crawford brings together key documents in the history of language debates over making English the official language of the United States.

Language policy and language rights, Retrieved June 14, 2008 from the Center for Multilingual, Multicultural Research, University of Southern California website: www-rcf.usc.edu/~cmmr/Policy.html
This collection of links represents a wide variety of perspectives and issues connected to US language policy and language rights.

10 Conclusion: Language policy and English language learners

Key terms

First language (L1)
Second language (L2)
Language transfer
Fossilization
English language learner (ELL)
Bilingual education
Limited English proficiency (LEP)
Immersion
English as a second language (ESL)
English for speakers of other languages (ESOL)
English as a second dialect (ESD)

Overview

This concluding chapter asks you to apply various concepts from previous chapters to the current debate over second language education in the United States. You will first review current linguistic theories about how people learn a second language. You will then learn about several of the most common approaches to teaching English as a second language, developed from research in applied linguistics. Finally, the Hot Topic asks you to explore the implications of teaching SAE to students who already use a nonprivileged dialect of American English.

Introduction

In previous chapters, you've learned about how linguists study language, and you've learned about the various components of American English, its morphology, syntax, phonology, and semantics. You've also come to understand how integral language is to our everyday lives, shaping the way we think and expressing our identities, influencing public policy, and allowing us to communicate with others. This final chapter introduces the idea of second language learning, a topic that brings all of these aspects of language together. As you'll see, second language learning is not solely a concern of students or teachers, but, rather, a matter affecting all Americans. Because this is an issue of public policy, intended to shape the future of the country, citizens frequently must vote on and pay taxes to support programs connected to second language learning. Today, across the United States, people are being asked to consider questions such as the following:

1.   Should all students be required to learn a second language?
2.   What's the most effective way to teach second languages?
3.   What is our responsibility to children in this country who need to learn English as a second language?

Most Americans answer the first question above in the affirmative: They believe that all students should be required to learn a second language, and they understand the benefits of knowing a second language, especially in the workforce. But answers to the other questions are more difficult to find and so generate more disagreement among Americans. This is why you need to have a basic understanding of the issues involved so that you can begin to make your own decisions on matters of public language policy and educational funding. This chapter will help you become more informed through its discussion of linguistic research in second language acquisition, methods of language instruction, and, finally, the politics surrounding second language learning.

> Recognizing the importance of second language learning, in 2006 President George Bush signed into law a multimillion dollar initiative to increase the number of Americans mastering second languages by starting instruction at younger ages and by increasing the number of second language teachers and resources in American schools.

Exercise 10.1

We noted above that many Americans support second language learning in the schools because they know that being multilingual is an asset in the workforce. Fewer Americans, however, have considered other benefits that arise from knowing a second language. For this exercise, do some research online and find out at least five benefits of studying a second language. Good websites to examine would include those of national foreign language associations, university departments of modern languages, and foreign language institutes. Be prepared to share your information with the class.

The second language acquisition process

The linguistic study of language development is divided into the fields of first and second language acquisition. Researchers in **first language (L1)** acquisition examine the development of the primary or mother tongue, while **second language (L2)** acquisition studies concern the learning of

Figure 10.1 *L2 learners have typically moved beyond the critical period for acquiring language*

nonprimary languages. As you learned in Chapter 1, linguists theorize that humans are born with an innate ability to acquire their first languages during the first few years of life, the period thought to be critical for successful language acquisition. Traditionally, the ability to *acquire* language has been distinguished from *learning* a language, which usually takes place at a much older age, for instance when a child goes to school, or even in adulthood. That L2 learners have moved beyond the critical period for acquiring language may explain why they generally have a much more difficult time becoming fluent in a second language (see Figure 10.1).

At one point, linguists thought that second languages were entirely learned: Students of any age who memorized vocabulary and grammar rules of a new language could eventually become fluent. Now, though, we know that second languages are also acquired, at least to some extent. Just as we saw with L1 acquisition, there is a critical age for learning second languages: In general, the younger a person is, the more successful L2 acquisition is. In fact, some adult learners may never become completely fluent in a second language, even after living for many years in the country where it is spoken. This also suggests that the innate ability to acquire a second language is linked to an earlier stage of biological growth and development, just as it is for a first language.

Other factors involved in the process of L2 learning also resemble those found in first language acquisition. For instance, L2 learners acquire their language in stages, just as L1 learners do, and in a similar sequence: Lexical morphemes are acquired before grammatical ones, inflectional suffixes before derivational ones, and so on. In addition, L2 learners also commit some of the same errors as L1 learners. Just as young children do, they might generalize past-tense endings to produce forms such as *he goed* or *they bringed*. And, because of limited vocabulary, they might use a more general lexical term than a specific one: the word "bus" to mean all vehicles larger than a car or "animal" to refer to all four-legged creatures.

Despite these similarities between L1 and L2 acquisition, many differences still exist. For instance, consider that an L2 learner already knows the complete grammar of his first language when he comes to learn a second, which will invariably assist his learning but may also hamper it. Linguists who study the phenomenon of **language transfer**, or the application of rules from one's L1 to an L2, have shown that this accounts for many of the errors that L2 learners make, especially in the beginning and middle stages of acquiring proficiency. These errors usually are most noticeable in a L2 learner's pronunciation. See Table 10.1 for a few examples of transfer errors. Linguists have also theorized that some of these errors may result in **fossilization**, that is, they may never be corrected despite intense instruction or drilling, and so remain forever in the L2 learner's internal grammar.

Table 10.1 *Examples of phonological transfer errors in English learner language*

L1	L2 (English)
Spanish: no initial consonant cluster [sp]	English: *spring* = [esprɪŋ]
Italian: rolled r = [ɹ]	English: *praise* = [pɹajs]
	trophy = [tɹofi]
Japanese: no distinction between [l] and [r]	English: *praise* = [plajze]
Russian: no final voiced fricatives and affricates	English: *badge* = [bætʃ]

Variables affecting L2 learning

In addition to a first grammar, other variables too influence one's learning of a second language. Some of these are internal factors, such as critical age, mentioned above. Other internal variables include personality traits: An extroverted person is found to have more success in L2 learning than an introverted learner, probably because the extrovert is willing to take risks, that is, to try new forms or attempt discussion in the target language. This factor may reveal another reason why children acquire a second language more easily than adults. Studies have shown that adults dislike the feelings of helplessness and disempowerment that often accompany L2 learning. Young children, who are typically less self-conscious than adults, may not experience similar feelings.

Exercise 10.2

Find out which second languages are the most studied and the least studied in American elementary and secondary schools by exploring websites such as those of the US Department of Education, the American Council on the Teaching of Foreign Languages, and others. Once you've found the information, discuss with your classmates possible reasons for some languages' popularity over others. Do you see any trends in the choice of languages? How might these choices be connected to political or social events, popular culture, or family heritage?

One's personal motivation for learning a second language also affects L2 learning: If the learner has a strong desire to become part of the second language culture, then he will be especially motivated to learn the second language. For instance, if the learner needs the second language to get a job, then his motivation may be higher than that of someone, say, who is learning a second language to fulfill a college requirement. Motivation to learn a second language is also strongly affected by feedback from the learning environment, including teacher praise, student peer responses, and grades.

Obviously many other variables factor into the success or failure of learning a second language. Because of their diverse characteristics, motivations, learning environments, and aptitudes, language learners develop individualized learning processes. Let's now see how research in L2 acquisition has influenced the creation of teaching strategies for these diverse L2 learners.

L2 instruction

In fall, 2000, approximately 6 million students, 34 percent of the total enrollment, in the secondary (grades 7–12) public schools of the United States studied a second language other than English (Draper and Hicks 2002). If we add to this the approximately 5 million **English language learners (ELLs)**, or the 10.5 percent of the national public school population who study English, we see why L2 learning in this country is a compelling issue of national importance (National Clearinghouse for English Language Acquisition 2006). And because these numbers are projected to keep growing, L2 learning becomes a crucial factor in the formulation of local, state, and federal education policies.

According to the National Clearinghouse for English Language Acquisition (2007), roughly 76.9 percent of school-age ELLs in the United States are native Spanish speakers, while 23.1 percent speak other native languages.

In the United States, both native English speakers who are learning another language and ELLs are considered L2 learners, and yet their situations differ in significant ways. The native English speakers have little opportunity to use their second language outside the classroom, while ELLs have a range of possibilities outside the academic arena for using American English. The difference between these two learning environments is one distinction made between what is often called "foreign language instruction" in the United States and "English as a second language" instruction. Because our focus in this book is American English, we will concentrate in this chapter solely on the process of learning American English as a second language, not on learning other second languages, but remember that L2 instruction refers to the teaching of any language that is not the primary tongue of the student.

Exercise 10.3

Research the number of ELLs in your state by exploring the website of your home state's Department of Education. If provided, also note their age ranges, countries of origin, number of years in the United States, economic levels, and other information. Next, think about the data you have gathered in light of the variables affecting L2 learning and make some hypotheses about these learners and their language acquisition processes, including their potential for success. Consider, for example, their age, possible reasons for coming to the United States, motivation for learning language, attitudes toward both the native culture and the target language culture, etc. Write up your data and hypotheses in a short report to be handed in.

Approaches to L2 instruction

In the United States, many approaches to teaching English have been tried over the years, but they can be broadly grouped under two types. One approach is **bilingual education**, or educational programs designed to incorporate both English and the first language of the learner. The delivery of bilingual education in schools varies widely in the United States, but, generally, students who are designated as having **limited English proficiency (LEP)** take some or all of their courses in their native languages while they learn English. The second approach, an alternative to bilingual education, is **immersion** in English, or a program in which non-English-speaking students take all their classes in English, attending alongside native English speakers.

A third type of language instruction is found in **English as a second language (ESL)** or **English for speakers of other languages (ESOL)** classes, which offer English instruction exclusively for LEP students and which are taught solely in English. ESL classes may be offered under both bilingual education and immersion programs.

Since 1968, when the first federal laws concerning English language instruction were passed, states have been offering forms of bilingual education in their schools, but in the last ten years these programs have come increasingly under attack. Critics claim that bilingual education isn't working and that other programs, such as immersion or ESL, are more effective in teaching students

English. In the discussion below, we explore this debate, beginning with a short history of bilingual education.

History of bilingual education

The history of bilingual education in America is similar to the history of the official English movement, principally because some of the same social and political forces are at work in both cases. You learned in Chapter 8 that during colonial times there was widespread language diversity, and as more and more immigrants settled the lands, they generally lived peacefully with their neighbors who often spoke different languages from them. By the mid nineteenth century, many of these settlements had formally organized into towns, and to meet the needs of the diverse language communities many began offering forms of bilingual education, that is, instruction in other languages as well as in English.

> At the end of the nineteenth century, many public schools had bilingual programs: German was taught in schools in Pennsylvania, Ohio, Maryland, Indiana, Illinois, Missouri, Nebraska, Colorado, and Oregon; Dutch in Michigan; Norwegian, Danish, and Swedish in Nebraska, Washington, Illinois, Iowa, and Minnesota; Polish and Italian in Wisconsin; Czech in Texas; French in Louisiana; and Spanish in many western states.

This situation would change at the end of the nineteenth century, as the federal government developed new policies concerning immigration and language. As you remember from our discussion of Native American languages in Chapter 9, during this period the federal government promoted the notion of cultural assimilation and thus, in the natives' case, outlawed the teaching of Native American languages on the reservations. This practice extended to other ethnic groups as well. With the belief that a stronger America should have one language and that language should be English came the demise of the early forms of bilingual education. "English only" instruction was mandated in many states, including in those that had previously had instruction in other languages.

This philosophy dominated the first half of the twentieth century but then gradually changed after World War II, when Americans began to see the importance of knowing and understanding other cultures, made even more imperative with the postwar surge of immigrants to the United States who needed language skills. Research into L2 learning increased in these postwar years and included specific inquiry into methods of English language learning.

In addition to more national attention being paid to immigrants' language needs, another major force in re-establishing bilingual education was the minority rights revolution of the 1960s and early 1970s. The establishment of national civil rights policy for the first time defined ethnic minorities in this country and then legitimized federal involvement in addressing these groups' concerns. A significant concern for minorities during this period was getting equal access to education, something that had been denied due to various barriers. For the Native American, Hispanic, and other populations, lack of English was an obstacle, in many cases producing substandard education for school children. To aid these students, in 1968 the Bilingual Education Act was passed, which offered money to school districts that wanted to implement programs to help LEP students. Federally funded bilingual programs became official in 1970 when the Office for Civil Rights *mandated* that these students be accommodated in the schools.

Reflecting their beginnings in the civil rights movement, bilingual programs have also provided a way of maintaining students' first languages and cultures in the United States. Notice that this idea is in direct contrast to the assimilationist notions dominant in the earlier part of the twentieth century, when the federal focus had been on homogenization of foreign cultures into an American ideal. Today in the United States, however, a return to this earlier assimilationist thinking may be taking place. The 2002 passage of President George W. Bush's No Child Left Behind (NCLB) Act, a comprehensive act designed to improve the educational levels of all children in American schools, effectively replaced the 1968 Bilingual Education Act. The NCLB Act contains no mention of bilingual education, neither forbidding it nor encouraging it. It also doesn't include any recognition and support for the preservation and maintenance of first languages.

Exercise 10.4

Today in the United States, the federal government supports special "heritage language" programs designed to preserve indigenous languages, such as Native American tongues, Hawai'ian, and Alaskan native languages. Look up information on one of these languages and find out its recent history, the number of people who currently speak it, and the programs available for its study. Given what you know about factors that contribute to successful L2 learning, consider whether preservation of this native language is a reasonable goal. As you consider possible responses, think also about the reasons for attempting to preserve indigenous languages in general. Why should a government and its people support this endeavor? Be prepared to discuss your ideas in class.

While the passage of the NCLB has complicated matters for those involved in programs of bilingual education, even before its passage extensive debate had taken place at both the federal and state levels about the merits of bilingual education. Let's now examine one state in particular where the debate on bilingual education has been wide-ranging.

Bilingual education: Focus on California

A state that boasts a high Hispanic population because of its history, California has been on the front lines of the battles waged about bilingual education. In the 1970s and much of the 1980s, the state adopted an extensive bilingual education program, but today state laws exist that prevent some forms of bilingual education. Why has this change in policy happened, and what has caused this backlash against bilingual education?

Like other states, California also succumbs to the unpredictable pressures of politics. After the period of civil rights legislation in the 1960s and 1970s that increased federal programs for minorities, the country shifted to a different political stance in the late 1980s. During this time, the national organizations of English First, US English, and others established themselves, and, as you saw in Chapter 9, began to campaign for English as the official language of the United States. Another movement was also started within this political climate, one that questioned the effectiveness of bilingual education programs.

> The percentage of California's population that is of Hispanic origin has dramatically increased over the last twenty years. According to the US Census Bureau (2007), California's population was 49 percent Hispanic in 2006. To give you a context for understanding these numbers, the Hispanic population for the entire United States in 2006 was 15 percent (ibid.).

Although the topic of bilingual education was being discussed nationally, in California it took on particular strength as an issue, probably because of the large linguistic minorities in that state. Those against bilingual education worked from an assimilationist position, one suggesting that all immigrants and citizens of this country should speak the same language, English, in the classroom. They also voiced other concerns about bilingual education, such as the amount of time required to learn English: Statistics had shown that many LEP students remained in bilingual education programs for years. The anti-bilingual education group endorsed an English immersion approach for LEP students, one that would immerse students in English in the belief that they would pick it up speedily (the goal was within one year) and succeed in their studies.

This same group proposed a measure to be put on the ballot, called Proposition 227, which would effectively terminate all bilingual education programs in the state. Parents who wished their LEP children to be instructed in their native languages would need to request a waiver to have their children put in bilingual classes.

Opponents of Proposition 227, including many linguists and educators, contested the claims of the pro-Proposition 227 side. They argued that effective language learning takes place over years, not just one year. Studies had shown that learning academic English, the English used in schools and on standardized tests, requires an average of four to nine years of study for the non-native speaker, very different from conversational English, which may be acquired in one to two years (Hakuta 2000; Collier 1989).

> A sponsor of Proposition 227, Californian Ron Unz (1999), claimed that in 1996 one-fourth of all children in California public schools were classified as not knowing English and that 95 percent of these had failed to learn English in any given year. In response to this charge, people against Proposition 227 pointed out that only 30 percent of the 1.4 million English language learners in California were enrolled in bilingual education programs at that time (Mora 2003). Thus they argued that the results of standardized English proficiency tests, which had been given to all schoolchildren, did not accurately describe the effectiveness of bilingual programs.

Contrary to the notion that "immersing" learners in the target language will naturally force them to learn, supporters of bilingual education argue that building an underlying language proficiency in a student's first language significantly helps language and academic development in the second language. Numerous linguistic studies have shown that students with previous education and literacy in their first language do much better at learning English than those who have not had any literacy training in their home language (Krashen 1996). Although the critical age for L2 acquisition is not agreed upon, it seems clear that cognitive processes developed through L1 acquisition are vital for learning a second language. Despite these objections, and after a heated campaign, in 1998 California voters passed Proposition 227 with 61 percent of the vote, and bilingual education programs were immediately dismantled (Unz 1999). Figure 10.2 articulates some of the main points used by each side in this controversy.

Bilingual education

1. Knowledge of the first language makes learning the second language more comprehensible.
2. Literacy transfers across languages.
3. Children feel more comfortable in the classroom using both the home and target languages.
4. Bilingual education programs create a sense of biculturalism – home cultures and languages are maintained.

Immersion programs

1. Children develop literacy and content knowledge in English.
2. English is the language of America, so students should use English at school.
3. Discomfort at not knowing the classroom language fades as children become proficient.
4. Immersion produces fluency in one to two years, a shorter time than that required in bilingual education.

Figure 10.2 *Arguments for Bilingual Education and for Immersion Programs*

What has been the effect of Proposition 227? The results of a five-year study contracted by the California Department of Education reveal that students across all language classifications in all grades have improved their performances on standardized tests (American Institutes for Research and WestEd 2006). The authors of the report, *Effects of the implementation of Proposition 227 on the education of English learners K-12: Findings from a five-year evaluation*, note, however, that since Proposition 227 was enacted alongside other legislative educational reforms, attributing these widespread gains to any one factor is impossible. Indeed, improvements in test scores may be a general effect of increased federal supervision of all aspects of education. The study also reports that the gap between native English and non-native English performance on standardized tests remains about the same as before Proposition 227 for all subjects (American Institutes for Research and WestEd 2006).

Because of limitations in the statewide data, the study does not conclude that one method of English language instruction is more effective than another.

Instead, affirming the findings of other researchers who have suggested that no single path to academic excellence among ELLs exists, the authors of the report declare: "The factors identified as most critical to [ELL] success were staff capacity to address English learners' linguistic and academic needs; schoolwide focus on English language development and standards-based instruction; shared priorities and expectations in educating English learners; and systematic, ongoing assessment and careful data use to guide instruction" (American Institutes for Research and WestEd 2006).

This study, as well as others that draw similar conclusions, recognizes that successful school programs use a combination of teaching approaches and methods geared to the needs of individual L2 learners. While the debates about bilingual vs. immersion methods will surely continue in state legislatures and individual school districts, teachers have been able to draw upon both approaches to help more of their students gain English proficiency.

The discussion of L2 learning in this final chapter reveals that policies enacted in education have far-reaching effects beyond the school walls. How students learn language, and hence become prepared to enter the workforce and live as responsible citizens, must be of concern to all Americans, not the least because they help to fund school programs through their taxes. From assimilationist to multicultural positions, people will hold differing philosophies about the best practices and purposes for L2 instruction in the United States. Fundamentally, however, they agree that they work for the success and well-being of all non-native speakers who seek to better their lives in America.

We have attempted to show you in this textbook not only the structure of American English but also the many ways in which American English penetrates social and cultural issues in the United States. From the discussions about English as a national language to the effects of IM on teenagers to the best means of instruction for ESL learners, language is an integral part of any cultural development in America. We hope that as you continue your college studies and then enter your life pathways that you will always remember the inherent implications of your own choices in using American English.

Chapter summary

In this chapter you have learned some of the major theories of **second language (L2)** acquisition research, including some of the variables enhancing successful L2 learning, such as age, motivation, attitudes, personality, and other factors. The chapter compared two prominent methods of L2 instruction, **bilingual education** and **immersion**, and examined the debates surrounding their use. To bring the debates into focus, the chapter explored their political ramifications in California, which is currently assessing the effects of its 1998 decision to drop bilingual education in favor of an immersion program.

Critical Thinking exercises

1.   Building on their victory in California, activists against bilingual education have transferred their work to several other states where they have been successful in getting legislatures in some cases to ban bilingual education, and in others to severely curtail or modify their bilingual programs. To get an idea of how widespread the movement against bilingual education is in the United States, research which states have bilingual education programs, which do not, and which are currently discussing the issue. To complete this research, work with at least three of your classmates. First, divide the United States by geographical region, and then have each person choose the states in one region to study. You will probably want to look first at each state's Department of Education website to find evidence of the issue, as well as current laws regarding teaching of English as a second language. Compare your results with your group mates and summarize your group's findings in a three- to four-page paper.

2.   In 2005, the US Census Bureau released data showing that Texas joins three other states in which non-Hispanic whites make up less than 50 percent of residents. It reported that 50.8 percent of all Texas residents are minorities: 32 percent are Hispanic, 11 percent Black, 3 percent Asian, and the rest declared as "other races." As a result of this demographic shift, the use of the term "minority," traditionally used to refer to Blacks and small ethnic groups, has come into question. Logically, some argue, the term is now obsolete, given the "majority–minority" populations in these states. But giving up the label is not a simple matter, since "minority" in this country can signify not only the size of a group but also an economically or physically disadvantaged group. Giving up this name might mean that a group would be forced to give up moneys distributed under current federal entitlement programs. Changing the name of this population will affect how Americans think about themselves and others. Form a small group with others in your class and discuss the implications of this demographic shift. Consider various meanings of the term "minority" and possible effects of living in states where "minorities" are now the majority. Be prepared to discuss your ideas with the rest of the class.

3.   Go online and read one or two blogs containing comments on English language learning and immigration. Blogs can be found all over the Internet and are often sponsored by organizations that seek reader input, such as news groups, opinion pages, political organizations, etc. Read as many of the blog comments as you can and then draw some conclusions about their content. Answer the following

questions in your response on the comments: How do the topics of immigration (legal or illegal) and learning/speaking English intersect? What are some of the beliefs people hold about immigrants and their desire to learn English? What other issues do these comments introduce, in addition to language? What is the tone of the comments you read? Be prepared to talk in class about your responses to the blog postings.

Hot Topic: Teaching SAE to native English speakers

In Chapter 2 you learned about World Englishes, or dialects of English spoken by people across the world that are learned as either a first, second, or subsequent language. The rise of World Englishes and continued high levels of immigration to the United States have created a challenge for the teaching of ESL in this country. Many persons who speak a dialect of World English now attend schools where they are put in English classes intended for non-native speakers. In addition to World English speakers, many students who speak dialects of American English are also commonly enrolled in ESL classes. Speakers of varieties that are less privileged in American society, such as African American English, Chicano English, and others, are often regarded as less proficient in English than those who use an English closer to SAE. As a result, they are placed in ESL classes, sometimes for years, as they struggle to learn the privileged standard dialect.

For many of the students and their families in these two populations, to be placed into English classes intended for non-native speakers is humiliating and insulting, given that in most cases English is their first language, or they have been speaking it as their second language for most of their lives. Nationally, groups such as Teachers of English as a Second Language (TESOL) have recognized this special group of learners by identifying them as **English as a second dialect (ESD)** learners, as opposed to L2 learners, yet little has been done to find practical ways in which to help these populations.

The situation of these students raises some interesting questions: Must all World English speakers learn SAE? To what extent should a speaker of World English alter her language to accommodate the American English standard? Should speakers of American English dialects be enrolled in ESL classes? What aspects of American English should both groups learn? Should ESL teachers be responsible for teaching these students, given that most teachers are trained in the instruction of students who have little to no knowledge of English? What are the most effective teaching methods for ESD populations?

For this assignment, working in small groups, consider and discuss some of the questions raised above. To help you get started, you might want to think about the effect of some practices. For instance, if you were the teacher of a student from Zimbabwe, Africa, and insisted that he speak American English and not his Zimbabwean-English dialect, how would you explain to him that his dialect, which he has spoken since birth, is unacceptable? In another instance, consider what might be the effects of having World English speakers, American English dialect speakers, and advanced second language learners all in the same ESL class. Imagine some scenarios, both positive and negative, that might take place. Once you and your classmates have discussed the questions above, write a paper of two to three pages in which you present your group's opinions about the current status of teaching English to these different populations. Be prepared to present your views in class and, possibly, to debate other groups that have reached different conclusions.

Learn more about it

The L2 acquisition process

Freeman, D. E. and Freeman, Y. S. 2001, *Between worlds: Access to second language acquisition*, 2nd edition. Portsmouth, NH: Heinemann.

Designed for future teachers, this book provides a clear and comprehensive review of L2 acquisition theories and research, while also discussing the social and political trends regarding the teaching of multilingual students.

Gass, S. 2000, "Fundamentals of second language acquisition," in J. W. Rosenthal (ed.), *Handbook of undergraduate second language education*, Mahwah, NJ: Lawrence Erlbaum, pp. 29–46.

The author succinctly describes the major theories of L2 acquisition research regarding the learning process, effects on learning, etc.

L2 instruction

Adger, C. T. 1997, "Issues and implications of English dialects for teaching English as a second language," *TESOL Professional Papers #3* (ERIC Document No. ED 420994).

Adger offers some perspectives on the use of English dialects, including World English and vernacular American English, in TESOL classes and argues that educational communities must formulate specific policies regarding their use.

Crawford, J. and Krashen, S. D. 2007, *English language learners in American classrooms: 101 questions, 101 answers*, New York: Scholastic Teaching Resources.

The authors present an accessible introduction to bilingual education for a general audience.

Bilingual education: Focus on California

Mora, J. K. 2003, "An Analysis of Proposition 227," retrieved June 14, 2008 from the *Cross-Cultural Language and Academic Development* website: http://coe.sdsu.edu/people/jmora/Prop227PPT/Default.htm

The author provides a detailed and clear analysis of the Proposition 227 controversy.

Ovando, C. 2003, "Bilingual education in the United States: Historical development and current issues," *Bilingual Research Journal* 27:1–24.

This article is a comprehensive survey of the history of bilingual education in the United States.

Glossary

Note: Words in italics refer the reader to a main heading elsewhere in the Glossary for further explanation.

Accent	The way that an individual pronounces certain speech sounds.
Acronym	An abbreviation that is created from the initial letter of each word in a phrase and then pronounced as a word.
Affix	A *morpheme* that can be attached either to the beginning (*prefix*) or the end (*suffix*) of both *bound* and *free roots*.
African American English	A general term that refers to a group of related *dialects* spoken primarily by a large population of Americans of African descent.
Alphabet	A writing system that pairs the specific speech sounds of a language with arbitrary *signs*.
American English	One of the many types of English that originated in England, traveled to America with British colonists, and then was adapted over time to fit the needs of its speakers in the United States.
Analytic language	A language, such as Modern American English, that relies primarily on word order, rather than on inflections, to indicate word functions.
Antonym	One of a pair of words with opposing meanings.
Arbitrary sign	A *sign* whose meaning has been assigned by an individual or a *language community*, rather than a sign whose meaning is inherent.
Assimilation	The act of being absorbed by or of converting to the customs and practices of a dominant culture; linguistically, the influence of a sound on an adjacent sound that minimizes their differences.
Backformation	When words come into a language through mis-analysis of their morphological histories.
Bilingual education	Educational programs designed to incorporate a learner's *first language* as well as the *target language*.
Blend	The combination of parts of two or more words to create a new word.

Bound morpheme	A *morpheme* that must be attached to another to carry linguistic meaning.
Bound root	A *root morpheme* that cannot stand on its own.
Cases	Categories of the different grammatical roles that nouns can play within some languages.
Chain shift	When a group of sounds changes their pronunciations at the same time.
Chicano English	An American English dialect spoken by people born in the United States who usually have a Mexican or Mexican-American heritage.
Clipped word	A shortened form of a word.
Code switching	Adjusting one's language to fit a particular *language community*.
Cognates	Words across languages that share similar forms and meanings.
Coined word	A newly invented word.
Communicative competence	The innate ability to use one's *first language* appropriately.
Compound	Two or more words joined together to form a new word.
Connotation	The additional meaning that comes with *denotation* when emotional shadings, attitudes, and opinions enter into the construction of meaning.
Consonant	A sound produced by constricting or completely stopping the airflow through the throat.
Constituent	A word that functions as part of a larger syntactic unit.
Covert prestige	Positive values associated with an entity that is otherwise stigmatized within the larger society.
Creole	A *pidgin* that develops into the *first language* of a *language community*.
Critical period	The most effective time in an individual's life span to acquire fluency in a language, roughly between birth and two years of age.
Danelaw	The territory in the north of England ceded to the Scandinavian invaders by Alfred the Great; Anglo-Saxon predominance remained in the south.
Dative case	When a noun or pronoun fulfills the role of an object of the preposition or the indirect object of the verb.
Decreolization	The process by which a *creole* becomes a *dialect* of the dominant language.
Denotation	The referential meaning of a word; the thing, person, object, idea, etc. to which a word refers.
Derivational morpheme	A *morpheme* added to other morphemes to form a new word that may or may not be of the same word category.
Descriptive grammar	A *grammar* that describes how a language is actually used.

Descriptive linguistics	The study of a language as it is actually used within a *language community*; might include both an analysis of structure and of the varieties within and between languages.
Dialect	A *language variety* common to a particular group of people.
Dictionary	A reference work containing an alphabetical list of words that explains each term's definition and usage.
Digraph	Two letters used together to represent a single sound.
Diphthong	Two sounds merged into one *phoneme*.
Discourse analysis	The study of a multi-line text.
Dissimulation	The act of making adjacent sounds less similar so that the sequence of sounds is easier to articulate.
Distinctive features	The unique characteristics of *phonemes* that create differences in meaning.
Ebonics	A term used to describe various *African American English* dialects.
Ebonics debate	A national discussion held in the 1990s over the use of *Ebonics* as a learning tool in the classroom.
English as a second dialect (ESD)	Classes for *ELLs* who speak lower-prestige forms of American English.
English as a second language (ESL)	Classes for non-native students learning English that are taught solely in English.
English for speakers of other languages (ESOL)	An alternative name for *ESL* instruction, in which classes are taught solely in English.
English language learner (ELL)	Someone learning English as a second or subsequent language.
Eponymy	The naming of things after the people associated with these things.
Etymology	The origin and history of a *lexeme*.
Euphemism	An expression used to replace a blunt or harsh word with a milder or less offensive word or phrase.
External change	An action of human behavior, such as moving, trading, learning, etc., that changes a *language community*.
Figure of speech	A word or phrase that carries a non-literal meaning; often occurring when very different ideas or objects are compared.
First language	One's mother tongue.
Fluency	The ability to articulate thoughts and concepts without effort.
Fossilization	A point in *second language* learning when the learner reaches a plateau and can't acquire some aspect of the *target language*.
Free root	A root that does not have to be attached to another *morpheme* to have linguistic meaning; all lexical morphemes are free roots.

Generative grammar	A *grammar* made up of a finite set of rules that would produce an infinite number of grammatical sentences.
Geographical isolation	One of the forces causing change in a language; occurs when speakers of a language become geographically separated from other speakers of the same language.
Grammar	The system of rules and relations that govern a language.
Grammatical function	Classification of a word according to its function within a sentence.
Grammatical morpheme	A *morpheme* that is *free* or *bound* and primarily carries grammatical meaning, that is, indicates the relationship between words in a sentence.
Great Vowel Shift	A major change in pronunciation occurring in English of the Middle Ages.
Hierarchy of constituents	The way users group words together in sentences to create units of meaning.
Homograph	A *lexeme* that is spelled exactly the same as another, but may or may not be pronounced the same.
Homonym	A *lexeme* that sounds like another but has a different origin and may or may not be spelled the same.
Homophones	Words that sound alike but whose meanings differ.
Hyponym	A word whose meaning includes the meaning of another word.
Icon or iconic sign	A *sign* that directly represents its meaning and so conveys it without the need for interpretation.
Idiolect	An individual's unique *language variety*.
Idiom	An expression of a particular *language community* whose meaning may not reflect the individual, literal, meanings of its words.
Immersion program	Education programs in which students take classes taught only in the *target language*.
Inflectional decay	A gradual process in which inflectional endings lose their distinct and different pronunciations.
Inflectional morpheme	A bound grammatical *suffix* (in English) that is joined to other *morphemes* to create a new word within the same grammatical category.
Initialism	A phrase reduced to its initials and referred to by these; an alphabetic abbreviation.
Internal change	Change that occurs within language structures, such as word and sentence forms.
Internal variation	The *language varieties* found within one language.
International Phonetic Alphabet (IPA)	The phonetic transcription system of the International Phonetic Association that represents the sounds of all languages.
Jargon	A specialized or technical language unique to a particular profession or workplace.

Language	A rule-based system of signs spoken by a particular community.
Language acquisition	The unconscious processes that young children undergo to attain use of their *first language*.
Language community	A particular group of language users who share the use of a specific language adapted to fit their needs.
Language conventions	The unspoken, unofficial rules within a particular community that are accepted and followed by members who may not even be conscious of them.
Language policy	A policy that controls language usage.
Language system	A language's organization, the way that the smaller elements of signs and symbols combine to create larger meanings.
Language transfer	The application of rules from a *first language* to a *second language*.
Language universals	Underlying transformational theories of grammar, the notion that all humans share certain features of the human mind that endow them with the same linguistic abilities.
Language variety	A specific use of language that exists within the diversity of any language, such as English.
Learner language	A non-native variety of a *target language* spoken by a language learner.
Leveling process	When the inflectional endings of a language become level, exactly like each other, and thus no longer convey grammatical meaning.
Lexeme	The smallest unit of *lexical meaning*.
Lexical ambiguity	When the meaning of a word or phrase is ambiguous due to a variety of possibilities in meaning.
Lexical category	Classification of a word by its identifiable meaning and its ability to be expanded by adding endings or being combined with other words.
Lexical meaning	The identifiable meaning of a word.
Lexical morpheme	A *morpheme* that primarily carries lexical rather than grammatical meaning; a *derivational morpheme*.
Lexical semantics	The study of the meaning of words and their relationships with other words in a sentence.
Lexicon	The vocabulary or wordbank of a particular *language community*.
Limited English proficiency (LEP)	A descriptor for people who are in the early stages of learning English.
Linguistic relativity	The hypothesis that language determines to some extent how we think about things.
Linguistics	The study of language and communication.
Loanword	A word borrowed from one language into another.
Manner of articulation	The way in which the airflow in the throat is modified when producing a sound in the mouth.

Meaning extension	When one *lexeme* gains several different meanings over time.
Mental grammar	The inherent knowledge that speakers have about the rules of their language.
Metaphor	A way of describing one thing in terms of another in which a name or descriptive word is transferred to an object different from but analogous enough to it to make a comparison.
Metonym	A word used in place of another to indirectly represent the same meaning.
Morpheme	A minimal unit of linguistic meaning.
Nominative case	When a noun or pronoun plays the role of a subject in a sentence.
Official language	A language formally identified as the national language of a country.
Onomastics	The study of names and naming.
Onomatapoeic words	Words created by the phonetic spellings of the particular sounds, such as *cock-a-doodle-doo* for the crowing noise that a rooster makes.
Orthography	The representation of sounds by written symbols.
Overt prestige	The positive values associated with a perceived superior entity.
Phoneme	The smallest distinct unit of sound that, when combined with other sounds, carries meaning within a particular language's sound system.
Phonetic transcription system	A system used to transcribe sounds by using one symbol to represent each significant sound in a language.
Phonology	The study of the unique set of sounds and sound patterns of a language.
Phrase structure rules	A set of *grammar* rules that represents not only all the actual sentences of a language, but all potential sentences as well.
Pidgin	A language that arises when people who do not speak the same language come into contact; a very simplified and basic language.
Place of articulation	The location in the mouth where a sound is produced.
Polyseme	A word with multiple meanings that are historically related.
Pragmatics	The linguistic subfield concerned with how meaning is created in particular contexts.
Prefix	A *morpheme* added to the beginning of a *root*.
Prescriptive grammar	A *grammar* that prescribes the use of language according to a privileged set of rules.
Prescriptivist	An individual interested in determining which dialects of a language are preferred, or considered "more correct," than others in a culture.

Privileged language	One whose speakers receive advantages not granted to speakers of other *language varieties* or to other languages; often the dominant language of a culture.
Prolonged contact	One of the causes of language change; when the speakers of two or more languages interact closely with each other for an extended period of time.
Psycholinguistics	The study of the psychological factors that allow humans to acquire, use, and understand language.
Punctuation	The written marks indicating how words combine together to create units of meaning, such as phrases, clauses, and sentences.
Rhetoric	The study of the effects of language upon an audience.
Root	A *morpheme* that cannot be analyzed further into smaller units of linguistic meaning.
Runes	Alphabet letters used by the ancient Germanic peoples, which were composed primarily of straight lines.
Sapir–Whorf hypothesis	A concept developed by Edward Sapir and Benjamin Whorf suggesting that language has the power to shape a person's reality.
Second language	A language learned after someone has become fluent in his or her *first language*.
Semantic fields	Categories of meaning used to classify words.
Semantic roles	The functions that *lexemes* take on in sentences.
Semantics	The linguistic study of meaning.
Semiotics	The study of *signs* and their conventions within a particular culture.
Sentence constituents	Words in a sentence that seem to belong together because their meanings go together.
Sign	Something that conveys meaning, such as an alphabet letter or a sound or a word.
Sign languages	Languages conveyed through physical gestures.
Slang	A specialized, informal language used by a subgroup within a larger *language community*.
Social isolation	A cause of language change, this occurs when day-to-day reinforcement of a culture disappears due to geographical isolation.
Sociolinguistics	The study of language as it affects and is affected by social relations.
Speech	The act of conveying ideas through the spoken word.
Speech act	An action carried out through language, such as promising, vowing, etc.
Standard American English (SAE)	The American English dialect privileged in the United States.
Stem	A *root* that has other *morphemes* attached.

Structuralists	Linguists concerned with describing the systems of language usage rather than making value judgments about usage.
Suffix	A *morpheme* added to the ending of a *root*.
Symbol	Something visible that represents something else, such as a word or an alphabet letter.
Synecdoche	Referring to a part of something to mean its whole.
Synonym	One of a pair of words that have the same or similar meaning.
Syntactic ambiguity	When the meaning of a sentence is unclear because the relationships between the words in a sentence or phrase are unclear.
Syntax	The rules of sentence formation; in American English this means word order.
Synthetic language	A language, such as Old English, that relies on *inflectional morphemes* to indicate the relationships between words.
Taboo	Used to describe something that is stigmatized by a community.
Target language	A second or subsequent language that is in the process of being learned.
Traditional grammar	The *grammar* based upon a Latin template that is usually taught in American schools today.
Transcribe	To transfer from an oral to a written medium.
Transcription	The transfer of sounds from an oral to a written medium.
Transformation rules	Rules about changes that can be performed on phrase structures to produce an infinite number of sentences.
Transformational grammar	A *grammar* developed from transformational theories of *syntax*.
Universal grammar	An innate grammatical structure that applies to all languages.
Vernacular	Everyday speech of the people.
Voicing	The vibration of the vocal cords when producing a sound.
Vowel	A sound produced with relatively little or no constriction of airflow in the throat.
Word	An individual unit of language that contains both lexical and grammatical meaning.
Writing	The act of conveying a language through the written word.

References

'Aha Pūnana Leo 2006, *History and timeline*, retrieved July 27, 2007 from the 'Aha Pūnana Leo website: www.ahapunanaleo.org/eng/about/about_history.html

American Civil Liberties Union 1996, "English only," *American Civil Liberties Union briefing paper number 6*, retrieved June 16, 2008 from the Center for Multilingual, Multicultural Research at the University of Southern California website: www.usc.edu/dept/education/CMMR/PolicyPDF/ACLUBriefEO.pdf

American Institutes for Research and WestEd 2006, *Effects of the implementation of Proposition 227 on the education of English learners K-12: Findings from a five-year evaluation*, submitted to the California Department of Education, retrieved June 16, 2008 from American Institutes of Research website: www.air.org/news/documents/227Report.pdf

Bailey, R. W. 2004, "American English: Its origins and history," in E. Finegan and J. R. Rickford (eds.), *Language in the U.S.A.: Themes for the twenty-first century*, Cambridge: Cambridge University Press, pp. 3–17.

Benson, L. D. (ed.) 1987. *The Riverside Chaucer*, 3rd edition, Boston: Houghton Mifflin.

Biber, Douglas, *et al. Longman grammar of spoken and written English*, Harlow: Pearson Education, 1999.

Cameron, D. 1998, *The feminist critique of language: A reader*, London: Routledge.

Chaucer, G. 1899, "The General Prologue," in Rev. W. W. Skeat (ed.), *The Canterbury tales: The complete works of Geoffrey Chaucer*, 2nd edition, Oxford: Clarendon Press.

Collier, V. P. 1989. "How long? A synthesis of research on academic achievement in a second language," *TESOL Quarterly* 23: 509–532.

Crystal, D. 1995, *The Cambridge encyclopedia of the English language*, Cambridge: Cambridge University Press.

Crystal, D. 2003, *English as a global language*, 2nd edition, Cambridge: Cambridge University Press.

Draper, J. and Hicks, J. 2002, *Foreign language enrollments in public secondary schools, fall 2002*, retrieved June 8, 2008 from the American Council on the Teaching of Foreign Languages website: www.actfl.org/files/public/Enroll2000.pdf

Eckert, P. and McConnell-Ginet, S. 2003, *Language and gender*, Cambridge: Cambridge University Press.

Finegan, Edward. 2003, *Language: Its structure and use*, 3rd edition, Boston: Heinle and Heinle.

Fought, C. 2003, *Chicano English in context*, New York: Palgrave Macmillan.

Gee, J. P. 1989, "Literacy, discourse, and linguistics: Introduction," *Journal of Education* 171 (1): 5–17.

Gibson, C. and Jung, K. 2002, *Historical census statistics on population totals by race, 1790 to 1990, and by Hispanic origin, 1970 to 1990, for the United States, regions, divisions, and states*, retrieved June 16, 2006 from Working Paper Series No. 56, US Census Bureau: www.census.gov/population/www/documentation/twps0056.html

Gordon, R. G., Jr. (ed.) 2005, *Ethnologue: Languages of the world*, retrieved August 4, 2005 from the SIL International website: www.ethnologue.com/

Graddol, D. 2004, "The future of language," *Science* 303:1329–1331.

Hakuta, K., Goto Butler, Y., and Witt, D. 2000, *How long does it take English learners to attain proficiency?* University of California Linguistic Minority Research Institute Policy Report 2000–2001. Los Angeles, CA: University of California.

Halliday, M. A. K. 1985, *An introduction to functional grammar*, London: Edward Arnold.

Krashen, S. D. 1996, *Under attack: The case against bilingual education*, Culver City, CA: Language Education Associates.

Labov, W. 1972, *Language in the inner city: Studies in the Black English vernacular*, Philadelphia: University of Pennsylvania Press.

Lincoln, A. 1863, *The Gettysburg address*, retrieved June 3, 2006 from the Library of Congress, *The Gettysburg Address* website: www.loc.gov/exhibits/gadd/images/Gettysburg-2.jpg

Molnar, Jr., A. 1997, *Navajo code-talkers: World War II fact sheet*, retrieved June 23, 2006 from the Department of the Navy, Naval Historical Center website: www.history.navy.mil/faqs/faq61 2.htm

Mora, J. K. 2003, "An Analysis of Proposition 227," retrieved June 14, 2008 from *The cross-cultural language and academic development website*: http://coe.sdsu.edu/people/jmora/Prop227PPT/Default.htm

Mufwene, S. S. 2001, *The ecology of language evolution*, Cambridge: Cambridge University Press.

National Center for Education Statistics 2007, *Table 6: Dropout rates in 9–12 by race/ethnicity, and state or jurisdiction: School year 2004–2005*, retrieved June 14, 2008 from the NCES website: http://nces.ed.gov/pubs2008/hsdropouts/tables/table_6.asp

National Clearinghouse for English Language Acquisition 2006, *NCELA frequently asked questions: How many school-aged English language learners (ELLs) are there in the U.S.?* retrieved June 8, 2008 from the NCELA website: www.ncela.gwu.edu/expert/faq/01leps.html

  2007, *NCELA frequently asked questions: What are the most common language groups for ELL students?* retrieved June 8, 2008 from the NCELA website: www.ncela.edstudies.net/expert/faq/05toplangs.html

Reyner, J. 1992, "Plans for dropout prevention and special school support services for American Indian and Alaska Native students," in P. Cahape and C. B. Howley (eds.), *Indian nations at risk: Listening to the people* (summaries of papers commissioned by the Indian Nations at Risk Task Force of the US Department of Education), pp. 47–53. (ERIC Document Reproduction Service No. ED 339 588.)

Smith. O. 1984, *The politics of language: 1791–1819*, Oxford: Oxford University Press.

Strom, D. 2006, "I.M. generation is changing the way business talks," *New York Times* April 5: G.4.

Tannen, D. 1993, *Gender and conversational interaction*, Oxford: Oxford University Press.

Thorpe, B. [1861] 1964, *The Anglo-Saxon Chronicle, according to the several original authorities*, vol. I, New York: Kraus Reprint.

Unz, R. 1999, *California and the end of white America, Commentary*, retrieved November 17, 2006 from the English for the Children website: www.onenation. org/9911/110199.html

US Census Bureau 2003, *The foreign-born population: 2003*, retrieved June 15, 2008 from the US Census Bureau website: www.census.gov/prod/2003pubs/c2kbr-34.pdf

2006a, *We the people: American Indians and Alaska Natives in the United States*, retrieved June 15, 2008 from the Census 2000 Special Reports, US Census Bureau website: www.census.gov/population/www/socdemo/race/censr-28.pdf

2006b, *2006 American community survey: Language spoken at home*, retrieved June 9, 2008 from the US Census Bureau website: http://factfinder.census.gov

[1890] 2006c, *Census of population and housing: 1890 census*, retrieved July 14, 2007 from the US Census Bureau website: www.census.gov/prod/www/abs/ decennial/1890.htm

2007, *Facts for features: Hispanic heritage month 2007*, retrieved June 9, 2008 from the US Census Bureau website: www.census.gov/Press-Release/www/releases/ archives/facts_for_features_special_editions/010327.html

US Citizenship and Immigration Service 2003, "Act 312: Requirements as to understanding the English language, history, principles, and form of government of the United States," *Immigration and Nationality Act*, retrieved June 15, 2008 from the US Citizenship and Immigration Services website:www.uscis.gov/propub/ ProPubVAP.jsp?dockey=39d68c6a6d6f2a792d6ebf343fce7116

US Senate 2006, *Affirming that statements of national unity, including the national anthem, should be recited or sung in English (S. Res. 458)*, 109th Congress, 2nd Session, retrieved April 25, 2009 from the THOMAS database in the Library of Congress: http://thomas.loc.gov/cgi-bin/query/D?c109:2:./temp/~c109bMSTON::.

Webster, N. ([1789] 1951), *Dissertations on the English language*, Gainesville, FL: Scholars' Facsimiles and Reprints.

Whittemore, K. 1998, "Saving California languages," in V. Clark, P. Eschholz, and A. Rosa (eds.), *Language: Readings in language and culture*, New York: Bedford/ St. Martin's, pp. 492–501.

Wolfram, W. 2004, "Social varieties of American English," in E. Finegan and J. R. Rickford (eds.), *Language in the USA*, Cambridge: Cambridge University Press, pp. 58–75.

Zorn, E. 1997, "Moves for simplification turn Inglish into another languaj," *Chicago Tribune 150th anniversary commemorative edition*, retrieved July 11, 2006 from www.spellingsociety.org/news/media/chicago2.php

Index